D0898210

Standing Up & Standing Out

How I teamed with a few Black men, changed the face of McDonald's, and shook up corporate America

by ROLAND L. JONES

Cover photo by
Todd Hildebrand, Nashville, Tennessee

Jacket & book design by
Axis Identification Systems, Atlanta, Georgia

For information write:

World Solutions, Inc.
4117 Hillsboro Pike
Suite 103-262
Nashville, Tennessee 37215-2728

ISBN
1-878095-99-4

Printed in the United States of America

Photo Credits

Selected photos courtesy of McDonald's corporation
Page 144, plus top left and bottom photos page 145

Photo courtesy of Antenor Adams
Page 146 bottom

Photo courtesy of Johnson Publishing Company
Page 150 top

Photos by Gil Williams Production
Page152 top right and bottom

Photo by J.R. Thomason
Page 153

TABLE OF CONTENTS

DEDICATION

This book is dedicated, with gratitude, to the memories of

RAY KROC
who inspired me and countless others to strive for perfection
in our work and to be true to ourselves in life

CARL OSBORNE
who paved the way
and never lost faith that the struggle would be won

My father, LEWIS CHARLTON JONES
who taught me by his example
to value personal integrity, live the Golden Rule,
and dignify every job

ACKNOWLEDGEMENTS

Standing Up and Standing Out is my first book, and writing it has been more challenging and more rewarding than I could have imagined when I began. I am deeply grateful to everyone who has helped me, and I am pleased to acknowledge them and their invaluable contributions.

To Martha Hailey, who has guided me throughout the entire process of writing this book, and to Richard Manson for his assistance on strategies and concept development and for his legal advice, thank you.

I'm especially grateful that my late mother, Mary Elizabeth Williamson Jones, was able to read much of the book before her death. She was a rock to the end. I also want to thank my aunt, Nanella Jones Johnson, and my cousin James Porter for their assistance with the family history; my cousins James Perry, a great reader and advisor, and Kenneth Jerome Jones for his research; and my brother, Carl E. Jones. To my cousin Carolyn Williamson Holder, who has been like a sister to me throughout my life's journey, thank you for your inspiration, superb instincts, and for reading everything, cover to cover, like the fine educator you are.

To my wife, Susan, thank you a million times over for your unwavering support, your wisdom, and your willingness to put up with your sometimes neglectful husband. Susan, from start to finish, you gave me the freedom and the loving support I needed and kept me on an even keel. I could not have done it without you.

In writing this book, I realized how very fortunate I am to have so many understanding friends. For their help all along the way, I thank Mitch Johnson for his moral and spiritual support; Al Golin for his strategic consultation, knowledge of McDonald's history, and generosity with his time; and Tom Burrell, whose support began

i

many years ago when I first conceived the idea of writing a book about my McDonald's experience. And to Ron Brown, Jim Caden, Ray Capp, Deborah Cole, Theda Day, Fay Ferguson, Janice Kelly, John Maupin, David Wilds, and Larry Womack, I give my sincerest thanks for being indispensable resources to me at every step.

I wish I had the space to describe the individual contributions of every person who shared their time and knowledge with me to make this project a reality. To the following members of the National Black McDonald's Owners Association (NBMOA), my friends and role models, thank you for sharing your stories and your insights with me and for enriching my life: Ernie Adair, Antenor Adams, Ben Alston, Bill Armstrong, Kenneth Brown, Darrell Byrd, Jim Byrd, Blanton Canady, Joan Clark, Sherman Claypool, Lonear Heard Davis, Lee Dunham, Leon Goodrum, Lanse Hyde, Chuck Johnson, Fran Jones, George Jones, Al Joyner, Ralph King, Yvonne Knox, Luther Mack, Rita Mack, Matthew Mitchell, Sam Munroe, Matthew Nichols, Carl "Reggie" Osborne, Jr., Roland Parrish, Osborne A. Payne, Bill Pickard, Bernard "B.J." Price, Wilson Rogers, Turan Strange, Yvonne and Hank Thomas, Gordon Thornton, Larry Tripplett, Artie Vann, Leroy Walker, Jr., Herb Washington, Reggie Webb, Craig Welburn, Ralph White, Mack Wilbourn, and Willie Wilson. A special thanks to Lozelle DeLuz for her careful reading and fact-checking and to Rosanna Wright for providing information about NBMOA.

It was a great pleasure to reunite by phone, e-mail, and in person with the original group of black McDonald's owners in Chicago. These pioneers will always exemplify for me the true meaning of standing up and standing out: Herman Petty, Edward L. Wimp, Walter Pitchford, our historian, Noel White, Cirilo McSween, and John Perry. Thanks also to Jim Cobham for his recollections of the early days in Washington, D.C. and Chicago.

I want to express my sincere gratitude to the following former McDonald's executives for their many contributions—verifying facts and incidents, recommending additional sources, answering questions, and always providing encouragement as the project moved forward—Marge and John Cooke, Mike Quinlan, Ed Rensi, Paul Schrage, and Tom Dentice. Other former and current McDonald's executives and owners who were so generous with their time and knowledge are: Dianna Alexander, Dean Barrett, Bob Beavers, Joe Brown, Lynn Crump-Caine, David Dandurand, James Daughtry, Rob Doran, Pat Flynn, John French, Clint Gulley, Pat Harris, Mel Hopson, Nick Karos, Barry Klein, Bill Lamar, Raymond Mines, Pat O'Brien, Mike Roberts, Shirley Rogers-Reece, Ed Schmitt, Jim Skinner, Annis Alston Staley, Horace "Stoney" Stonework, Don Thompson, Bob Weismueller, Karen Wells, Bill Whitman, Cosmo Williams, and Herb Williams. I am also very grateful for the assistance of McDonald's administrative staff members Rose Lane, Barb Balle, Brenda Elliott, Judy Johnson, Deanna Jevremov, Joyce Molinaro, and Adrainia Nieto.

As a McDonald's owner in Nashville, I had terrific crews, and I thank the following former employees for their remembrances of those good days: Jemice Cross Cheatham, Donna Myers Jones, Duane Rucker, Nancy Vincent, and Edward Vinsang. More recently, I was invited to New Orleans to hear the stories of current owners, crews, and McDonald's executives working under the extraordinary challenges of the post-Hurricane Katrina recovery, and I thank them very much for their time and their forthright accounts of courage under fire: Chris Bardell, Henry Coaxam, Jr., Rick Colon, Denise Harris, Gloria and Kurt Holloway, and Terry Scott. Thanks also to Kathy and David Wolf, who were victims of Katrina and provided me with further information about the storm and its aftermath.

There are a number of special friends and advisors who have helped me in countless ways at each stage of the development and writing of this book. I cannot thank them enough for their expertise and their patience: Seawell Brandau, David Condra, Holly Cooper, Ron Corbin, John Finch, Boyd Griffin, Bill Hudson, Sally Kilgore, Pam Stone Klein, Liah Kraft-Kristaine, Ed Carl Neal, Ben Rechter, Mary and David Rollins, Jim Schenk, Tom Scott, Mike Shmerling, Art Smith, Calvin Sydnor, Steve Travis, Cal Turner, Jr., Stephanie Williams, and Vernon Winfrey. In addition, I want to recognize Bonnie Kamis, Edna Maple Perry, Keith Rinehard, and Fred Tillman for their assistance in filling gaps and providing perspective about certain times and events.

I have researched various texts and historical documents to check the accuracy of my memories, especially in connection with the Civil Rights movement and the history of McDonald's Corporation, and I wish to acknowledge these authors: Elizabeth Gritter for her excellent "Local Leaders and Community Soldiers: The Memphis Desegregation Movement, 1955-1961" (2001: American University senior honors thesis); Juan Williams for *Eyes on the Prize: America's Civil Rights Years, 1954-1965* (2002: Penguin Books) and *My Soul Looks Back in Wonder* (2004: AARP/Sterling Publishing); John F. Love for his comprehensive *McDonald's: Behind the Arches* (1995: Bantam Books); Max Boas and Steve Chain for *Big Mac: The Unauthorized Story of McDonald's* (1976: E. P. Dutton & Co.); and Ray Kroc and Robert Anderson for Mr. Kroc's autobiography, *Grinding It Out: The Making of McDonald's* (1987: St Martin's Paperbacks).

iv

In the preparation of the manuscript, I am indebted to Debra Wright for her meticulous proofreading, and Jon David Alexander, Axis Identification Systems, for his design and layout, and Todd Hildebrand for his photography.

Roland Jones,
Nashville, Tennessee
April 10, 2006

FOREWORD

Roland Jones, a best friend for more than thirty years, is finally telling the story I encouraged him to tell many years ago. *Standing Up and Standing Out* includes twenty-five years of previously untold history that changed the way business is done in America. Except for a few people in McDonald's Corporation who were there at the time, virtually no one knows what was going on inside the company and the effects those days would have for African Americans, other minorities, and business in America.

Before Roland Jones, corporate America was harvesting crops without tilling the soil. Roland taught McDonald's corporation *how* to till the soil and grow bigger and better crops. Many other corporations have since followed McDonald's lead.

Standing Up and Standing Out documents history and tells how one person can achieve great results by working with others. This book is a blueprint for self-improvement, training, organizational progress, and for developing a business culture where everybody wins. Other significant contributors to this illustrious history are also getting recognition in this book. McDonald's Corporation can take pride in the true story of those important days.

In 1972, I resigned from the New York Police Department to open my first McDonald's franchisee on 125th Street in Harlem. It was the first McDonald's in New York City and the beginning of a successful McDonald's tradition in the Big Apple. While I was getting up to speed on the running of my new enterprise, I met Roland, the first black on the McDonald's corporate scene in Chicago. He was a strong advocate for McDonald's, African American franchisees, and black consumer advertising. A couple years later, when I was elected to the National McDonald's Operator Advisory Board, I attended quarterly meetings in Chicago, and I made it a priority to meet with Roland before and after every meeting to discuss key agenda issues, especially those affecting store operations, black franchisees, black consumers, and urban markets. He was known throughout the company as an operational expert and was McDonald's sole expert on inner-city markets. Roland and I shared a lot of common interests, and once he accepted the position of corporate director of Urban Operations, I got to know him even better. He was a strong leader and nonpolitical in his role as an executive. He focused on mission and absolutely refused to compromise the mission for the sake of climbing the corporate career ladder. I supported that mission and recommended several potential black franchisees to the company. I was an active participant in organizing the New York Black Hispanic McDonald's Operators Association (BHMOA), a self-help group similar to an organization formed by Roland and the Chicago black franchisees. When he organized a national convention in Kansas City for minority franchise owners, our entire New York chapter attended. Roland continued to work with minority owner-operator groups throughout the country, and his leadership led to official formation of the National Black McDonald's Operators Association (NBMOA) one year later in Cherry Hills, New Jersey.

When Roland left McDonald's Corporation to become the first black franchisee in Tennessee, I was there working with him during this transition. A couple of years later, he became president of the NBMOA, and I was a member of the leadership team that worked with him. We achieved much during his administration. When he decided not to seek a second term, he and other members, without my knowledge, chose me as his successor. I found this out when Roland said to me at an NBMOA convention luncheon in 1982, "Lee, it's your time in the barrel." As soon as Roland said the word "barrel,"

Carl Osborne, the president who preceded Roland, and other members started passing out "Dunham for President" buttons. I think everybody knew I was going to be the next in line, except for me.

Roland's continued support was important in making my administration successful. He showed us how to lead and how to follow. He always seemed to know which role to play in every situation. We stood together and continued to provide quality services to our members, our businesses, and the communities in which we operated. Roland was there with me when the TV cameras rolled, when the newspapers called, or when we met with McDonald's corporate management, with the powerbrokers on Capitol Hill, and with national figures like Ben Hooks and Jesse Jackson. Roland's knowledge, experience, and understanding of the company made him a perfect sounding board and leadership partner. When I was nominated to be the first two-term president in the history of the NBMOA, the decision to accept was easy. We were effective in creating a better life for ourselves, our employees, and our communities and in making McDonald's corporation a better company. That's the mission I bought into with Roland back in his days as director of Urban Operations.

Standing Up and Standing Out tells the story of the mission and a journey that changed many lives along the way. It is still changing lives. I am glad that my friend is setting the record of history straight, and I believe his book will have a positive impact on readers in every walk of life.

R. Lee Dunham
Chair Emeritus, NBMOA, and McDonald's Franchisee

INTRODUCTION

Trouble is only opportunity in work clothes.

HENRY J. KAISER, INDUSTRIALIST

All of us have lived through personal events, such as the first day of school or an important promotion, that remain etched in our minds with crystal clarity. Sometimes we share our memories with hundreds, thousands, even millions of people—unforgettable events forever attached to a day and a date. Few Americans today do not know where they were and what they were doing on the morning of September 11, 2001.

I remember April 5, 1968, in such high detail. The previous evening, April 4, we had gotten the news that Dr. Martin Luther King, Jr., had been shot as he stood on the balcony of his motel room in Memphis, Tennessee. Later that night, our worst fears were confirmed. Dr. King was dead, and at first, the shock was too great to sink in.

The next morning, I went to my job as manager of the McDonald's restaurant at 3510 Duke Street in Alexandria, Virginia. We opened the store; we served the people who came in. I guess that those of us who showed up for work were seeking a kind of security in tending to business as usual, although my own actions during the early part of that day are a blur. Only the unanswered questions that my colleagues and I asked ourselves again and again remain vivid: *Why had Dr. King been slain? Who could have done such a thing? What would happen next? How would the people of my race respond? Would this hideous tragedy tear our country apart? Would there be a new civil war?*

I was very concerned about my family: my parents and grandfather, who lived in Memphis, and my brother in Mississippi. I thought about myself too. *How would this affect my life? Would I still have a job? Had my move to Washington been for nothing?*

My memories become sharper as I recall hearing the reports of rioting and looting in Washington. I decided to close the restaurant early and send everyone home. I locked up the store and got into my car for the drive back to my apartment in southwestern D.C.

It wasn't long before the acrid smell of burning and the unnatural haze of smoke filled the air. What had started as a clear spring day was now a dirty gray, but not because of a change of weather. As I drove into the city, I realized that Washington was on fire, and I didn't know how close the chaos was to my home.

The smoke grew thicker and darker; it made my eyes water. I caught whiffs of what I thought was tear gas. Sirens screamed above the honking traffic. It became almost impossible to see farther than a few feet ahead. I was driving on instinct, and if I hadn't made the trip so many times before, I would never have found my way.

I couldn't have explained my thinking that day; I had no idea that I was at a personal turning point. Like everybody else, I was afraid of the violence. I was enraged at the senseless murder of a true man of peace. A decade-old memory hit me: I was back in my college dorm, and my friend Barney Hawkins Pace and I were having one of those "what if" discussions that students engage in. One of us asked, "What if someone tried to kill Dr. King?" We knew even then that he was a target of the hate-mongers, but we didn't want to contemplate what might result if he were taken from us. Now it had happened, and I felt deep grief for Dr. King and for all of my people. I had a troubling sense of disorientation, not knowing what might come next. To this day, I can't sort out the welter of emotions that assailed me. But I understand now what impelled me toward my apartment that afternoon.

I was twenty-nine years old, a college graduate, and a military veteran. Almost three years earlier, I had left the Deep South and come to Washington. I'd been hired as a management trainee by the largest McDonald's franchisee in the country and had risen to the position of restaurant manager. I was one of a small number of black men for whom doors were beginning to open in what had been, until recently, an all-white company (and was, at that point, still 'whites only' inside the corporate echelons). Even more important, I loved the work I was doing, and an assassin in Memphis wasn't going to make me turn my back on the opportunities that had begun to come my way.

This book is my story, but it is also the story of how one of America's largest and most successful corporations changed itself from the inside and for the better. I was a witness to and a participant in the change. From that dreadful day in April 1968, my future was wedded to the McDonald's Corporation and its growth.

I didn't really think of myself as a pioneer. But like the handful of African American men who preceded me in the company and mentored me as my job became a career, I was heading straight into uncharted territory.

The civil rights movement, personified by Dr. King, had challenged the nation's long history of moral blindness to its black citizens. A lot of progress was being made in attaining legal equality, but changing hearts and minds was another matter. The business sector lagged far behind the lawmakers—often from blatant racist (and sexist) motives and also because the traditional all-white, all-male power structure of American business wasn't convinced that it needed to do anything different. For the most part, private businesses, including the country's largest and most profitable corporations, considered themselves immune to integration, especially at the management level, where negative stereotyping of people of color and women abounded.

There were exceptions. Some farsighted executives—including Ray Kroc, founder of the McDonald's Corporation—sensed the way the country was moving and knew the time had come for a new kind of thinking. To continue to ignore the newly united and therefore economically significant African American market, which comprised one-tenth of the national population in the 60s, would sooner or later be bad for business. By the closing years of the decade, McDonald's had come to the brink of change, and the question was if and how it would take the next step forward.

The McDonald's system is famous for its efficiency, but within that system in the late 1960s and 1970s, African Americans would be needed if the company was to break new ground. We found ourselves at the forefront of expanding McDonald's from a primarily suburban fast-food operation to one that would serve urban customers in cities across the country, in locations where the population was often largely or predominantly black. What sold hamburgers, French fries, and Cokes in comfortable, middle-class, suburban, and predominantly white communities could not simply be imposed on cities. From necessity rather than by design, the company was taking its first baby steps toward transforming its consumer base from mostly white suburbanites to one that reflected the country as a whole—the whole 'stew pot' of racial, ethnic, and cultural diversity. In the process of enlarging its geographical reach into urban America, McDonald's had to attract and retain a new kind of customer. Whatever their personal feelings about integration, smart people at the top of the corporation realized that McDonald's well-established systems and hardcore attitudes had to be revised and adapted if the company was to succeed in new and even some of its existing territories.

McDonald's, by moving to inner city ownership, needed to attract new markets, and this created opportunities for men like me (and eventually for women and other minorities) to come in by the front door. The company's challenge gave us the chance to use our abilities and our experience to develop new business practices and models and to modify the franchise program in ways that would literally change the face of McDonald's.

There was no career path for blacks when I first came to McDonald's in 1965; nobody had heard of "affirmative action" yet. Maybe a person with a different temperament and a different upbringing would have abandoned the effort. But events had conspired to put McDonald's and me together, and I was going to take my best shot at making the relationship work. I had no idea that being hired as a management trainee would propel me into the corporate offices and, after more than a decade, into the entrepreneurial realm of restaurant ownership.

I didn't do it by myself. The ground was broken by a couple of black men who preceded me in McDonald's and who became my role models, my supporters, and my colleagues. Their efforts opened the way for me and other African Americans to rise in the company and eventually to stand up for change with a unified voice. I was accompanied on my journey by a group of men—the first black restaurant owners in McDonald's—whose courage and determination inspire me to this day. How we managed our relationships with the corporation, how we supported each other and organized ourselves for self-help, and what we all learned along the way is one of the major subjects of this book.

My goal is that telling my story may provide incentive and

encouragement for others who face seemingly insurmountable barriers to success. And by success, I don't mean money, though that can be one of the rewards for achievement. The bookshelves are already full of guides to financial success, and there's little need for one more.

Neither is this book intended to be a history of race relations, though I owe an incalculable debt to the civil rights movement and its leaders, whose heroic battle for fairness and equality paved the way. I'm a black man, and my life has coincided with one of the most significant struggles this country has been forced to confront. There have been times when my race has been a barrier to equal access and financial opportunities, but overall, the benefits have far outweighed the difficulties. When I've faltered, it has usually been my own fault because I wasn't being true to myself and my core values—values I'd been taught since childhood and which have, for the most part, guided my business as well as my private life.

The most important lesson I've learned and want to share is that most of the obstacles we confront in life are also opportunities—the bigger the obstacle, the bigger the opportunity. Nobody knows what each new day will bring, but we can control our attitudes, prepare ourselves for whatever happens, and then do the right thing.

Back on April 5, 1968, when I finally reached my D.C. apartment, it was hard for me to see any opportunities in the violent aftermath of Dr. King's death. Still, I had decisions to make. I could give in to my anger and frustration by making myself into another bitter victim of racism, no different from the irrational mob that was burning and looting just four blocks away from where I lived. Or I could give up my hopes and ambitions and seek safety back with my family in Tennessee. Or I could go on with my life, adjusting as necessary to circumstances I could not, on that night, begin to predict.

As I watched television and tried to sort through the anger and violence erupting in cities across the country, I was also thinking about my options. I realized that I was too much of an optimist to give in or give up. So I would go on. I'd hang tough and hold on to my dreams. I wasn't naïve; I knew that everything had been altered by Dr. King's murder. I just didn't expect how my own life would change. Yet out of the literal ashes left behind by the riots in Washington, I would soon be offered a job that everybody, even the man who made the offer, considered impossible. That job would lead me to an opportunity no black man had ever had before.

How I handled the challenges and conflicts that followed was grounded in lessons I'd learned years before there was a McDonald's Corporation. I can look back and see how my family and my early experiences have influenced my thinking and decision-making. I put a lot of stock in education and training, but I also think that our current emphasis on advanced degrees and specialized credentials, essential as they are in an era of lightning-fast technological change and globalized commerce, can lead us to underrate our most valuable resources—the moral principles and ethical underpinnings that strengthen our efforts to stand out without selling out.

A few years ago, when I first decided to write a book, I ran into all kinds of obstacles. I can sum them up as too little time and too many ideas. So I finally put the whole project on a back burner and let it simmer. Unconsciously, I was taking the first step in the problem-solving process that I've followed successfully throughout my business career and that I'm sharing now. By letting my ideas simmer for a time, I was able to focus on what was most important. With focus and clarity, I went to work again.

I don't intend this book to be an exact blueprint. Each of us has to carve out his or her own path to success. Rather, I offer my story as a source of support, encouragement, and practical guidance. I also want this book to stand as my tribute to the many men and women I worked with in McDonald's, who didn't let race stand in their way and who cleared the obstacles of prejudice and discrimination for those who have followed us.

Though my McDonald's years are in the past, I'm still active in business, still finding better ways to get the job done and to improve on what is by visualizing what can be. I continue to refine my personal definition of success and to strive to do the right thing for myself and for others. Over time, I've learned that there are many advantages to getting older. There's a saying that you hear a lot after you pass forty: "You're not getting older. You're just getting better." I don't know about "better," but experience is an excellent teacher. With persistence we gain perspective and grow in wisdom, learning to honor the past and to draw on our own history for guidance. We can look backward, see our successes and our errors, and use the past to shape the future.

My history—and the story of my experiences inside one of this country's most successful corporations—begins at the beginning, among the hard-working people of a small West Tennessee town just north of Memphis.

Almost Everything You Need to Know

A problem is a chance for you to do your best.

DUKE ELLINGTON, MUSICIAN AND COMPOSER

In 1939, the year I was born, no one dreamed that a black child from rural western Tennessee might someday climb the ladder of success in one of America's largest and most influential corporations. No one would have dreamed it because that wasn't how things were done.

Back in 1939, the best a child like me could reasonably hope for from corporate America was the possibility of a skilled job in a factory. Members of my own family had moved north to industrial cities like Cleveland, Buffalo, and Detroit to find such jobs in the blue-collar workforce. But an office in a major corporation's headquarters? Not likely. The corporate ladder was for white men only and strictly off-limits to people of color (and to most women). The idea of a "black executive" in the power structure of white corporate America was unthinkable.

I didn't know much about this reality when I was a kid. Like most children born in rural America in the waning years of the Great Depression, I grew up within a fairly small and well-defined community. Most of the adults I knew had grown up in the area and stayed there to raise their children, who, it was expected, would stay on and repeat the cycle. Back then, leaving home for good was an exception to the rule.

Mason, my hometown, is a farm community in Tipton County on the far western border of Tennessee, where the state comes up against the Mississippi River. In the late 1930s, Mason was a typical Southern country town—maybe 4,000 people, with blacks and whites fairly evenly divided. Everything we thought we needed was there: schools, churches, stores, restaurants, a movie theater, a baseball field that adjoined my parents' property. (Like so many rural communities, Mason has since seen its population shrink with the decline in individual farming and the departure of younger generations to find their opportunities elsewhere. The 2000 census reported a population of just over a thousand people, slightly more than half of them African American.)

At some point when I was a boy, I became conscious of divisions between blacks and whites. We didn't attend the same churches and schools; we got used textbooks while the white kids got new ones; our schools weren't allowed to compete against white schools in sports. These were the kinds of differences a boy noticed and wondered about, though they didn't seem to limit my life that much. But I also remember when my father's youngest brother was killed in World War II. My dad rarely showed anger, but on this occasion he pitched a fit when the county newspaper refused to run a picture of my uncle, as it did when white soldiers died in the service of their country. Though I don't think anyone used the word "racism," that's what it was, pure and simple. Even though the newspaper finally did run the photo of Uncle Booker, after Daddy's protest, I'd never seen my father so mad. Maybe that's when I began to understand something about the hurt of discrimination.

Still, I didn't think of myself as being a member of an oppressed minority. My playmates came in all shades, and we were tight with our white neighbors. Our house was always a gathering place, and lots of the neighbor kids called my mother "Mom." For a long time, my parents had the only telephone and the only radio in the neighborhood. People's color didn't matter much when they needed to make a phone call or got together in our home to listen to the broadcast of one of Joe Louis's prizefights.

Segregation was a fact of life for all of us, black and white, and there could be trouble when anyone "got out of place." But most people we knew tried not to let it get in the way of getting along with one another. The hurricane of change that would blast Jim Crow out of the South in the 1950s and 60s was beginning to form elsewhere, but it barely made a ripple in Mason while I was growing up there in the 1940s.

Mason was rural but not isolated. Trains stopped in town every day, taking on travelers and the mail and transporting them to distant places. Greyhound buses pulled into the Esso service station each day, picking up and letting off passengers. Private automobiles were not numerous in the war years, and most rural folks still relied on their horses, buggies, and wagons until well into the 1950s. But my family had a car—a blue 1941 Ford—and my father often drove us to the next county to visit my grandparents. Sometimes we went up to Covington, the county seat of Tipton, or we headed thirty-eight miles south to Memphis. In my school years, my parents took my younger brother, Carl, and me on road trips to see the historic sites of Nashville and Chattanooga and St. Louis. Then in 1950, when I was eleven, our family moved to Memphis, in large part because my parents wanted my brother and I to have better educational opportunities and to

3

broaden our horizons. But the geography of my early years was mainly the dusty clay roads and the ball fields of Mason, the rural countryside that surrounded it, and the homes of my family and friends.

Looking back, I realize how fortunate I was to be born into my family. It's not something I thought about when I was a boy, but as I grew older and moved beyond the confines of Mason, I began to see just how much I'd learned there: life lessons taught by my parents and grandparents and drawn from the model of their behavior. They were what Southerners call "good people"—a simple phrase that encompasses a wealth of positive characteristics and worthy habits: generosity, honesty, loyalty, faith in the Lord, concern for others, self-reliance, a strong work ethic. "Good people," in the Southern mind, aren't perfect by any means. Education and material wealth have little to do with it. "Good people" are the kind of folks who try hard to practice the Golden Rule, who can be trusted to do right by others, and who aren't afraid to get their hands dirty when there's work to be done.

Some years ago, Robert Fulghum wrote a book titled *All I Really Need to Know I Learned in Kindergarten.* The book was a huge success, staying on *The New York Times*'s best-seller list for almost two years. The reason for the appeal of Fulghum's book, and the continuing popularity of similar collections of homely wisdom, seems straightforward enough. We Americans sometimes feel the need to reconnect with our roots and the values we learned before we got caught up in the day-to-day demands of our hectic and often ethically ambiguous culture.

I didn't learn all I need to know in kindergarten; we didn't even have kindergartens then. But I learned my core values when I was young. That's nothing unusual; most of us acquire our sense of the world and our place in it when we are children. What continues to amaze me is how apt those teachings from my youth have always been, no matter where I've gone or what I've done. The moral and ethical lessons I learned as a boy growing up in a small Southern town are just as valid today as they were in the middle years of the twentieth century. Throughout my career, there were plenty of chances to set those values aside and maybe climb the corporate ladder a little faster and a little higher. But I don't think I ever missed a genuine opportunity because of my values. I can look back over my life, particularly my life in business, with a sense of satisfaction: I didn't get where I am by abandoning where I came from.

With the death of my mother not long ago, the people who shaped my values are mostly gone now. Yet they live on, not only in my memory but also in the way I see the world and deal with it. I owe them a debt that can only be repaid by continuing to honor their teachings and passing them on. The story of my experience in corporate America and as a business owner begins with my family.

ENDURING VALUES

There's a tradition of bootstrap entrepreneurship that runs on both sides of my family. My paternal grandfather, James Willie ("Jimmy") Jones, inherited nine acres of Tipton County farmland from his father, a freed slave. Over time, Grandpa Jimmy increased his holding to 251 acres, a substantial farm on which he grew cotton and sugar cane and raised cattle and pigs. He acquired some profitable gravel pits, and he became a prosperous businessman.

Jimmy also served as an unofficial bank for the community. White banks were not inclined to make many loans to black folks, so people would go to Jimmy. He was careful about lending, and he charged a fair interest and expected full payment. He believed that every debt should be repaid; he would say that "you're not free until you're debt-free," and he held himself and everyone else to that standard.

People still recall the story of Grandpa Jimmy's loan to his local church. The church needed a new building and was able to secure a bank loan for part of the costs. But when the congregation was unable to raise the rest of the funds, they approached Jimmy, and he agreed to lend the full amount needed. After the construction was completed, the congregation dutifully lived up to its commitment to the bank, but they never got around to repaying Grandpa Jimmy—hoping, I suppose, that he would forgive the debt. So after waiting a reasonable time, Jimmy started foreclosure proceedings. The church people were shocked, and some were angry, but they knew Jimmy wasn't kidding, and the loan was soon paid. Then Jimmy surprised them again; he gave everything back to the church. What mattered to him was not the money but the obligation. A loan was a responsibility, and Jimmy wasn't the kind of man to shirk his responsibilities or allow others to ignore their obligations to him.

My grandfather understood the value of money, and he made his money work for him. He took his business seriously—refusing even to joke with people he did business with to avoid misunderstandings. Clear communication was something he always emphasized. As an employer and a business owner, he took the time to make his meanings clear to the people who worked for him. I doubt that Grandpa Jimmy thought of verbal clarity as a management technique. To him, it was just wrong to expect anyone to do what he wanted if he didn't explain himself well.

Though he was a small man who never raised his voice, people knew that Jimmy Jones wasn't a soft touch. He was tough but fair, and he understood that money wasn't an end in itself. He taught us to be cautious with what we had—I still remember the time when, as an object lesson for his grandchildren, he raked through the ashes to recover a penny dropped in the fireplace—but not tight-fisted. Like so many people of his generation, Grandpa Jimmy had little formal schooling, finishing only the third grade. Yet he was smart and determined. He said, "Sometimes you have to make something from nothing," and that's exactly what he did all his life.

My grandmother, Totcy Pete Jones, was unlike her husband in both appearance and personality, and their marriage was an example of opposites attracting. Tall for a woman at the time, she stood a good six or seven inches above Grandpa Jimmy, and her nearly limitless enthusiasm was a good balance for his quiet ways. She was "Mama-Totcy" to us grandchildren, and she was the glue that held our family together. She believed with all her heart that families have to stick together—loving and protecting one another—and she would do what it took to keep every member of the family interacting. I guess she gave us our first lessons in teamwork because, to her, the family was a team, and everybody had to pull in the same direction.

It might seem like a contradiction, but Mama Totcy was also a great believer in not following the crowd. She respected individuality, and she didn't want us to be like everyone else. Again and again, she told us, "Stand out; don't blend in." Even now, when I'm faced with choices, I can hear her saying those words and telling me to do what I know to be right. From her I learned that loyalty to the team and staying true to yourself aren't mutually exclusive. A person can be a team player and a leader at the same time.

Jimmy and Totcy had eight children, and my father—Lewis Charlton Jones—was the eldest. He inherited his enthusiasm from his mother, and his keen sense of responsibility from his father, though my father followed a different path. Daddy was a school principal and a Baptist minister. His faith was grounded in the commandment to "love your neighbor as yourself"; nothing made him happier than being of service to someone else.

Daddy loved people, and he loved learning. As a teenager, he walked eleven miles each way to attend school in Shelby County. At that time, there wasn't a black high school in Tipton County that ran on a split-session schedule. A split session meant that a school operated basically year-round and followed the farming calendar, with breaks throughout the year so students could do field work during the periods of planting and harvesting. Like so many boys back then, my father might have been forced to drop out of school if he couldn't get the time off to work the family farm. But education was too important to him. So he walked through the searing heat of Tennessee's Julys and the icy cold of January and February, to earn his diploma—and I don't think he ever considered not making the effort.

After graduating from high school, Daddy went on to LeMoyne (now LeMoyne-Owen) College in Memphis, a historically black institution that traces its beginnings to the Civil War. When my father attended, it was still called LeMoyne Normal and Commercial School, and one of its primary activities was the training of Negro teachers.

When he finished at LeMoyne, Daddy returned to Tipton County to teach. He became the principal of the black public elementary school in Gainesville—a bump-in-the-road community a few miles west of Mason. There were three teachers, including Daddy, and they made the best of conditions that would be intolerable today. Supplies were always short for black schools, and most of the materials they received were hand-me-downs from white schools. Once, when Daddy's school received a shipment of brand new textbooks, presumably delivered by mistake, he immediately had the children write their names in each book, so this unexpected bounty couldn't be taken away when the white county supervisors came to collect the books.

Daddy had high expectations of himself, just as he would for my brother and me and all the children he mentored. Though he was a teacher and school principal, his focus was not on getting the highest grades but on doing the best that we could. He would say, "God bless the child who does his best," and he meant it.

Daddy was one of the most respected men in our community. He was an educator; he was a minister—positions of authority. But he really earned respect because of the way he treated people. Everything he did was guided by his religious faith; his vision was biblical. He acted out of the belief that it was not up to people to judge their fellow humans. To judge others was, in his ethic, a case of "the blind leading the blind." He preached understanding. He taught the importance of getting to know other people and their circumstances before setting expectations for them, and his commitment to that approach was what made him a fine teacher and role model for his students, his congregation, and the community. He got joy from helping people when he could, and he was one of those rare individuals who didn't make distinctions. Black or white, well-off or poor—our father just didn't think in those terms. He'd say, "Find the good," whatever the situation.

Daddy met my mother, who was from neighboring Fayette County, when he was living and working in tiny Gainesville. My mother's name was Mary Elizabeth. Her family nickname was "Sudder," but Daddy always called her "Rosey." She was eight years younger than he, and though she had only one more year to complete high school, she left to get married. I don't think she regretted dropping out at the time, but Daddy made a commitment to help her finish, which she did eleven years later.

Her father, Gentle Yerger Williamson, was a farmer—a sharecropper for much of his life, working land that belonged to someone else. He didn't seem to mind working for others, because he loved farming and what he earned supported his family. Hattie, his wife, had the entrepreneurial spirit. She had inherited eighteen acres of land from her father, but there was no dwelling on the property. So she grew vegetables and raised chickens, and she built up a business selling her produce and eggs. She saved and saved until she had enough to finance the construction of a house that was just what she wanted. When my grandparents moved into their own home on their own land, my Gran-daddy was able to give up sharecropping.

Hattie, whom we called "Gran-dear," and Gran-daddy Williamson were typical of farming people back then. They worked hard, reared their family, and bore their burdens with dignity. But they weren't immune to the racism of the time and experienced it in a particularly terrible way. One of their sons was wrongfully accused of the murder of a white sheriff, and before his trial, a mob of white men (most likely Ku Klux Klan) tried to seize my uncle from the local jail. The lawmen took him out of the county, probably saving his life. There was at least one witness to the murder, so people had a good idea who had actually committed the crime. But a black man accused of killing a white man didn't have much hope of justice. In spite of a vigorous defense, my uncle was convicted and sentenced to thirty years. The family stuck by him, and so did his lawyer—a white man who fought for my uncle long after most lawyers would have given up—and after thirteen years in prison, my uncle was finally freed. It's hard to imagine the pain and grief my grandparents must have felt. I knew what was happening, but adults back then tended to keep such matters to themselves. They protected children as best they could from the harsher realities of life.

I wish I'd had more time to know my Gran-dear. She died when I was nine years old, but I remember her forceful personality, her determination, and her work ethic. We had Gran-daddy with us much longer. He was a quiet, gentle man, and independent in the way of country folk. A near-fatal accident brought him to live with us some years after Gran-dear's death. The house he was living in then caught fire, and he was badly burned when he ran inside to retrieve something. He had never been to a doctor in his life and had no intention of seeking treatment, until my mother stepped in. We were living in Memphis by that time, and when someone called her about the fire, she rushed to her father and took control. Paying no attention to his objections, she took him to the hospital, and after he finally recovered, she brought him to live with us.

That was how my mother always did things—decisively. When I was in elementary school, Mother decided it was time for her to finish high school, and she did. Then she decided it was time for her to go to college, and she did. She applied to Lane College in Jackson, Tennessee, forty-five miles away from our home. We only had one car, which my father needed, so Mother couldn't drive back and forth each day. Instead, she stayed in Jackson to attend her classes on weekdays and returned home most weekends. My brother and I would always go with Daddy to meet her bus at the Esso station. After we moved to Memphis, my mother's weekly journey to Jackson was nearly doubled in length, but she kept up the pace, graduating from Lane College when I was a sophomore in high school and becoming a teacher in the Memphis school system.

She expected the men of the family—my father, brother, and me—to manage for ourselves when she wasn't there, and Carl and I knew better than to let her down. Mother was the disciplinarian in our household. Daddy could talk a good game, but Mother was the enforcer. She set the limits, and Carl and I soon learned that not much got past her. My father didn't rely on physical punishments, though Mother sometimes spanked us. Usually when Carl and I got in trouble, we could expect to lose some privileges, but our parents tried to make their lessons stick by appealing to our consciences. Whatever the infraction (I often tried to get out of doing my chores, while Carl was prompt with chores but inclined to skip his homework), Mother and Daddy would talk to us about doing what was right. They talked about the effects of misbehavior on ourselves and others, and they would use a minor incident to make a larger point.

Daddy was especially adept at making a lecture seem more like a lesson worth learning. He was a good-humored man, and he could joke about faults in a way that didn't make a boy resentful. I was the kind of kid who hated getting out of bed in the morning, and the family would say that I was "as slow as cold molasses coming out of a barrel in wintertime" when there were chores to be done. Daddy teased me by calling me "old gray man" because of the way I'd drag my feet and delay doing what had to be done. From that, I got the nickname "Grady," which was fun but also a reminder to improve my procrastinating habits. Eventually the lesson took and was reinforced later by my years of early rising and prompt response to commands in the Army.

My mother, as I said, set the limits. Mason was a safe place, and Carl and I had a lot of freedom to go where we wanted without supervision. We could walk the mile from our house to the center of town and go to a couple of stores, a restaurant, and the movie theater. There were other businesses we weren't allowed to enter. In those days, some great musicians, like B.B. King, came to perform in a large club just outside the Mason town limits, but the areas with the honky-tonks were strictly forbidden to us boys. Mother didn't always explain these restrictions, but we trusted our parents to be right. Besides, there were plenty of places for boys to explore and play.

Of course, Mother kept a sharp eye on us, and when she wasn't around, there were neighbors and friends who watched out for us and other kids. Adults did that for one another because we were like an extended family. I don't remember anyone quoting the African proverb that "it takes a village to raise a child," but that's the kind of community Mason was.

I was lucky enough to know my mother's grandmother—my great-grandmother Henrietta Porter. From Grandma Henrietta, who died when I was fourteen, and from my mother and her siblings, I learned about my great-grandfather, Dennis Porter, who also passed the entrepreneurial spirit down our family tree. A former slave, he became a landowner, farmer, and successful horse and livestock trader. It was his business philosophy to get exactly what a trade was worth—no more and no less. I heard stories about his method of dealing, and they stayed with me. He thought it was a waste to trade for a cow and milk her dry. A smart man would get enough milk to make the trade worthwhile; then he would sell the cow or trade for a better one. A dry cow had no use as trade; a cow that gave milk did. You have to give value to get value.

He had a reputation for integrity; people knew they could trust him to deal fairly. That, plus a talent for making sound investments, was how he built a good life for his family. When he died—dropping dead in a field at the age of fifty-two—he left his wife a house and seventy-five acres, and each of his seven children inherited eighteen acres of farmland, a remarkable legacy for a black man in the early years of the twentieth century. My great-grandmother was able to live

13

the rest of her life in financial security.

Great-grandmother Henrietta was a religious woman, and she used to hold regular prayer services. We'd go to her comfortable house, and the adults would join in the prayers, while the children were admonished to stay quiet and listen. Grandma Henrietta's faith was unwavering, and when she spoke to the Lord, her prayers were always very focused. It seemed to me that most of what she prayed for, whether for herself or someone else, was sooner or later accomplished. Like a lot of preachers' kids, I didn't grow up to be a church-going man; my spiritual beliefs are more universal and deeply personal. But in Daddy's church and on my knees during my great-grandmother's prayer sessions, I got a real sense of the power of faith. To achieve anything, a person has to believe in what he's doing and stay focused.

When your father is the principal, school naturally plays a big role in your life. I was five years old when I entered the first grade at Gainesville School, but it wasn't long before the teacher skipped me to the second grade. I can't claim to have been the smartest child, but because of the early education I received at home, I was already reading and writing and was well ahead of my classmates. From that time forward, I was always the youngest person in my classes, graduating from high school at age sixteen.

When my father became the minister of St. Matthew's Church in Mason, he also took over the running of the public school affiliated with the church, and I transferred with him. St. Matthew's was an all-black school with around 150 students, and most of them lacked material advantages, but we had some great teachers. Segregation was a terrible thing, but it did create a few advantages. With most professional careers closed to blacks, the best and brightest of my race gravitated to the ministry, medicine, and education. Our teachers were smart and well trained, and I can see now that they were also sensitive to the obstacles that the majority of their students had to overcome. For the most part, they shared my dad's focus on enabling and encouraging every child to make the most of his or her abilities.

I was inclined to goof off; I did what was necessary to keep my grades up, but I wasn't a dedicated scholar. My attitude ran counter to my father's philosophy of doing one's best, so he made personal responsibility a frequent theme in our conversations. When I would ask him why I had to go to school, he'd say, "You go to school to prepare yourself to meet the demands of the future." He would tell me, "There's no future in just getting by." He often quoted from Galatians 6:7: "for whatsoever a man soweth, that shall he also reap." Sometimes he emphasized his point by telling the biblical parable of the sower. Nothing came of the seeds that fell on the path and the rocks and among the thorns, but the seeds sown on good earth yielded a crop. He encouraged me to make a greater effort, and he made certain that, at the least, I was at school every day. I had a perfect attendance record through the eighth grade, but I can't take credit. When your father is the school principal, you get to school and stay there.

Maybe my dad knew that the day would come when I really understood the value of a good education. He didn't chastise me for my somewhat lackadaisical attitude. But he made it perfectly clear what he wouldn't allow—cheating in any form. At home, at school, from the pulpit, on the basketball court (he coached the school team), Daddy always insisted on fair play, and he made it clear that cheating was never tolerated. Cheating might seem like an easy way to get something you wanted, but the consequences were never worth it. Daddy had a saying: "People who take short-cuts get short-changed."

Like every kid at some time or another, I suppose I was

tempted to cheat. But thanks to my father and my mother, I knew in my young conscience that it would be wrong. It would violate the central value my father taught us—the Golden Rule. Daddy would say that we could control what other people thought of us by consistently treating others as we wanted to be treated. I didn't have to understand the fine points to know that I did not want people to think of me as a cheater.

From Mason to Memphis

We moved to Memphis in 1950. As my parents hoped, the move definitely widened the world for my brother and me. Memphis was *a real city*, and though small compared to New York or Chicago, it was humongous to us. Carl and I didn't get into a lot of mischief, but we would sometimes risk big trouble with our parents by sneaking off on our bikes to explore parts of the city that were off-limits for us. Memphis was segregated into white neighborhoods and black neighborhoods in a way I hadn't experienced in Mason, and we realized pretty quickly that black boys didn't hang out in white residential areas without a reason for being there.

Memphis is located just eight miles north of the Tennessee-Mississippi border, in cotton-producing Mississippi River Delta country. It was always more of a Deep South city than Nashville, Chattanooga, or Knoxville, and Carl and I saw "Colored Only" signs sprouting everywhere, like cotton bolls in an unpicked field—something else that hadn't been so obvious in Mason. In those days, Memphis had the only real zoo in the state, at Overton Park, but in a city with a nearly 40 percent African American population, the zoo was open to us only one day each week—Thursday, which was also the traditional day off (or more usually afternoon off) for domestic workers in the South. Since most black women who worked were employed as maids and cooks, I presume the logic was to admit blacks to the zoo on the one day when mothers and grandmothers could take their children. The one part of central Memphis that blacks literally owned was Beale Street, renowned for its blues clubs but also the center of black-owned businesses and professional practices. On Beale Street, black men and women walked tall. Everywhere else, we were separated and roped off from the white citizens, and access to public services—from water fountains to seats on the buses—was strictly limited.

For a couple of years, Carl and I were spared from many of the harsh realities of city segregation. Daddy stayed on as minister at St. Matthew's, and he remained as principal of the St. Matthew's school until Tennessee's public education system was integrated and consolidated in 1965. Carl and I continued to attend school with our friends in Mason, commuting with my dad for two years. In 1951, I entered Gaylor Industrial High School in Tipton County. Gaylor had formerly been an Episcopalian school but was converted to a public school. The student body was co-ed, and the school operated on a split-session schedule. We'd get a month off at planting time, for example, just as Daddy had when he was a boy. Mr. Lewers, my homeroom teacher, also taught agriculture, and partly because of his influence, I became active in the Negro Farmers of America. I don't think I ever wanted to be a farmer, but at Gaylor, I gained tremendous respect for what is not just a job but a way of life.

In my one year at Gaylor, I also had a couple of those "lights turned on" experiences that improved my attitude toward my education. Mrs. Priscilla Cochran taught English, and she infused her classes with such enthusiasm that I was mesmerized. She loved her subject, and she loved her students. She transmitted to us a sense of pride in learning—and pride in ourselves. Her husband, John Cochran, was the principal and taught math and science. In his classes, I discovered the elegant logic of those subjects, a new awareness that would affect the rest of my high school and college years. I didn't become a mathematician or a scientist, but the principles of logic and organization that I learned from Mr. Cochran were to prove fundamental many years later in business.

The commuting back and forth to Mason came to an end when I reached the tenth grade and entered Booker T. Washington High School in Memphis. That was in 1952, two years before the Supreme Court of the United States would hand down what is arguably the single most important legal decision of the twentieth century—*Brown v. Board of Education*. Because of the Brown case, few children today can even imagine what it might be like to attend schools divided by race. But when I was almost fourteen and going off to my first urban school, segregation was still the law in the South, under the principle of "separate but equal." The "separate" part was rigidly observed, but "equal" never got much attention from the white-run school system.

I was too busy adjusting to my strange, new academic environment to be aware of the upheaval that would occur before I graduated. First of all, I had never attended a large school. There had been fewer than 200 students at Gaylor. The student body at Booker T. Washington was more than 3,000, and it was easy to get lost in the crowd. Being two years younger than my fellow sophomores, I was smaller, and the girls especially looked on me as "that cute little boy." I made good friends among the guys, but I never got past that "little boy" image with the girls—even when I shot up to nearly six feet in height during my senior year. I would grow several more inches in college and finally escape the "little boy" tag, but it shook my social confidence in high school.

18

Luckily, there were other things to do, and I found new interests in school. I took woodworking and met the man whom I still regard as the most influential teacher in my life. His name was Fred Jordan (we called him "Flash Jordan" behind his back, though it was meant as a compliment), and he taught me about the real-world meaning of producing a quality product at a reasonable cost. Initially, I admired Mr. Jordan because he had been a standout athlete during his college days. Under his instruction in the workshop, my hero worship was quickly replaced by genuine respect for the man.

Mr. Jordan loved to repeat the aphorism "waste not, want not," and in his class, we learned to apply the old saying to the items we made and the tools we used. We spent a lot of time on preparation, learning to estimate the amount of wood required for a project with accuracy. Poor preparation was an open invitation to wasted materials and wasted time. Mr. Jordan also made us responsible for the care of our tools. There was no sloppiness, no carelessness, in his shop. Woodworking was a craft that required attention to every detail, down to the last nail.

At the same time, Mr. Jordan encouraged us to think of better ways to get something done. Progress, he told us, depended on knowing what we didn't know, and he taught us to keep our minds open to new ways of thinking. Mastering the basics was the first step; then we would be ready to experiment for ourselves and to appreciate the innovations of other people. I remember him saying, "Be ready—ready to leave somewhere and ready to go somewhere." Years later, I would think about that admonition when I was deciding whether to alter my old ambitions and tackle new challenges.

Under our principal, Mr. Hunt, Booker T. Washington High School was an on-going course in developing confidence and pride. Our school motto was "We lead and others follow," and we took it seriously. Our teachers expected us to make our best efforts, and most of us tried our hardest to live up to their goals. There was an emphasis on collaboration as well as individual achievement in academics and in sports. We were encouraged to work together for shared goals. That may not sound like a novel approach to take with teenagers, but it was a powerful incentive for young black people who were reminded at every turn that in American society, they were excluded from full participation.

Booker T. Washington had terrific football and basketball teams, but we were not allowed to compete with white schools. We couldn't even dream of becoming state champions because we were only permitted to play against other black schools (and in that limited league, our teams were consistent winners). Interestingly, some of the white schools resented this aspect of segregation almost as much as we did, and there were rebellions. Outside the control of the official system, arrangements were made and games were played between black and white teams. I think many of us, regardless of our color, enjoyed defying the established authorities even more than playing the actual games. I couldn't tell you now who won those games, but our teams played hard, and we cheered hard. Win, lose, or draw, I think a lot of us learned from those events. Black or white, we were more alike than we knew.

My new life in Memphis also included jobs. Soon after we moved to the city, Carl and I started our first business—delivering groceries on our bikes. We were paid in nickels and dimes, making maybe fifty cents a week, and to us, that was rich. What we didn't realize was that we were also learning lessons about responsibility and service. We earned our nickels and dimes by doing more than our customers expected and doing it on time. We also discovered that being friendly and polite might be rewarded with a little tip. Most of our customers didn't have much money to spare, but they appreciated dependable and courteous service.

Once I was in high school, Carl and I worked as caddies at Chickasaw Country Club, an elite all-white enclave. On the golf course, I chased balls, cleaned clubs, and learned the game inside and out. The more I knew, the more helpful I could be to my players, and an impressed player was generous to his caddy.

Then we got jobs making deliveries for Speedy's grocery store in south Memphis. On my grocery routes, the lesson of reward for service was affirmed. I earned $12 a week, plus tips. I'd knock at my customers' doors and call out "Speedy, Speedy boy!" The customers liked my smiling cheerfulness, and again, good service won good tips. We began doing so well that the owner of Speedy's, a German immigrant and my first Jewish friend, talked with my brother and me about the importance of saving. Following his advice, I began putting some of my earnings aside—the start of a habit that has served me well ever since.

My next job was my first experience working side by side with adults, and I liked it a lot. I was hired at Baptist Memorial Hospital— the Memphis hospital where Martin Luther King, Jr., would be taken on that awful April night in 1968. My job was cleaning doctors' offices, and I was paid fifty cents an hour, which was good money for a schoolboy in those days. Miss Parker, my supervisor, demanded a very high standard of cleanliness, and for once I was glad about all the household chores my mom made me do. Thanks to Mother, I knew the meaning of "neat and tidy," and my work won the approval of my employer. My only regret about that job is that I lied to get it. The cleaning service wouldn't employ people who were still in school, so I told them I was a dropout. As my dad always taught, a lie hurts the teller most of all, and that lie troubled my conscience for a long time.

My favorite job was unpaid and not really a job. Every Friday, I went along with my friend Doug Williams when he collected the weekly revenues from his paper route. We'd go from house to house, and I had a great time meeting Doug's customers. I never got bored with the routine. I loved the variety of people and the chance to chat with them for a minute or two every week. I wasn't making a penny for my time, but I was gaining insight about myself. Like my father, I found my joy in other people and the opportunity to be of service. Getting to know so many folks—and helping my friend in the process—became its own reward. It made me feel good. Really good. Unknowingly, I was learning another lesson that would affect my entire life. To be successful, the first goal is to determine what you enjoy doing. Then make a living at it, and have fun at what you're doing.

I wasn't ready to make a living for myself when I got my high school diploma. I was just sixteen, and I had years of education and training ahead of me. But self-awareness was dawning. The lessons of childhood and adolescence were beginning to come together and form a pattern for my future.

Chapter 2

The Business of Learning

No race can prosper till it learns there is as much dignity in tilling a field as in writing a poem.

BOOKER T. WASHINGTON, EDUCATOR

The principal of Booker T. Washington High School insisted that our diploma ceremony be called a *commencement*. To his graduating students in June of 1955—all 531 of us dressed up in our caps and gowns—graduation seemed like an ending. We were finally done with high school. But Mr. Hunt wanted us to think of that day as a beginning. Whatever our plans for the future, we had reached the commencement of our adult lives, and that meant new opportunities, new privileges, and new responsibilities.

I got the message about opportunities and privileges; I was less inclined to worry about the responsibilities. I thought of graduation as the sign that I was now grown up, but because I was still sixteen years old, that was a stretch. I didn't think too deeply about my future. Some of my friends were headed for college and others for the military. I wanted to go into the service, but my parents weren't about to let me sign up yet. As I was underage and needed their written permission to enlist, I lost the argument. I would follow their wishes and continue my education. So my family and I spent the summer after my graduation deciding which college I would attend.

There were a number of excellent black colleges in and near Memphis, including my parents' alma maters, LeMoyne and Lane, but I was determined to follow my friends to Tennessee Agricultural and Industrial University (A&I), now Tennessee State University, in Nashville. A&I was the best-known all-black school in the state. It was a public university and—unlike its close neighbor, the private Fisk University—A&I was a powerhouse in the segregated world of collegiate athletics. My favorite high school teacher, Fred Jordan, had been a star football player for A&I, and my respect for him extended to his university. Sports, plus the presence of my friends and the distance from home, was the big attraction for me, and I made up my mind to major in physical education.

I had always loved sports, especially baseball, and Jackie Robinson was my hero. There had been a lot of commotion when he broke the color barrier in the major leagues in 1947, but I wasn't surprised by his triumphs in the previously all-white arena of the majors. I had grown up watching the black men of our local Mason team play with power and brilliance at the ball field behind our house. I'd read avidly the reports of the Negro League baseball games. I knew that we had more than our share of great athletes, and Jackie Robinson was earning us the chance to show it to the world.

My own ambition was to become a coach rather than a player. Because I had been younger and smaller than my classmates, I wasn't able to play varsity sports in high school. But I always had great coaches, starting with my dad. Coaching was a way to combine sports with what was a vague intention to make my living as a teacher. My grandmother Totcy would have understood my thinking; coaching offered the chance to be both a team player and a leader.

When my parents had won the argument over what I would do after high school, they were probably inclined to let me have some leeway about where I would go. I applied to and was accepted by A&I. My dad and I packed up my mother's new red Pontiac—we had recently become a two-car family, which was a big deal for any family in the 1950s—and we all set off on the 200-mile drive east to Nashville. I arrived too late to get into a dormitory, but a school housing officer found me a room in a home on Eaden Street, a short walk from the campus. My parents moved me in, imparted some final wisdom, and said good-bye.

Almost as soon as I waved them farewell, rebellion set in. I headed straight for the nearest grocery, bought a pack of Pall Mall cigarettes, and tucked it into the breast pocket of my nylon shirt for everyone to see. Back in 1955, cigarettes signified rebellion in the same way tattoos and body piercings do now, and the easiest way for a young man to flaunt his independence was to have a cigarette dangling from his mouth. I thought I was a big shot, even though smoking went against everything I had learned from my family and church.

I'm not sure how I could afford cigarettes. My weekly allowance was five dollars, sent from home. It was a reasonable amount for my needs, but not my 'wants,' and I figured out very quickly that I had to find a job. This realization led me to Eugene Story, a man who remains one of my most admired role models. Gene was a twenty-four-year-old Korean War veteran who ran his own dry cleaning business. He hired me part-time to drive his truck and pick up and deliver cleaning, but the most important aspect of my employment was the opportunity to learn from watching Gene work. He was a real pro, dedicated to providing excellent service. He did it by paying close attention to his customers and anticipating their

25

needs. Gene was the genuine article: an ethical businessman who measured his success by the quality of his work and the satisfaction of his customers. He often talked to me about the meaning of service—rarely about money.

I guess I impressed Gene because after a while, he offered to teach me the dry cleaning business from the inside. But I had another plan; I wanted to buy my own vehicle and then contract with Gene to do his deliveries. I talked it over with him, and he thought I had a good idea. To purchase a van, I needed to earn more, so I quit my delivery job (with Gene's approval) and went to work as a dishwasher at Nashville's Baptist Hospital, which was located less than two miles from the A&I campus. It was backbreaking labor and my supervisor was tough, but the pay was good, and I often went beyond the call of duty to establish my value as an employee. Fortunately, my college rebellion hadn't undermined the work ethic instilled in me by my family. The truth is, my rebellion never progressed much further than smoking and some swaggering when I was with my peers. Still, like so many kids on their own for the first time, I was soon burning my candle at both ends, and under the pressures of work, classes and study, and social activities, something had to give. The time I was putting in at Baptist Hospital finally took its toll on my studies, and I had to resign.

In my sophomore year, reality set in—in the form of my father. After I started at A&I, Daddy would pay me periodic visits. He was checking up on me, and he never disguised his motives. Normally, he told me when he was coming to Nashville, and I looked forward to seeing him. But one night he arrived without notice to find me away from my room. He was waiting when I got in at about eleven o'clock, and he was not happy when I told him that I had just been messing around with my friends. He reminded me that I had come to

Nashville to attend school, "not to be out on the street." The next day, he talked to all my instructors, and he asked each of them the same question: "Do you think my son is doing his best in school?" Some said my work was okay; others told him that I could do better. What my dad heard from my teachers didn't square with his philosophy of succeeding by doing one's best.

The upshot was that when I finished the spring quarter of my sophomore year, my parents decided not to send me back to A&I. I didn't entirely agree, but I had little choice since they were paying my bills. Looking back, I think I was also relieved by their decision. Deep down, I probably knew that I had bitten off more than I could chew. I hadn't failed at anything, but neither had I taken full advantage of the opportunities I'd been given.

Once again, I considered military service, but my parents encouraged me to continue college. They wanted me to complete my education, but they also wanted me closer to home—under a tighter rein until I could learn to resist peer pressures and follow my better instincts. They again suggested their own schools, LeMoyne and Lane. Then one of my dad's friends recommended Rust, a liberal arts, United Methodist college in the small town of Holly Springs, Mississippi, about fifty miles south of Memphis. We visited Rust College, and while we were there, we also toured Mississippi Industrial College, which was located across the street. On that tour, I found my academic home.

A POSITIVE CHANGE IN MIDSTREAM

Mississippi Industrial College (known as M.I.) was founded in 1905 by Bishop Elias Cottrell under the auspices of the Christian Methodist Episcopal (CME) Church. Its goal was to educate young men and women in the liberal and industrial arts within a framework of Christian principles. The spiritual emphasis pleased my parents, of course, but it also proved to be of great benefit to me in the sense that I was able to re-focus on my fundamental values and redefine my academic goals in terms of achievement.

I still wasn't a grown-up; I had just turned nineteen when I started at M.I. as a third-year student in January of 1958. I'd almost caught up with my classmates in age, however, and I was much more serious about what I was doing, so the school was a perfect match for me. At A&I, my best education had been outside the classroom—learning about business from Gene Story and several other businessmen I met during my time in Nashville. But at M.I. and at Rust College, where I took required education courses in my senior year, I found myself too focused on what I was learning in my classes to let my schoolwork slide. Back in Mr. Cochran's classes at Gaylor High School in Mason, I had discovered my interest in math and science. Then in my first semester at M.I., I took biology; it fascinated

M.I. was the best of all worlds. The student body was small, fewer than a thousand students. The president knew each of our names within a week or two of our arrival on campus. Believe it or not, he even drove students who were working for their education to their jobs. He, like all the faculty and staff at M.I., understood how difficult it was for their students, many from poor, rural communities, to support themselves (and in some cases, their families) while also pursuing their degrees. Compared to college students today, the young men and women of M.I. might seem very old-fashioned. We dressed conservatively, and the upperclassmen wore ties every day. We went to chapel. We took tremendous pride in our school and in ourselves. And from the top down, the attitude at M.I. was one of mutual respect, regardless of our backgrounds or economic situations.

me. When I mentioned to one of my buddies in the dorm that I might major in biology, he had a good laugh and told me that I couldn't make it through such a rough curriculum. I couldn't let a challenge like that pass, so biology it was.

My rebellious stage had run its course in Nashville, and at M.I., I threw myself into my studies and campus life. Athletics were still important to me, and I found a part-time job officiating for high school girls basketball games. This led to an unforgettable experience: refereeing for the New York Harlem Satellites, a professional team that was an offshoot of the famed Harlem Globetrotters. The Satellites toured the South, playing local college teams, and the games were fantastic. I also did volunteer fundraising for the school's athletic department—by picking cotton. One reason I avoid stereotypes is that they are so often wrong. It's commonplace now to regard picking cotton as a demeaning occupation, something slaves had to do because they had no choice. But my father grew up picking cotton on his father's farm, and Daddy loved it. He was a champion, able to pick more than 500 pounds in a day. When he was a young schoolteacher, he would pick cotton during his fall vacations. The physical nature of the work must have been exhilarating for a man who spent most of the year in a schoolhouse (like the feeling of well-being I now get from long-distance running). I learned to pick from him, and I was good at it, though never as good as my dad. From my parents and my grandparents, I'd learned that *honest work, well done, always dignifies the worker*. So when the M.I. athletic department held cotton-picking contests to raise money, I didn't hesitate to compete. It was a challenge, just like biology.

My father continued to pay visits and to check on my progress with my professors. But what he heard was an entirely different story from the fair-to-middling reports he had gotten at A&I. When he asked if his son was doing his best, my teachers told him "yes." Even in the subjects that were most difficult for me—chemistry and genetics—I was trying hard. The news pleased my father, and it pleased me as well.

There was a time when I worried that black colleges and universities like M.I. were below the standards of white academia, but I was dead wrong. Segregation didn't end in Southern higher education until the late 1960s, and it applied to faculty as well as students. As a result, black intellectuals were clustered in the black colleges and universities—schools without the high profile of the Ivy League but with first-rate professors and instructors whom the white universities would, after integration became the rule, recruit for their scholarship as much as their color. I don't think I could have asked for a better education. At M.I., I learned that there's a big difference between learning how to live and learning how to make a living. My two years there gave me proof of one of my father's teachings: "Figure out ways to make the wrong right." There was nothing right or just about institutionalized racial discrimination, but our African American forebears had beaten the system by establishing and privately funding schools, like M.I. and Rust College, which were extraordinary by every standard that made a difference in the quality of the education.

In May of 1960, with my new diploma in hand, I went home to Memphis, where I lived with my parents until I made some very big decisions. I was twenty-one years old, and I knew that the choices I faced would influence the course of my life. With my science background, I gave a lot of thought to going to medical school. A career in teaching, following in my parent's footsteps, also appealed to me. But a meeting with a friend of the family reminded me of another option.

A.A. Latting was one of Memphis's first black lawyers, and he was widely respected in the community. My dad, who had been in college with Mr. Latting, made an appointment for me to see him. My parents accompanied me, and after Mr. Latting heard my ideas about medical school and teaching, he recommended that I enter the military. This might seem odd advice today, but in 1960, all young men were subject to the military draft. Military service was considered an obligation, and healthy young men like me were sure to be called up sooner or later. There were some deferments available, but they only postponed the inevitable. Mr. Latting reasoned that the best plan was to enlist and complete my obligation before I began a job or graduate study that might be interrupted by a notice from the draft board. By enlisting, I could choose the branch of service I wanted, have more control over the kind of duty I wanted, and add some heavy-duty job experience to my resume.

His logic made sense to me and my parents, so I went to the local Army recruiters and signed on the dotted line. As an enlisted soldier, I committed to a three-year tour of duty. Draftees were called up, on very short notice, for two years, but they had fewer choices and were more likely to wind up as foot soldiers.

I was sent to Fort Jackson, near Columbia, South Carolina, for boot camp and training. Then I was assigned to another company at Fort Jackson, working in personnel, my specialty, for more than a year. But like a lot of soldiers, I was itching to go abroad and see the world. Although Germany was considered the plumb assignment back then, I wanted to go to Laos—an area of the Far East that heated up just before the United States became entangled in Vietnam. There were no openings for my specialty in Laos, so I didn't get my first choice, which was probably a lucky break, and I went to Korea instead. We were sent over by way of Hawaii and Guam—three weeks

31

aboard ship that seemed like the longest weeks of my life. I spent a little more than a year in Korea, at a post about fifteen miles south of the DMZ (de-militarized zone).

Personnel in the Army is similar to an administrative assistant position in business. The reason I was first selected for personnel work was simple: I could type. In the 1950s, typing was considered a woman's job, and most men couldn't do much more than hunt-and-peck—slow, two-fingered, error-prone key-tapping. But with some help from my aunt Nan Johnson, I taught myself to type while I was in high school, and I could accurately turn out sixty words per minute. The Army put my skill to good use.

At Fort Jackson, I started as a clerk for the company commander. By the time I went to Korea, my official designation was "personnel administrative specialist," one of a number of "military operations specialists" involved in support services for the frontline headquarters of my infantry division. My primary responsibility was to make troop assignments and transfers and also to reassign our guys when they returned to the States. My other duties included making temporary duty assignments, administering tests to personnel eligible for proficiency bonuses, and authorizing leaves. It wasn't the most exciting work, but it taught me a lot about the importance of organization and personal discipline.

I really enjoyed my time overseas, being in a part of the world that I would probably never have experienced otherwise. Though the truce that concluded the Korean War in 1953 was generally being observed, there were flare-ups along the DMZ, and the sense of danger was always present, even for those of us who weren't on the front line. The South Koreans were friendly, gracious, hard-working people and glad for our presence in their country. They made us feel welcome. In Korea and also in Japan, where we took our rest-and-recreation leaves, I got my first real-world lessons in the value of ethnic diversity. Despite the language and cultural barriers, I saw that people were more alike than they were different.

By the time of my service, the Army was integrated. Individual service people and officers certainly continued to draw distinctions based on race, but the U.S. Army's official policy was institutionally color-blind. The Army was the first place I experienced integration on a day-to-day basis, with blacks and whites working and living together. Initially, this mixing felt strange, but before we finished basic training, most of us had figured out that it's hard to hate or resent a fellow soldier when you're both enduring the same demands and discipline from drill sergeants who couldn't care less about your skin color. Break 'em down and build 'em up again—the military has a particularly harsh way of turning individuals into a unit. But I didn't miss the lesson: *Successful teams are grounded in common purpose.*

The Army taught me other lessons and firmed up habits I had begun to cultivate in high school and college. One lesson was to be an early riser and to make maximum use of the most productive time of the day. When I was a kid, my mother had to haul me out of bed in the morning, but there were no moms in the military. I had to get myself up and get to work or face the wrath of my superiors. Another lesson was in the value of a structured schedule. There I was, one of literally millions of "employees" of an institution that functioned virtually worldwide. And what made it work was a structure by which everyone knew what he was supposed to do and when he was supposed to do it. It surely wasn't a perfect system; there were plenty of snafus. "Snafu" itself is a word that comes from soldiers' frustration with problems in the structure—the acronym for "situation normal, all fouled up."

I learned almost immediately that it wasn't hard to foul up; intentional or not, mistakes had consequences. I had showed up for my first morning of basic training wearing a mustache, and my sergeant ordered me to shave it off before the next inspection. I thought he meant the next day, but there was another inspection that afternoon, and I hadn't shaved yet. My sergeant took no excuses. I had disobeyed him, and as punishment, I was ordered to scrub out the latrine. It was not an experience I wanted to repeat.

I wound up cleaning the toilets because I failed to clarify the sergeant's order. Grandpa Jimmy's teachings about the importance of clear communication came back to me, and I realized that a message goes two ways. If the sergeant hadn't been clear, it had been *my* responsibility to ask, respectfully, about the time of the next inspection. An order comes down the chain of command, but the soldier at the bottom of the chain has the duty to be sure he understands the order and to ask questions if he doesn't.

Years later, I heard Fred L. Turner, who was then president of McDonald's Corporation, ask a question of a senior manager and then ask the same question of a person on a lower tier of management. He told me that he always went to the top and the bottom for answers; then he squeezed the middle for accuracy. His method affirmed my own approach—what I called "bottom up management"—which traced partly to my Army days. To get the best information and ideas, communication has to flow upward as well as downward in any organization. The person in charge has to be clear about what he wants and open to ideas from below. People down the line must be empowered to speak up, seek clarification, and express their ideas without fear.

Back on that first day in boot camp, I had no idea that I was getting a lesson in command structure that would influence my management philosophy when I supervised others. I just knew that if I had asked one simple question, I wouldn't be on my knees in the latrine.

I served in the Army for two years and eleven months. In June of 1963, I boarded another ship for the first leg of the journey home, going again to Hawaii by way of Guam, then on to the West Coast. (My return trip took only two long weeks.) After my official discharge at a reception center in Oakland, California, I headed for the San Francisco airport to get a plane back to Memphis. That trip is something I'll never forget—my first flight on a jet. While I was serving my tour, the commercial airlines had replaced many of their old prop planes with these sleek, jet-powered birds that crossed the country in astonishingly short time. Being in the Army is something like being in a cocoon; you are so focused on the duties at hand that what doesn't affect you directly seems distant and remote. That jet flight from San Francisco was my first real taste of the United States in the extraordinary decade of the 1960s. I would quickly learn that, as a Bob Dylan song of that decade proclaimed, the times were a changin' for my country and for me.

John F. Kennedy was at the helm, bringing in what seemed like a new era of youthful idealism and hope. The first U.S. astronaut had flown in space. The Peace Corps had been created. The country had also faced down major crises under his presidency—the Bay of Pigs debacle; the construction of the Berlin Wall as the most concrete symbol of the Cold War between the western democracies and the Soviet Union; and Kennedy's face-off with the Russians over the installation of ballistic missiles in Cuba. Meanwhile, our government was quietly ratcheting up its involvement in Vietnam.

The civil rights crusade was expanding, and barriers were beginning to crack. Following on the Supreme Court's 1954 ruling outlawing segregation in public schools, courts across the country were demolishing legal obstacles to equality. Under the passive resistance doctrine espoused by Dr. Martin Luther King, Jr., people my age and younger were demanding change. The "sit-in" movement had been launched in February of 1960 when four black students were refused service at a Woolworth's lunch counter in Greensboro, North Carolina. Within a year, sit-ins were being staged throughout the South, and "freedom riders" were traveling the region in old buses to protest segregation in the national transportation system. In the autumn of 1962, James Meredith had enrolled in the University of Mississippi—the first black student at that all-white Southern bastion. But it had taken 3,000 troops to quell the riots that preceded his admission.

At about the same time I was making my way home from Korea, Governor George Wallace was resisting the integration of the University of Alabama and backing down in the face of the National Guard. A day after Ole Miss was integrated, civil rights activist Medgar Evers was assassinated in Mississippi. I had just returned from what was considered one of the most dangerous places in the world, yet it was the escalating violence against peaceful protestors in my own country that truly shocked me.

I was living in my parents' home on August 28, 1963, when nearly a quarter-million people assembled in Washington, D.C., to present their demands for passage of the omnibus civil rights bill that was languishing in Congress. Under a sweltering sun, they gathered on the Mall and around the reflecting pool before the Lincoln Memorial. Under the bronze gaze of the statue of "the Great Emancipator," who had freed the slaves a hundred years before, they heard dozens of speakers calling for absolute equality under the law. But the moment everyone was waiting for—those on the Mall and all

36

of us watching our black-and-white TVs—came when Dr. King stepped to the lectern. He began speaking in quiet, solemn tones about the debt owed by the nation to its Negro citizens. As his speech progressed, he chronicled the abuses suffered by black people every day of their lives and in every part of the country. He laid out the grievances, and then, in a rising voice, he said, "I have a dream that one day this nation will rise up and live out the true meaning of its creed: 'We hold these truths to be self-evident; that all men are created equal.' "

I had followed Dr. King's career, but I hadn't seen him speak before. It was electrifying. The speech wasn't long, but I had never heard the case for equality, and for restraining the impulse to meet violence with violence, made with such power and eloquence. Dr. King's dream became our dream: an America in which all people "will not be judged by the color of their skin but by the content of their character."

I hadn't been totally isolated in the Army. When the sit-ins began in 1960, I was at Fort Jackson, and some of my friends and I wanted to get involved with local civil rights groups during our off-duty hours. It didn't occur to us that the United States Army, which took great pride in its own integrated status, would have problems with our plans, but we were soon set right. No member of the military was allowed to participate in any civil rights activities. The ruling angered us, but short of risking court martial, there was no way to fight it.

Once I was a civilian again, I found myself following the news more closely than ever before, and as I read about and watched the events of the summer unfold, my own consciousness was being raised. Things that I'd accepted when I was younger now grated on my sense of right and wrong. In the Army, people of every color had lived together and shared facilities. Why should it be different in the rest of the country? Why were restrooms and water fountains legally separated as "Whites" and "Colored"? Why were blacks not allowed to try on clothing in the fitting rooms of white-owned stores? Why did blacks have separate entrances to stores and restaurants and movie theaters? Why, if they worshipped the same God, were black people excluded from worshipping in white churches? All the divisions and distinctions I had taken as normal when I was a child now hit me with the force of a slap in the face.

I had served my country, and in the process, I had gained confidence in my abilities and my social skills. I'd shed the shyness that had dogged me since boyhood, when I was always the youngest kid in class. Now, home again in Memphis, I was ready to decide what I wanted to do with my life. It didn't take long for me to see that segregation would affect my choices. For all the good that the civil rights movement was accomplishing, life in my corner of the South hadn't changed that much in my absence. If I wanted to achieve my own goals, I had to understand, as I never had before, that the system was against me. Could the system itself be changed? I wasn't sure.

Chapter 3

Mapping Out a New Course

*Human beings, by changing the inner attitudes of their minds,
can change the outer aspects of their lives.*

WILLIAM JAMES, PHILOSOPHER

After my military service, I spent two years figuring out what to do next. In the Army, I'd learned new skills, adapted to a new way of living with people, and built up my self-confidence. But I still wasn't sure about the direction I wanted to take. I was twenty-four years old, and I had a number of interests that might turn into careers. I needed to give myself time to experiment and explore my options.

From the summer of 1963 to the next summer, I lived with my parents, and by day, I taught school. My mother and father were both teachers and loved what they did, so it seemed a natural choice for me. My old ambition to coach surfaced again, and I was employed by the Memphis school system in what amounted to a full-time substitute position as a physical education instructor for grades seven and eight. I also taught square dancing, which was included in the phys ed curriculum—don't ask me why. Substitute teaching took me into a number of schools, and I often spent many weeks with my classes when a regular teacher was out or no teacher was available—enough time to get to know the kids and the system. I really liked working with those young people, and from them, I learned a great deal about how to instruct with a combination of discipline, clarity, and respect.

I had been teaching for just a couple of months when President Kennedy was assassinated in Dallas on November 22, 1963. That's when I saw how important teachers are in times of crisis. Over almost five days, from Thursday afternoon through the following Monday, the nation watched as the president's body was brought from Texas to Washington, laid in state in the rotunda of the U.S. Capitol, and then taken to its final resting place in Arlington Cemetery. Many of us also saw the presumed assassin, Lee Harvey Oswald, murdered before our eyes on television. The whole country was in shock as we tried to figure out what was happening. It's difficult to say who suffered most, but I think it was young people, adolescents and teens like my students. They were the first generation of Baby Boomers; they had grown up under the cloud of the Cold War, but for most of them, violence was still something isolated and rare. John F. Kennedy was a hero to many of these children, and for black youths especially, he seemed to embody the promise of change. Suddenly he was gone. A new man was in his place, and most of us knew little about him. As it turned out, Lyndon Johnson would be the great ally of the civil rights movement, spearheading the passage and enforcement of the Civil Rights Act of 1964 that at last guaranteed equal rights to all Americans, regardless of race, color, or creed. But that was in the future.

My school assignment at that time was Hyde Park School. I wasn't teaching on the day of the assassination, but my fellow teachers told me how the kids had reacted—the bewildered confusion when everyone heard about the shooting, the fearful waiting for more information. Then came the announcement that the president was dead. A friend of mine still remembers how she and the other teachers had no time for reflection because they were too busy helping the children. Some of the kids were racked with sobbing, and some became physically ill. Others were dazed and wandered from their classrooms into the school corridors. Nothing like this had ever happened before, and there was no protocol for handling the outpouring of fear and grief and panic. Those good teachers ministered to their children with love and compassion that day, just as teachers were doing in schools all across the country. It saddens me that in the years that have followed, we have become accustomed to such horrific events and that today, we see nothing odd in the fact that school systems rush in trained grief counselors to manage such tragedies.

By the time I went back to Hyde Park School, everything was calm again, but I could sense the change in my students. I saw the sadness in many eyes and the anger in some. The president—a man in whom their parents and other black Americans placed so much hope and whom the children themselves had come to love—was dead. Nobody knew why he'd been murdered, though all kinds of half-baked theories were going around. But Kennedy's killer had robbed us of his optimism and shaken our still innocent faith in the peaceful resolution of the country's ills. That's a dreadful thing to do to anyone, particularly a child.

Despite the pleasure I got from my students and my colleagues, I decided over the course of the school year that formal teaching wasn't for me. Unlike my father, I didn't feel called to teach and couldn't picture myself making it my career. To be honest, money was a big issue. Teaching was not lucrative, and in those days, blacks were paid much less than whites, no matter how far they rose in the profession. Single or married, most male teachers I knew had to take

41

one or more additional jobs to get by.

I was also wary of the bureaucratic nature of the public education system. I guess I'd had my fill of paperwork and regulations in the Army. Full-time employment in a large school system offered security and a little chance for advancement. With integration in its early stages, there might be more opportunities ahead for blacks, but there wasn't much room for creativity. My dad had a lot more freedom as principal of a segregated, small-town elementary school in a rural county, where the powers-that-be were not too interested in the quality of the education black children received. With nobody looking over his shoulder, he had been able to set a standard of excellence for himself and his teachers and to cultivate the virtues of honesty, integrity, and diligence among his pupils. He could develop methods that really suited his students, without having to dot every *I* and cross every *T* just to satisfy some bureaucrat. But that kind of creative problem solving was disappearing, just like one-room schoolhouses were. As I saw it, the school system that was evolving in the 1960s was becoming too rigid and too political for my taste.

It was my cousin Erman Porter who pointed me down another road. Like me, Erman had recently completed his military service and returned to Memphis. He told me about a local trade school, Keegan's School of Radio Broadcasting and Television, that he was attending. Keegan's School was well known in Memphis and other parts of the South. Johnny Cash had graduated from there, and so had a good number of the on-air and behind-the-scenes people in the region's radio stations.

A radio career sounded interesting to me. At Mississippi Industrial College, I'd had my first serious public speaking experiences, and I had enjoyed standing up in front of people and having my say. Shy at first, I'd learned to control the normal nervousness and focus on the message I wanted to convey. Also, I grew up listening to radio, and even after my family got our first TV set, radio was the medium that brought us our music and sports and news. Television back then had almost no black faces, except for a few athletes and character actors. If we wanted to hear black voices, we turned our radios to the black-owned stations that were flourishing across the South. The idea of being one of those voices appealed to me, and I signed up for the course.

The school was segregated. White students attended classes during the day; classes for blacks were taught at night and in a different location. In this instance, segregation worked for me, because the evening classes suited my teaching schedule. But a problem came up almost immediately that might have ended my effort. The school's tuition was expensive, and after several classes, only two students, a young woman and I, had paid in full. The president of the school met privately with both of us and told us that he was going to dismiss the class until the other students paid. When they didn't pay up, the class wasn't reconvened. The two of us who had paid never got our money back, and it might have been a bitter lesson, except for the integrity of our teacher, a young white man named Tom Davis.

Mr. Davis worked at two Memphis radio stations, one black (WLOK-AM) and one white. His sense of fairness was challenged by the school's decision to cancel the class without refunding our money, and he was determined to do the right thing. Instead of writing us off, he continued our class at his own home. Our 'laboratory' was the studio of WLOK, which was one of the first black-owned radio stations in the country. He wasn't compensated for his time, but he saw to it that we completed the course. (Keegan's eventually re-opened the training program for blacks and changed its policy to allow monthly installment payments of tuition.)

I have never forgotten Tom Davis. His personal decision to fulfill the contract we'd made with the school was one of the most valuable lessons I ever got in the true meaning of service. Without asking anything in return, he went the extra mile and more to see that we got full value for our investment. I learned a lot about radio from him; I gained a great deal more from his example.

Going on the Air in Mississippi

My brother, Carl, had graduated from Alcorn State University and moved to Greenville, Mississippi, where he was the director of the colored YMCA. Around the time I completed my training at Keegan's, Carl called me about a possible job at a Greenville station, WESY. One of their announcers was moving to a larger market, and Carl thought I should apply for the position. I had been on air only once, at WLOK during a class, but I was ready to try. I drove down to Greenville, an old Delta town about 140 miles south of Memphis. Carl introduced me to J. Brown, the announcer who was leaving, and I visited him at the station. J. and I talked, and then he called the station manager, Paul Ottman. Mr. Ottman wanted to hear me, so he told J. to put me on the air. I had done thirty minutes of broadcasting when Mr. Ottman called back, asking J. to keep me at the station until he could get there. Within an hour, I was hired and would start the next day. All of a sudden, I had a new job, a new town, a new direction.

It would be too easy to say that getting the job at WESY was a case of being at the right place at the right time. I wouldn't have known about the opening if Carl hadn't been friends with J. Brown. Nobody called it "networking" back then, but that's what got me the chance. My network at that time was my brother, but it made me think about the importance of developing friendships in business as well as in one's personal life.

Before I could take over, I had to get my broadcast license, so I spent my first day on the job studying for the test and another day driving down to New Orleans to take the test. I passed, and soon I was on the air every day with "The Roland Jones Show." I was an announcer/disc jockey; my job was to select and play music that I thought my listeners wanted to hear and to fill the breaks with talk. In those days, radio wasn't rigidly formatted as it is now, and DJs attracted listeners as much with their personalities as the music. DJs also read the news and many of the commercials and sometimes wrote selected copy. There was a strong component of public service in broadcasting back then, and radio was a primary medium for breaking news, which we could get on air before the town's newspapers hit the streets. "Live" meant something; aside from the records we played, virtually everything was broadcast in real time. If I made a mistake, it was out there for everyone to hear. There were no second takes or tape delays, so a DJ had to be able to think fast, stay on his toes, and handle lots of tasks at once—all the while keeping his patter lively and interesting.

WESY featured music that appealed specifically to a black audience, mostly a mix of rhythm and blues, jazz, and gospel. That was a great time for R&B, which was at last making inroads into the mainstream, especially among white teens and college kids. Radio was bringing the music to a wider audience, but the clubs were the real home of R&B then. Musicians whose names are legendary today—James Brown, Ray Charles, B.B. King, Ike and Tina Turner before their split—made their living and honed their talents on the black nightclub circuit. The payment for all but a few black performers was still low, so the clubs in Greenville could afford really

45

fine musicians. The town's then all-white leadership liked to play up Greenville's antebellum and Civil War history (skirting the slavery issue), its Delta traditions, and its status as "the towboat capital of the world." But with a majority black population, Greenville was also a great music town, and in the clubs I often heard and met the performers whose music I featured on my program. Now, when I hear anyone say, "Those were the days," I know just what they mean. My radio days were something else.

Soon after I joined WESY, Carl discovered a neighborhood grocery store that was for sale. We pooled our resources and bought the store for $500. We re-named it Jones Food Market, and we made it a success by offering a level of service that our competitors couldn't or wouldn't match. When we weren't at our regular jobs, we were at the store, doing everything we could to please our customers. We made home deliveries; we stayed open late; we gave out free candy to the children whose parents shopped with us. We were known for selling "the coldest beer in town," and as a fringe benefit of my job at WESY, I got to do two radio ads a day for the store. Word went around about the Jones brothers and their service, and it wasn't long before folks would pass by their usual shopping places to come to our store.

The importance of good service was something Carl and I had learned years before from our Grandpa Jimmy Jones and our Grandear Hattie Williamson, the entrepreneurs in our family. We'd had our own boyhood experience working together when we'd delivered groceries for our neighbors in Memphis and earned our tips by being prompt and courteous. It had been reinforced by the jobs we took during high school and college. For me, the Army had also been a kind of service-oriented job, because personnel, by definition, means working with people and doing one's best to keep them happy. I also thought about the businessmen in Nashville who had befriended me when I was a greenhorn college student. I remembered how Gene Story emphasized personal service: When you were selling something that is basically the same as what other people are selling, it's the way you treat your customers and the extra attention you pay to each of them that gives your business the edge.

Jones Food Market was Carl's and my first chance to put all the pieces together, drawing on our own experiences and the examples of others. We had always worked well together. We can be very different in the way we think, but our individual strengths tended to complement each other. It's a good thing we got along, even when we had our disagreements, because in Greenville, we were almost always together, except when I was at the radio station and Carl was at the Y. Looking back, I realize that we didn't have much of a social life; our time was consumed by our jobs and our store. But we had a terrific time.

We lived in a rented house with several other guys, and we often had friends staying with us. We were also carrying a secret that none of us dared to tell. A number of our houseguests were strangers when they first came to stay, and just having them in our house put everyone in jeopardy. They were young white men, mostly college students from the North and East, who were among the hundreds of civil rights activists pouring into the South to work for the black cause.

For a couple of years before my move to Greenville, Mississippi had been a special target in the struggle to achieve voting rights for blacks. In 1962, local civil rights groups had joined with the major national organizations to form the Council of Federated Organizations—COFO. This new body recruited students from Harvard and Stanford to come to Mississippi for their summer breaks and train black citizens in their rights and the process of voting. The success of their first efforts—in spite of attempts to intimidate the students with threats and actual physical assault—led to an expanded push for black voter registration and establishment of an official political entity to counter Mississippi's segregated Democratic Party. Additionally, the movement planned to open "freedom schools" for black children and centers where poor blacks could get free health care service and legal help. The summer of 1964, when I moved to Greenville, was designated Freedom Summer.

The white power structure was determined to quash the project and rid the state of "outside agitators," one of the nicer terms for the student activists. Laws were passed that made the "freedom schools" illegal and effectively banned economic boycotts. Law enforcement agencies, from local police to the state highway patrol, increased their numbers and their armament—and not to protect civil rights workers. The eight hundred young activists who volunteered to come south that summer were warned of the dangers, but they came anyway. Almost as soon as they arrived, they got a terrible lesson in the meaning of justice in Mississippi.

In late June, three young men—Andrew Goodman and Michael Schwerner, both from New York, and James Chaney, a Mississippian—set out from Meridian to investigate a church burning in a nearby community. Goodman and Schwerner were white; Chaney was black. They were picked up for speeding by a deputy sheriff in Philadelphia, Mississippi, and released. Then they disappeared. As the search for the three men continued through July, the U.S. Congress passed and President Johnson signed the 1964 Civil Rights Act, further infuriating Mississippi's segregationists.

I clearly remember the day in August when the bodies were found buried in an earthen dam on a farm near Philadelphia. All three men had been shot; Chaney, the black man, had also been beaten. On air, I read reports about the murders and the subsequent charges against twenty-one white men, including the deputy sheriff who had arrested the three activists. (The state charges were dismissed, but six of the men were eventually tried and convicted under federal civil rights law.)

The fact that white supremacists were violent was not news to us. Stories of blacks being harassed and beaten and of black churches and meeting places being bombed and burned out were all too frequent. In Mississippi, whites had long been able to literally get away with murder when the victim was African American. In 1955, two NAACP organizers had been killed when they tried to register black voters. That same year, fourteen-year-old Emmett Till had been brutalized and murdered for the "crime" of speaking disrespectfully to a white woman. There had been other deaths and other failures of justice in the years that followed. But somehow the murders of Goodman, Schwerner, and Chaney galvanized the national press and influenced public opinion across the country. Maybe it was because two of the victims were white or because even in dying, the black man had been singled out for special pain and degradation. But for right-thinking Americans, whatever their color, it was no longer possible to regard Mississippi as just an embarrassing backwater. The state was now a battleground where an army of people committed to non-violent action were engaged in a life-or-death struggle against the forces of ignorance and evil.

When I look back on those days, I'm still awed by the bravery of those volunteer civil rights workers and of ordinary Mississippians, black and white, who resisted every threat and stood firm in the face of every violent act. A few of the volunteers left the state after the murders, but more came to help and many stayed on after Freedom Summer ended. They were always in danger, especially when they traveled from place to place, and they needed safe places to stay. Our house became one of those places, and we felt privileged to help the volunteers. Getting to know those young white men from all parts of the country affected my thinking, as the Army had. When you are sharing space and secrets with guys from New York and Ohio and California, it widens your world and opens your mind to new possibilities.

I enjoyed my job at WESY so much that I thought I had found my career in radio. But something began to happen that troubled me. As the year went on, the station management seemed to become more timid about reporting on civil rights activities. One day, just after I had broadcast a United Press wire story concerning Dr. Martin Luther King, Jr., the station manager called me. He said that we would no longer be including news about Dr. King or any civil rights stories. There was some kind of justification, as I recall, that the station shouldn't appear to be taking sides—"not with MLK or the KKK or any of them." But it was clear that management was scared. I could understand the fear, but I just couldn't accept letting our listeners down by depriving them of information. I had always ended my news segments with these words: "You've just heard the world's best coverage of the world's biggest news." Apart from the obvious exaggeration, that statement was true in my experience. Until that day, we hadn't censored ourselves, and we'd served our audience well.

For the most part, I conformed to the station manager's directive, but I wasn't happy about it. As 1964 turned into 1965, I came to the decision that I wanted to stay in radio but not in Mississippi. I was sure I could find better opportunities outside the South. I talked it over with Carl, and he understood. The store was going well, and he would keep it running. I planned to resign in the spring; then I learned that J. Brown, the announcer I had replaced, was coming back to Greenville and WESY was hiring him again. Before I could hand in my resignation, I was fired—the only time I was ever fired. I don't remember being too upset about it, since I was ready for another move. I didn't have a job to go to, but I was pretty sure I could find something better. The truth is, I was thinking more about *where* I'd like to work and live. St. Louis, Milwaukee, and Chicago were high on my list.

MOVING ON, AND OUT OF THE SOUTH

I went back to Memphis briefly, and my parents were supportive of the change I was making. I had a 1958 Chevy at the time, but Daddy wanted me to take his new '65 Impala as I set out on my job search. I think he knew that I would be leaving the South for good, and he wanted to be sure I was safe on my journey, wherever it might take me.

My dad was going to a church conference in Oklahoma, and I made the trip with him. After we returned home, I took his car and drove on to St. Louis. Before we parted, Daddy had some advice for me. He realized that it might not be so easy for me to find just the job I wanted right away, so he reminded me that I was responsible for making the most of whatever work I did. "You don't lower yourself by doing any job," he said. "You dignify the job by doing your best." He made me promise to drive carefully and call home every night. Then he repeated one of his favorite sayings: "Autograph your job with excellence." I had heard him say the same thing hundreds of times, but the message never lost its impact.

In St. Louis, I set up my first interview at a radio station, and it was going really well—until the interviewer, a white man, addressed me as "boy." Maybe he didn't realize he'd said it or how

51

condescending that term is, but I had served my country, taken on a man's responsibilities, and run my own business. His remark seemed to express the kind of casual, ingrained bigotry that I wanted to put behind me. I hadn't left Mississippi to be anybody's "boy." I finished the meeting politely, and the interviewer arranged a second meeting. I probably could have gotten the job, but I didn't go back. I had already decided that St. Louis wasn't for me.

I was going to try Chicago next, but I had been talking with a cousin of mine, John Perry, who was working in Washington, D.C. John asked me to come visit him and look for employment there. He said that jobs were plentiful in the capital city, so I figured it was worth a shot. I was anxious to get back to work, and when I got to Washington, I quickly applied at several radio stations. There were no openings for announcers right then, so I decided to find something else, just to fill in until a radio position became available. I had no intention of changing my direction.

It's funny how things happen. I only wanted work so that I could support myself for a little while. I went to an employment agency on Friday, July 2, 1965, and was assigned to a counselor, Miss Page. At first she wasn't sure she could place me. As a college graduate and military vet, I was over-qualified for most of the jobs she had. Then she saw something she thought might suit me—a management trainee spot with Gee Gee Distributing Corporation, the largest franchisee in the McDonald's system. I wasn't sure about a restaurant job, but Miss Page was persuasive. She arranged for me to see a man named Bud Dawson in personnel on the following Monday, July 5. That was the first year when national holidays were observed on the closest weekday, and Miss Page wondered if I minded meeting on a day that most people had off. I didn't mind at all, and I was glad to have the weekend to do some 'detective work.'

I knew little about McDonald's, which had relatively few locations in the South at the time. Once, some friends and I had gotten hamburgers at a McDonald's in Memphis, but only after we'd agreed to go to the store's back door to pick up our purchase. I also remembered a trip I had taken to Birmingham with my parents. We had driven past a McDonald's, and I'd been impressed by the long line of customers being served at the side window. (Years later, when I was an executive in the corporation, I visited that same McDonald's during a business trip to Alabama. I noticed a glass window on the side of the red and white tile building and asked about its operational purpose. My question got a laugh, and finally somebody explained that it was the old "Colored" window and hadn't been used in years. I got more laughs when I told the story of my first sight of this particular restaurant and my realization, in retrospect, that all the customers waiting in that long line were African Americans.)

I used the weekend before my interview to visit several McDonald's restaurants in the D.C. area. I observed service that was consistently superb, and, more important, I didn't see a single incident of discrimination. As a result, I looked forward to my interview at Gee Gee. The interview was good, and when Mr. Dawson, the director of personnel, offered me the trainee job, I accepted without a second's thought. There was a downside, though, and Bud was upfront about it. Gee Gee was not going to pay the employment agency's placement fee. Basically, for the $383 I owed to the agency, I'd bought myself a job that earned $100 a week.

Though unexpected, it was a debt that I was willing to assume. I had grown up on my Grandpa Jimmy's philosophy: "You're not free until you're debt-free." So far, I had borrowed little and paid my own way. I'd paid cash for my Keegan's School tuition, used my own money to finance my part of the store in Greenville, and paid off my

53

car. When I got to Washington, I was free of debt but cash poor, so my mother sent me the money for the employment agency. She meant it as a gift, but I considered it a short-term loan. Mother was always more free with financial help than Daddy, when she decided the need was a worthy one. But she had made so many sacrifices for Carl and me when we were in school, and I wasn't about to let her do it again. Even when someone at McDonald's suggested that the company might be able to help with the fees, I appreciated the offer but declined it because I didn't want exceptions made for me. I wanted to stand on my own. My family's ethic was now my personal ethic, and I would pay my mother back by myself. (A year later, Carl sold our Greenville grocery, and we made a small profit. We kept some for ourselves, but it was two proud sons who presented most of the proceeds to our mother, in gratitude.)

When I was visiting those McDonald's restaurants over the July holiday weekend, I was aware of other teachings from my family. I watched closely how each store was run. Though I knew nothing about the restaurant industry, I got a strong sense that here was a company providing a consistently superior level of customer service. If my grandmother Totcy had been with me, she would have liked the way the managers worked with their young employees and the efficiencies they achieved with teamwork. She'd probably have said that McDonald's was a company where a person could "stand out and not blend in."

I had liked working with kids when I was teaching, and that would be essential to the job. McDonald's restaurants were staffed almost entirely by teenagers—boys only back then. I was definitely overqualified for a trainee, and I later learned that all the black managers in Washington were college-educated while most of the white managers were high school graduates. That didn't matter much to me. Somehow, I knew that I had been handed an opportunity to do what I wanted—give service, learn with and eventually teach younger people, and if I succeeded, become a leader.

Fate, luck, necessity—whatever had guided me to the office of Miss Page, the employment counselor, set me on a path I had never considered before. I understood that the work would initially be lowly and demanding when I accepted Bud Dawson's job offer. But whatever I was expected to do, I was determined to "autograph my work with excellence." Just like the time in college when my friend said I couldn't handle a hard major like biology, I was challenged by this new opportunity that had dropped into my lap. When Bud told me to report the next day to a store in the D.C. suburb of Alexandria, Virginia, I was ready to get started. Whether I was truly prepared for the role of a trainee was another question.

Chapter 4

The Bottom Line Is Service

Real success is finding your lifework in the work that you love.
DAVID MCCULLOUGH, HISTORIAN AND BIOGRAPHER

I was out in the parking lot, up to my armpits in soap and dirty water, and I was not happy. *I got a college degree for this?*

My first assignment on my first day as a McDonald's management trainee was outside maintenance, cleaning and scrubbing the restaurant's trash cans. This might not sound so bad, but the year was 1965, and nobody used can liners then. It was July, and in the D.C. area, that meant very hot and very humid. Discarded food stewed in the red and white plastic cans until it was dumped, leaving a stinking, disgusting mess. I had cleaned plenty of garbage cans as a kid, but I didn't expect to be doing the same job after finishing college, completing a three-year hitch in the Army, teaching for a year, and spending another year as a radio announcer and owner of a successful grocery store.

Earlier that morning, I had reported at the restaurant on Duke Street in Alexandria to find myself one of three trainees—me and two young white men named Brad and Brian. The restaurant manager was

56

out on vacation that week, and John Zimba, the first assistant manager, greeted us with some frustration. Having a black trainee in the all-white restaurant didn't faze John. He was a great guy who really cared about the store and its employees. But he'd never had to deal with three new trainees at one time; usually Gee Gee Distributing sent just one trainee to a store. With the manager away, John had the restaurant to run, so he turned us over to the second assistant manager and gave him a list of tasks for us. The second assistant manager got to decide who did what. The white trainees were assigned inside jobs; I got the trash cans. The second assistant manager wanted them cleaned to perfection—something that hadn't been done in a while—but he didn't tell me what materials and equipment to use. I found those answers for myself in the McDonald's operations manual.

At the time, I assumed that I got the trash cans because of my color. But later on, I was told that the people at the store had formed a totally off-base impression of me that first day, and it was all because of my car. I was driving my dad's sharp new Chevy Impala, and when they saw me park it, some of them assumed I was a 'rich guy.' So having me scrub out garbage could have been the second assistant manager's way of testing me to find out if I was up to the job. Or it might have been just the luck of the draw. I'll never know what he was really thinking, but over the years, I have learned not to make too many snap judgments about other people's motives.

At any rate, a couple of hours of hot, grimy work made me angry enough to quit, but giving up—even when it was justified—didn't fit my work ethic. My dad had taught me to "autograph your work with excellence." It was up to me to dignify the job, not the other way round. So I scrubbed those cans until they looked like new, and it paid off in an unexpected way.

I was still hosing out the garbage cans when the vacationing restaurant manager stopped by to check up on the store. Unlike John Zimba, the manager didn't seem pleased to learn that his store had a black trainee. Alexandria was an old, historic, and nearly all-white suburb. The area was undergoing a wave of restoration and renovation, and it attracted upwardly mobile, white government workers, middle managers, journalists, academics, and students. African Americans, who made up the majority of people living and working in D.C. proper, were rarely seen in Alexandria, except when they were coming and going from their jobs in low-end service and domestic positions.

The manager made his feelings obvious by talking with the other trainees and pointedly ignoring me. I think he may have wanted to let me go, but since I was employed by Gee Gee Distributing, the franchise owner and his boss, he had no authority to fire me. What I didn't know at the time was that Gee Gee—owned by John Gibson, a Miller Beer distributor and former Assistant Secretary of Labor, and Oscar Goldstein—was actively trying to recruit black employees for management slots. Gibson and Goldstein had the exclusive McDonald's franchise for all of D.C. and northeastern Virginia, plus several Maryland counties in the D.C. area. They were smart men, and I figure they knew which way the winds of change were blowing. They already owned a number of inner-city stores, and it made sense to employ black managers for their holdings in urban and predominately black D.C. neighborhoods. Bud Dawson, the man who hired me, had been brought in from Pennsylvania with a specific mandate to upgrade restaurant management and find black men with management potential.

I'd just finished the cans when the manager was leaving the restaurant. Clearly, he didn't intend to speak to me, but a woman customer stopped him in the parking lot.

I heard her tell him, "That young man has got those trash cans so clean! I've never seen cans so clean. You ought to give him a raise."

That woman's unsolicited praise was the reward I needed. She must have impressed the manager too. When he returned from his vacation the next week, he treated me with cordiality, even when he was correcting my work. He never got involved in my training, though, and that was just fine, since John Zimba took a genuine interest in me. John was later promoted to director of training, and we became friends. After I became a manager, he and I would often discuss the realities of the newly integrated McDonald's workforce and my role in it. I also got to be friends with my two fellow trainees, especially Brian Jillson. They didn't have any problems with my color. We were just three guys in the same boat, and that was a tight bond.

Our training lasted about four weeks, and then I was assigned to a store on Annapolis Road in Landover, Maryland—another white suburb. Now I was a second assistant manager. At the Duke Street store, we had been trained in all the areas of operations, but I was especially happy doing work that brought me in direct contact with customers. I'd worked all the restaurant stations—fries, grill, shakes, and so on—but what I really enjoyed was counter service, taking orders, ringing up sales on the cash register, and getting customer responses. (The cash register was the old-fashioned kind, a metal monster that did little more than tote up numbers, and it really did make a "cha-ching" sound when the cash drawer sprang open.)

There had been a terrific kid at Duke Street, a high school student named Clarence Hoop, who showed me how to use the register. His approach to counter service was remarkable: genuine enthusiasm and courtesy combined with accuracy and speed. I never saw him let down; he had a smile and pleasant words for everybody. Clarence was all of sixteen years old, but he taught me so much about the meaning of service and professionalism that, to this day, I consider him a role model. It was from him first of all that I really saw how important it is to be open and to seek opportunities to learn from anybody, regardless of their age or position.

I think now that one of the Duke Street manager's issues with me was his fear that white customers would react badly to being waited on by a black man. He needn't have worried; if any customer ever had a problem with me, I never heard about it. There were no complaints when I was in training and none when I was at the Annapolis Road restaurant.

Although I worked in Maryland for only five weeks, I quickly got a reputation for giving good service. Clarence Hoop had shown me the bottom-line benefits of enthusiastic service, and I followed his example when I moved to the Annapolis Road store. Pretty soon, customers were looking for me when they came into the restaurant— the black guy with the big smile who assembled their orders rapidly and bagged them correctly, presented their meals cheerfully, made sure they received the right change in return, and always said "thank you." McDonald's didn't allow tips, but some people insisted on leaving money for me, and my co-workers began to joke that the customers were "throwing their money at Roland." I was just doing what I enjoyed—giving a level of service that impressed the customer. Without really thinking too much about it, however, I had stumbled onto one of the basic business principles underlying the success of the McDonald's Corporation.

QSC—The McDonald's Way

Ray Kroc, founder of the company, was one of the most astute business leaders of the twentieth century, and he was famous for stating his ideas in folksy language that everyone could understand and relate to. He said, "Every job at McDonald's depends on customers coming into our stores." He believed, with a rare kind of passion, that all customers should be treated with "tender loving care."

His original McDonald's restaurants were easily recognized by their huge golden arches—two bright yellow, arc-shaped, lighted structures that rose high above each store and stood out in even the most visually cluttered suburban and urban landscapes. (Though the architecture of McDonald's stores has been toned down since the 1970s, the arches remain prominent in the company logo and signage.) But what truly set McDonald's apart was Mr. Kroc's golden rule of service: Every employee at every level should "look at everything we do from the customer's perspective." Customers must always *feel* that they are right; that was our job.

Sounds obvious, but it's amazing to me how many businesses fail because their customers are treated as an afterthought. Mr. Kroc understood that when customers are impressed by the quality of both the product *and the service*, they are happy. Happy customers generate money, not the other way around. They may be inclined to order more—fries with their burger or fish sandwich, for example—thereby increasing sales and profits. Customers who are impressed by standout service also tend to be repeat customers and 'recommenders,' bringing in new customers through their word-of-mouth recommendations.

In the restaurant business, from the most expensive

establishment to the local short-order diner, success depends on three fundamentals: good food, good service, and a clean and wholesome environment. The most delectable food in the world will rarely compensate for poor service in a really unpleasant setting. Excellent service can sometimes make a less than satisfactory meal acceptable. A customer who feels comfortable and is treated respectfully might give a restaurant a second chance after she has a mediocre or poor meal. But a customer is unlikely to return if the service has been rude or inept or the restaurant itself is filthy. Mr. Kroc preached QSC—quality, service, and cleanliness—in everything. "Do it first class," he said. Never compromise on the fundamentals.

My own growing focus on the importance of service was affirmed by my next assignment—an inner-city McDonald's on Good Hope Road in a part of D.C. that was considered in transition. It was a working class neighborhood, once predominantly white but rapidly shifting to a majority black population. I was brought on as first assistant manager, which involved more responsibility (first assistant managers normally handled the night shift and would run the stores whenever the managers weren't on hand) and greater exposure to the business side of operations. During my six months at the Good Hope Road restaurant, more often than not, I had to shoulder the full weight of responsibility. My manager was a drinker, and even when he came to work, he frequently wasn't fit to do his job. The first assistant, whom I was replacing, wasn't in much better condition. By default, their duties fell to me. It was a trial by fire; I learned how to manage by managing.

Almost from the start, I was putting in really long hours, sometimes coming in at 7:00 a.m. and not leaving until I closed the store at 1:00 a.m. The five-and-a half-day work week was standard then, but I found myself working two weeks at a stretch before I could get a day off. I had to run both the day and the night shifts because no one else was up to it. I hired and trained nightside workers, did inventory, spent hours helping out on the line, and cashed out at the end of the shift. Most McDonald's managers and assistant managers are expected to be hands-on. But with my manager and the other assistant either on a binge or sleeping one off, I was it.

The store didn't lack customers, but without real leadership, the service was hit-or-miss. Most of the employees were black, but we also had maybe a half-dozen white teens. They were a good bunch, and a few were really sharp. I was sure that, with the right kind of guidance and supervision, they could become a first-rate team. I began thinking seriously about motivation. Great service depends on a great staff. How does a manager get his mostly young, male employees excited about their work? How could I inspire my crew to value the work they did and the people they served? How could I transform a group of individual employees into a cohesive team?

The problem was that I literally didn't have the time to work on building a team. When the other assistant manager left, a new man came. I thought I would get some relief, but the new guy was a number-crunching desk jockey. It seemed like the only time he wasn't sitting at his desk was when he walked into the store and when he walked out. As a result, I had to pick up more slack.

I already trained my night crew; now I was responsible for dayside training as well. If I hadn't been so loaded down with work, this could have been the perfect opportunity to put some of my new ideas into action. For instance, I thought there was too much separation between the day and night shifts. Each crew depended on the work done by the other; problems that had not been resolved by the day crew were passed on to the night crew, and vice versa. Yet there was hardly any communication between them. The crews literally passed each other like ships in the night. This led to all sorts of difficulties, including lost time, wasted product, needless repetition of chores that had already been done, and lack of attention to necessary tasks. Since I was at the store day and night, I could see the inefficiencies. I was sure we could improve productivity if everyone thought of himself as part of one team. It meant breaking down the wall between day and night workers, and I thought it could be accomplished through shared training and emphasis on cooperation and coordination between crews. But I was too busy putting out other people's fires, and I didn't have the authority to make radical changes. Still, I had some memorable successes in the area of hiring. One of the young men I brought on board and trained was Earl Smith—we called him "Smitty"—and he was good at every job. But at the milk shake station, no one could match him. In those days, McDonald's criterion was that each shake was supposed to weigh between 10¼ and 10¾ ounces when they came off the Multimixer spindles to assure the proper air-to-shake-mix ratio and guarantee that the customer got full value. Most employees could get close, but Smitty came in at exactly 10½ ounces every time, filling cups right to the cap seat (the slot where the paper top fit into the cup). It was amazing.

My best cashier was McArthur, one of the few white employees. Crew members often addressed each other by their last names only, and I regret that I can't recall McArthur's first name. But I remember clearly that he set a standard for courtesy that few could equal. His good manners were so reliable that people who knew him sometimes tried to annoy him or make him laugh, just to see him slip up. McArthur never did.

I've also never forgotten Oswald Jackson. Even though I didn't hire him, I recognized immediately that he was a superstar. He was my fastest employee, turning orders with astonishing speed and accuracy. He never seemed to lose focus. Other employees joked that you put your life on the line if you got in Oswald's fast lane when he was assembling an order.

The thing that set Smitty, McArthur, and Oswald apart was attitude. As young as they were, they really got it. They weren't just "burger-flippers"—a term I dislike because it trivializes the nature of the work and the people who do it—they were providing service. The kind of positive attitudes they brought to their jobs was the raw material of team building. I have hired thousands of employees since my days at Good Hope Road, and I remember many of them. But Smitty, McArthur, Oswald, and several others stand out. I can teach almost anybody to do specific tasks, but the qualities I was looking for were a lot harder to define than mechanical skills. When hiring employees, I had to rely more than I expected on my gut instincts. Smitty, McArthur, and Oswald showed me that I should trust my instincts.

Another experience taught me that not everybody is suited for the demands of the fast-food industry. Apart from four or five hours of sleep, I was spending all my days and nights at work, and I was desperate for help. My cousin John Perry was working as a computer programmer at the Pentagon, but I convinced him to come in part-time to give me a hand with counter service. John only lasted a few days. He was embarrassed when some of his Pentagon friends came into the store, and leaving customers standing in line, John quit on the spot. Counter service wasn't his kind of work at that point in his career, although he and his brother, Jim, eventually became McDonald's franchisees. Later, while I was still in D.C., another of my cousins, Ken Jones, came into McDonald's as a management trainee. After his training, Ken worked for me as a second assistant manager while I was at Good Hope Road, and he was a natural at service.

Peter Drucker, who became the leading exponent of common-sense business management in the 1970s and 1980s, said, "Hire for enthusiasm." From John and Ken, I learned that different folks have different enthusiasms, just as they have different aptitudes and talents. In hiring, a manager has to be on the lookout for that spark of enthusiasm. It's not the kind of thing that shows up on a job application.

PUTTING MY PRINCIPLES TO THE TEST

My first year with Gee Gee Distributing was an intense education. I was learning the McDonald's restaurant operating system from the ground up and formulating my own philosophy of effective management. My chance to put my ideas into practice came in the spring of 1967. After six months at the Good Hope Road store, I was sent back to Virginia. I was more than glad to leave Good Hope Road, though I missed my workers a lot. I left the restaurant more stable, fully staffed, and more efficient than when I arrived. Several key people in the company were aware of what I had achieved, in spite of the lousy conditions and miserable hours. But I was exhausted, frustrated, and ready for a change.

My next assignment was as first assistant manager of the McDonald's at 3510 Duke Street in Alexandria, down the road from the Duke Street store where I had trained. The manager was being promoted, and I went into the job with the expectation that I would take his place, but that didn't happen, not at first. I can't say for certain whether the delay in my promotion was because of racism, but it did bring about a reunion with Brian Jillson, one of the two white men I'd trained with. Brian was sent in to manage 3510 Duke Street, and when he discovered that I was his assistant, he couldn't believe it. "This should be your job," he said. "You'd be better than me."

Brian and I had gotten along really well when we were trainees, and we could be open with each other. Since 3510 Duke Street was a low-volume store, the pressure was on to increase customer traffic and sales. Brian honestly didn't feel ready to manage a problem store, and he said that he really needed my help. He wanted another assignment. When I said that I wanted to manage 3510 Duke Street, we came up with a plan to accomplish both our goals. Basically, we agreed to share the manager's responsibilities—to be a two-man team. If we could show improvements, we figured that Brian could ask for another position, and I could take his job.

Looking back from the perspective of more than three decades of business experience, I have to laugh at how naïve we were, thinking that we could conspire to manipulate the system. But what is really amazing is that it worked! And I added another key principle to my management philosophy: *positive collaboration and teamwork for the good of all.* As it turned out, Brian's and my plan had good outcomes for everyone. The store, the employees, the company, and the customers all benefited when Brian and I got what we wished for. After about four months, traffic at the restaurant was picking up, Brian got a new assignment, and I was promoted to store manager. I had been a good student for the past year; now I was in charge, and I was determined to prove that I could lead.

The neighborhood we served at 3510 Duke Street was mainly working class and, like the rest of Alexandria, white. Though the restaurant was well known in the community, it had serious problems. The store had an average sales volume at best, but it didn't earn enough to be consistently profitable at a level acceptable to the owners. In fact, it was one of the least profitable restaurants in the Gee

Gee franchise, a poor performer regarded within the company like a troublesome stepchild whom everyone prefers to ignore. One of the reasons I got the opportunity to manage the store when Brian moved on was that no one with my experience wanted to tackle the job. I say "opportunity" because this was my chance to demonstrate not only my management skills but also my abilities as a problem solver. Together, Brian and I had improved volume at the restaurant, and I had no doubts that I could keep the store at that level. But I wasn't satisfied with just treading water. I wanted to rescue 3510 Duke Street and make it stand out.

The challenge was made easier by my employees. They were a great group, mostly kids, and I had already discovered what hard workers they could be. It helped that I was still young myself—twenty-seven when I first set foot in 3510 Duke Street. It didn't take long for me to see that my color made no difference to these white teenagers. It was almost 1967, and American culture was being forever altered by its young people. Teens and young adults were relating in new ways. A popular motto of the time was "Never trust anyone over thirty," and I was on the right side of that divide. The kids were willing to accept my leadership and learn from me.

With good employees, I had the most important ingredient in my recipe for change. Our new emphasis would be service. Service would set us apart from the competition and bring more people to our counter.

Ray Kroc always said that McDonald's should strive for perfection, and he meant perfection in everything. He once said, "You've got to be demanding. Emphasize and have enthusiasm for details. No detail is too small." I realized that striving for perfect service involved a lot of work that customers may not be aware of. I had learned that on my first day as a trainee manager, when I scrubbed those filthy, smelly garbage cans. That day, a customer saw something she hadn't expected. I won her approval, and she spoke up. Other customers probably noticed too, and though they didn't say anything, it's a sure bet that their goodwill transferred to the entire store.

So I got down to the business of pulling my employees together as a real team. We talked a lot about the importance of every job. I needed to build up their enthusiasm for all aspects of the work. It was important to me that the workers have some fun, so I began to encourage some friendly competition—who could speed up their counter service and similar challenges—that promoted the concept of making our best better. One time, I got three of my standout crew members and my cousin Ken Jones from Good Hope Road to come in and work with us; the point was to model top-notch performance without making my Duke Street employees feel that their work habits were inferior. I also had my employees visit other stores, so they could make comparisons and learn from what was working elsewhere. Open communication was essential, so I asked the employees for their ideas, and they had good ones. They knew where many of the problems lay. I welcomed their observations and suggestions because they saved me a great deal of time.

My father always taught by example. If he expected his students to do their best, he had to do his best. Mr. Jordan, my high school woodworking instructor, had done the same. I learned more from *watching* him work than I could from any book of instructions. I had adopted this method when I was teaching back in Memphis, and it had served me well, so in my Duke Street store, I turned again to example. I was the manager, but I made a point to work alongside my employees as often as possible. In some measure, I was being selfish; I got such pleasure from interacting with customers that I didn't want to give it up. But mainly, I wanted to demonstrate to my team 1) that there's a correct way to get things done, and 2) that all tasks are interrelated. That's also when I started referring to day work and night work as "dayside" and "nightside" rather than "shifts." I wanted my team to think of themselves as two sides of the same coin, both working together to achieve the same goal.

I knew the McDonald's manual of operations backward and forward, so it would have been easy simply to lecture to my young employees on systems and procedures. But by rolling up my sleeves to mop the floors and clean the equipment, I really got their attention. They were smart young men and learned quickly.

One thing I always liked to do was go outside every day and observe customers who were eating in their cars in order to gauge their reactions. When feasible, I would talk with customers to get their opinions about our food and our service. I would also empty the trash cans; this chore enabled me to inspect the contents. If there was something unusual, like an excessive quantity of unconsumed fries, I knew we might have a problem and could correct it immediately. These kinds of activities were my personal brand of market research. But they had another benefit: My employees saw me practicing what I preached. Details mattered, and service didn't end when we handed the food to the customer.

I couldn't expect my employees to strive for perfection, whatever the task, if I wasn't willing to talk the talk *and* walk the walk myself. Teaching by example worked for me and achieved my immediate objective: 3510 Duke Street was soon the cleanest restaurant in the area, with a highly productive staff and consistently efficient service. My workers had a new sense of cohesion among themselves, and we were attracting some new customers, but we were still in the profit cellar. How could we build a loyal customer base?

I wanted us to think seriously about who our customer was.

Soon after coming to 3510 Duke Street, I saw that the store's low-volume/low-profit difficulties were largely traceable to lack of interest among our potential customers. The store was there, but people had few expectations of it. Our restaurant was little more than a place to go when you needed a meal fast or when you'd run through all other options. I was convinced the store could turn the corner, so I studied operations carefully to determine what was off-track. It became obvious to me that the store's reputation for personal service was sub-par. Under previous management, not enough attention had been given to details. Lackadaisical attitudes from the past were reflected in the overall quality of service. It wasn't the employees' fault, but as a consequence of past leadership (or lack of leadership), customers perceived that the store was generally low on energy and enthusiasm.

Once I put my finger on the main problem, I again consulted with my workers. After all, they were members of the community we served and knew the people far better than I did. Invited to share their thinking, they came up with solid insights that greatly helped me develop a strategy.

The fundamental responsibility of every member of the team (myself included) was to provide the customer with what he or she asked for, quickly and accurately. Every successful burger restaurant does that. But what would set us apart was providing *more* than the customer expected. I thought about what had worked when my brother, Carl, and I were operating Jones Food Market in Greenville. It was going the extra mile. We hadn't just sold beer like other markets; we'd sold the *coldest* beer in town. Now, I had to do something similar in Alexandria. We had to sell more than burgers and fries. We would sell ourselves—the best, fastest, and friendliest service in town.

71

Instead of simply waiting for customers to step to the counter and give their orders, we would greet our customers when they stepped in the door and ask how we could serve them. It's called "threshold service," and it's the McDonald's way. We would avoid long lines by directing customers to what we called our express service. We'd know our products so well that we could answer most any question. We'd look our customers in the eye and read their expressions; if we saw annoyance or confusion, we would do whatever was necessary to impress them with our willingness to make things right. We'd pay attention to everyone who walked in the door. We'd be nice to little kids. We'd help anyone who needed assistance. If a tourist just wanted directions and didn't purchase anything, we would treat him with the same courtesy as a paying customer; he might return for a meal on his next visit and send other folks our way. We would keep our counters and floors spotless, our restroom clean (only one restroom in those days, outside and behind the store), and our parking lot neat. No detail was too small to overlook.

In short, our new method was to treat every customer as a guest—a special guest. With quality food, clean facilities, speedy service, and personnel who were consistently competent, courteous, and *enthusiastic*, we would raise expectations in the community. Instead of trailing along in the wake of the other fast-food restaurants in the area, we would generate business by setting the standard for everyone else. I began to think of this strategy as "barefoot service"— *service so good that it would knock the customer's socks off!*

To make it work, I understood that I needed to empower my employees with a degree of decision-making authority that was unusual for young workers. To impress customers, the workers as well as the assistant managers had to be able to address problems when they arose. We discussed the kinds of situations when servers could

72

act on their own and circumstances when an assistant manager or I had to be called in. I was expanding their authority, but I also had to establish the parameters; young people are more likely to take responsibility when expectations are carefully and clearly defined. I wanted them to feel comfortable seeking help when the situation was more than they could handle.

As we made operational improvements and enhanced our service, our business was increasing. It was slow at first, as I anticipated, but word-of-mouth was our best marketing tool. Customers talked about the new way we were doing things, and as word spread, our daily volume grew. Profits rose, and the store climbed steadily in the ranks. By the time I left 3510 Duke Street in April of 1968, the restaurant was consistently in first, second, or third place on the company's monthly profit statements.

I was working day and night to pull the store out of the doldrums, but strangely, I didn't feel the fatigue and frustration that dogged me at the Good Hope Road store. Progress is a great energizer, and what we were accomplishing made the long hours more than worthwhile. I was also coming to understand that my personal sense of success wasn't measured by the size of a paycheck. It was grounded in achievement.

The only personal problem I had was that my hours made it nearly impossible for me to socialize with family and friends. On one occasion, my mother came to visit me, and I just couldn't get the time to show her the city as I'd hoped to. We had both looked forward to the visit, and although Mother didn't complain about our having so little time together, it was a huge disappointment for me. I did, however, manage to get one full week off, and I returned to Tennessee to get married. I'd known my fiancée, who was a schoolteacher, for a number of years, and we kind of drifted into the marriage. It lasted for almost a decade, but practically from the start, I think we both knew the foundations were too shaky to hold up. It was a mistake that I won't dwell on.

I was happiest when I was working, but there was one fly in the ointment, my supervisor, Stan Jeter. Stan became supervisor after I'd been made manager. The previous supervisor had promoted me and another African American, Bob Beavers, as managers of stores in suburban Virginia and Maryland—a good thing since Stan probably wouldn't have let any black man have such authority. Stan didn't appear to approve of black managers in white markets, and he seemed to find any excuse to come down on me. He nearly drove me nuts with his nit-picking. He'd look for the one bad potato in a multitude of good ones, and hold me accountable. He also used the security time locks on the store's doors to check up on me. McDonald's didn't serve breakfast then, and there was no morning shift. Most managers arrived at their stores around 8:00 a.m., but I liked to start early, about 7:00 a.m. That time was *my choice*; as manager, I didn't punch the clock. But Stan would review the time locks every week. If I had opened the door a few minutes after seven, he'd berate me for being late!

All the time we were working so hard to increase sales and profits at 3510 Duke Street, he was giving me no more than average performance ratings. He used to say that it was too bad the one thing I did well—turn a profit—wasn't listed on the performance review form. I'm sure he meant that as a compliment, but it didn't make up for his criticisms. The weird thing was that profitable stores earned higher bonuses for supervisors, so increasing volume and profits at 3510 Duke Street benefited Stan Jeter personally. Instead of encouragement and support, however, I got a constant stream of negative comments. Stan complained repeatedly that the store was dirty (it wasn't) and at one point, he recruited a cleanup person for me. I was informed that this new employee was his father-in-law. Though I was told I could fire the guy if he didn't work out, Stan had put me in a classic Catch-22. Who would fire his supervisor's father-in-law?

Initially, I was shocked and angered by the mediocre reviews. I wondered if I should complain to a higher level in Gee Gee. Or maybe I should just quit. But those two options would be counterproductive. On one hand, I probably couldn't win in a fight with my immediate superior and would sacrifice my progress in the effort. On the other hand, I didn't want to leave a job that, in every other way, I had come to love. Most important, I didn't want to sever my relationship with McDonald's. So when I cooled down, I decided that the smartest course was to continue to do my best and find ways to work with Stan. I could see that he wasn't such a bad guy, however misguided, and that I could actually learn from him. Stan had knowledge about operations that I needed; in fact, his constant nit-picking alerted me to details that did require more attention. For instance, he harped on the importance of storage, and he was right. When we reorganized our inventory to suit him, it was a better system.

I began inviting Stan to visit the store. Knowing that I couldn't control his reactions, I tried to anticipate his needs. I listened respectfully, made necessary changes, and always gave him credit, which was important to him. I made a real effort to separate his high standards for the business from his seeming prejudice against me. In the end, I never compromised my basic principles, but I gained a lot of insight about the too common problem of dealing with a difficult supervisor. By attending to his priorities, when they made good sense, I didn't give him many opportunities to complain.

Though Stan and I related well later when we were peers, I

doubt that I could have totally won him over as his subordinate. But history intervened, and I didn't have any more time to try.

A CRISIS AND UNEXPECTED OPPORTUNITIES

The murder of Dr. Martin Luther King, Jr., on the evening of April 4, 1968, set off a wave of violence in D.C. The anger unleashed in those chaotic few days brought a major problem to a head for McDonald's corporate management. Most of their high-volume restaurants in the riot areas of Washington were then managed by whites, and it suddenly became truly dangerous for white men to enter black neighborhoods. A national tragedy had created a crisis for McDonald's in D.C.

We had been living in volatile times well before the assassination. The civil rights movement was divided into two camps: those who followed Dr. King's strategy of peaceful resistance and those who were calling for direct confrontation with the violent forces of racism. Opposition to the war in Vietnam was heating up, and people were taking to the streets to demand an end to America's involvement in Southeast Asia. Many folks—particularly young people—came to the conclusion that the real enemy was "The Establishment." How one defined "The Establishment" tended to be personal. It could be the government, big business, racist society, the military, colleges and universities that cooperated with the Defense department, churches that remained passive in the face of human suffering. There was a lot of crossover between the civil rights and anti-war movements, and the seeds were being planted for new movements that would continue to shake the whole country in the 1970s—feminism, gay rights, rights for the elderly, environmentalism. Small groups of extremists, who invariably got the lion's share of attention from the press, were calling for the total overthrow of established institutions. The hottest buzz words of the time were "alienation" and "revolution."

Since joining McDonald's, I had been so preoccupied with work that I hadn't followed events as closely as I might have if my job had been a nine-to-five routine. Dr. King's assassination was shattering. It was impossible not to wonder if the racist establishment hadn't won. But I didn't think so. I've always been one of those people who think that if a system has problems but is basically sound, the best way to fix it is from the inside. As a black man, I wasn't ready to abandon my faith in America's founding principles of equality and justice. More than a decade earlier, Dr. King had said, on the eve of the bus boycott in Montgomery, Alabama, "We are here because of our love for democracy, because of our deep-seated belief that democracy transformed from thin paper to thick action is the greatest form of government on earth." I believed those words, and I still do.

As a young man who had finally found the work that I loved, I also wasn't prepared to leave a company that I believed to be fundamentally decent. Big corporations tend to change their ways slowly, but they do change—or they die. In the nearly three years since I had started at McDonald's, I'd become convinced that the company had the potential to change more rapidly than most. I admit that my thinking was self-centered; I was happy where I was, and I didn't want to leave.

In the traumatic days after Dr. King's death, I took a long, hard look at my own situation and made several pivotal personal decisions. Despite the new uncertainties of life in the capital, I would stay in Washington. All thoughts of a career in radio were gone; I was committed to the restaurant business. And I wanted to remain with McDonald's, which had recently purchased the Gee Gee franchise for the then enormous price of almost $17 million in cash. I had a strong sense that doors were opening in the corporation, and I planned to be standing on the doorstep, ready to walk inside.

I knew myself a lot better than I had on my first day as a trainee. Yes, I'd had to deal with racism and a few hardcore racists since I started with the company. But most of the problems I'd encountered resulted from the frailties and failures of *individuals*. I had seen no evidence that McDonald's *as an institution* was any more racist than society in general. I'd been able to deal with individual racism pretty effectively, training myself (because it sure wasn't in any of the manuals) how to work around other people's prejudices without losing my cool. As I evaluated my progress so far, I realized that every setback—like initially losing out on the manager's job of 3510 Duke Street—had turned into an opportunity for advancement. Patience, persistence, and hard work had gotten me this far, and I just knew that more opportunities lay ahead.

Ten days after Dr. King's death, Carl Osborne, a man I had gotten to know while I was working at Good Hope Road, came to see me. He had been the second black trainee and the second black store manager in D.C., and when I was struggling at the Good Hope Road store, Carl Osborne had encouraged me to stick it out. My time was coming, he'd told me more than once. He would say, "Roland, you've got to pay the cost to be the boss."

Carl had recently been promoted to supervisor—the first African American supervisor in the entire McDonald's system. His territory comprised the inner-city McDonald's restaurants in D.C. Though most of the white-owned retail businesses in the riot area had been burned out, only two of McDonald's inner-city restaurants were damaged. Still, it wasn't safe for white managers to go back to their stores, and Carl was scrambling to grab black managers who could take over.

Most managers didn't work on Sundays, but I was behind the counter at Duke Street when Carl walked in. He asked me to go for a ride with him. He had something to discuss, in private. We drove around Alexandria while he explained the situation. Carl had been "selling" me to Stan Jeter for months, and my most recent review had been better. But now Carl was afraid that Stan would use the violence in the city as an excuse to fire black managers in Virginia, me included. Rather than waiting for the ax to fall, Carl wanted me to transfer to one of his D.C. stores. He had a location for me. The address was 1164 Bladensburg Road, in one of the roughest parts of D.C., and the store had been in serious trouble even before the riots. Despite high volume, it was not making money at an acceptable level. Carl didn't downplay the difficulties. There were problems in just about every aspect of operations. Food, labor, and maintenance costs were especially high; pilferage and frequent robberies were draining money; and the store was basically out of control. Carl said that he doubted if anyone could make better than an average profit in such a troubled store, but he'd already seen what I had accomplished at Good Hope Road and was well aware of the turnaround at 3510 Duke Street. He asked me if I was up for a new challenge—a big one.

I don't remember hesitating more than a few seconds before I gave him my answer.

Chapter 5

Out of the Frying Pan and Into the Fire

I don't sing a song unless I feel it. The song don't tug at my heart,
I pass on it. I have to believe in what I'm doing.

RAY CHARLES, SINGER AND COMPOSER

There was no avoiding the devastation caused by the April riots. Driving from my apartment to my new assignment at 1164 Bladensburg Road was like going into a combat zone. This was not the D.C. that tourists came to see. The most obvious casualties of the riots were the burned out and partially burned buildings, primarily retail establishments. Here and there a building stood intact. The mobs had taken out their rage selectively, on white-owned businesses. Black owners had not entirely escaped the post-assassination rampage, but in general, white owners had paid the heaviest price.

I couldn't help thinking how Dr. King would have grieved over this destruction. In the days after his death, the whole country had learned why he had been in Tennessee—to generate support for Memphis's sanitation workers in their nonviolent wage strike against the city. We'd read or heard the speech Dr. King delivered on the night before he died. His final words to the crowd assembled in the Mason Temple had been eerily prophetic: "Like anybody, I would like to live a long life. Longevity has its place. But I'm not concerned about that now. I just want to do God's will. And he's allowed me to go up to the mountain. And I've looked over. And I've seen the promised land. I may not get there with you. But I want you to know tonight, that we, as a people will get to the promised land .... "

In my own heart, I knew how the riots would have saddened Dr. King. He had been battling for some time against hotter heads in the civil rights movement who wanted "an eye for an eye" retribution for every unjust act against black people. On the last night of his life, Dr. King had urged the protestors in Memphis to use their legal and economic power and to resist the temptation of violent response as they exercised their "right to protest for right." But what I saw on Bladensburg Road was a negation of everything Dr. King stood for.

The Bladensburg Road McDonald's restaurant had escaped the destruction, but as I approached the site, it was painfully clear why Carl Osborne had warned me about the place. There were broken and missing panels in the store's signature arches. The store's red and white tile exterior was dirty, the lot was littered with debris, and the trash cans were overflowing. In those days, only a few McDonald's restaurants had inside seating, and there was no drive-thru service. Purchases were made at walk-up windows, and customers could sit on outdoor benches attached to the building or in their cars to eat or they could take their meals with them. City stores served a largely pedestrian clientele, and because most people ate on or near the property, litter in the lot and on the street required constant attention.

The restaurant, like its surroundings, suffered from an overall dinginess that was depressing. Other businesses were still operating in the immediate area: a home improvement store that also sold lumber, a liquor store, a Sunoco service station, a tire store, and a used car dealer. Down the block was a mom-and-pop grocery. On one side of the McDonald's property was a sign shop. But our other next-door neighbor was a rundown house where adult winos and drug-users hung out day and night. I learned about their activities by finding empty bottles and broken syringes in our dumpster. Behind the restaurant were low-income apartments; I could say they were "poorly maintained," but I never saw evidence of any maintenance.

Inside the store, I immediately noticed a number of the younger workers wearing street clothes instead of McDonald's uniforms. In the afternoons and evenings, when teenagers frequented the store, the absence of workers in their uniforms gave the restaurant the appearance of a teen hangout—an image that could put off and even intimidate the adult clientele we wanted to attract. An assistant manager was supposed to be in charge, but there was precious little supervision. Without leadership, the employees' work habits, like their clothing, were uneven and unpredictable.

The facilities and equipment were functional, and the speed of service was okay, but the general quality left much to be desired—a long way from meeting McDonald's QSC standards. Things were far from clean and organized. I saw a lot of obvious waste: too much food and paper products tossed out, misuse of towels and aprons. The employees wore paper caps, white for staff and red for managers, which they were using and losing at a ridiculous rate. The food wastage was even more serious. It was most evident at night; without strict quality control, too much food was being prepared and thrown away. When I reviewed the books, I found a pattern of ongoing wastage and employee pilferage. There were excessive cash shortages and unaccounted-for inventory. The day before my arrival, the restaurant had been robbed, a common occurrence in the area. The problems were everywhere, raising controllable costs and cutting into the store's profits.

If I had given a grade to the restaurant I first encountered, it would have been an overall D at best, with maybe a D+ in a few areas. It wasn't a total failure, but it was barely passing. When Carl Osborne offered me the store, he'd been straight about the problems, but I hadn't fully comprehended what I was getting into. To call the Bladensburg Road restaurant a "challenge" was an understatement.

That first day, I set my number-one priority. We had to get the place cleaned up and make it into a physical standout. I wanted the store and the personnel to be impressive, even if the neighborhood wasn't. The team building and service training I'd done at 3510 Duke Street would take precedence later on. But my personnel skills were tested immediately. It wasn't long before I figured out which of the existing staff had to go. With all the hard work ahead, I didn't have the time to rehabilitate anyone. I couldn't afford to keep employees who were lazy, arrogant, unwilling to take direction, or who wouldn't participate in a team effort.

It has always been my theory that if a manager hires carefully, then he'll have little need to fire. It's a theory that has been born out in practice, and for most of my career, firing employees—instantly for theft—has been an infrequent necessity. I had inherited the staff at Bladensburg Road, and in those early days, I only fired one person, for deliberate abuse of store equipment. But when I made my expectations clear, a number left on their own accord. Basically, I implemented and enforced policies and standards that they couldn't or didn't want to meet. Each week, I would upgrade my expectations. Everyone had a chance to prove himself, but workers who didn't keep up with the pace were scheduled for fewer hours, which lowered their income. Through a process of attrition, the deadwood cleared itself out. Bob Beavers, another of the black managers brought into the inner city stores after the riots, used to say that we have to strengthen the weakest links in the chain. The weak links who refused to change their ways pretty quickly chose to go elsewhere. In the end, only one guy from the night shift, and three or four dayside workers made it through, and they had earned their jobs.

On the other hand, hiring was a pleasure for me, but not all that easy. I was looking for honest workers with that intangible spark of enthusiasm, and when I found them, I was ready to pay good wages to retain them. I took heat from some of my superiors (criticism delivered through Carl Osborne, although he agreed with my approach) for paying higher starting wages than any other McDonald's in the city. So I decided to start all new employees at minimum wage. After they had completed their training and demonstrated their commitment to the new standards of service, they were quickly rewarded with a raise within the next two days to two weeks—whenever the next pay period began. The better they worked, the higher their pay. Linking raises to performance in this way was a positive incentive, especially for young workers who are motivated by quick gratification. It was hard to argue with the results. Over the next few months, my staff of new hires and holdovers melded into a trustworthy and loyal team. Turnover and absenteeism were dramatically reduced, and productivity went up. We cut employee theft to zero, eliminated shortages at the cash registers, and reduced all controllable costs. The savings more than made up for the fatter paychecks, and eventually the store's labor costs as a percentage of net sales were below the company's expectations for all McDonald's stores in the D.C. market.

There was one hire I didn't make, and I have always regretted it. A young man applied for work, and he was clearly well qualified. In our interview, I was very impressed by his intelligence, his eagerness, and his sophistication. I sensed that he was the kind of person that Carl Osborne, a racing fan, called "a horse"—an employee who would go the distance and come home ahead of the field. I offered him the job on one condition: The applicant had to cut his hair. He wore an Afro, a hairdo that was just beginning to be adopted by young black men and women. His hair wasn't wild, and today it wouldn't cause anybody to bat an eye; in fact, I wore an Afro in the 70s. But in 1968, an Afro was unusual and had associations in the public mind with the "Black Power" movement. I thought the hairdo would be a distraction, and it might not go down well with the few white customers who were part of our lunchtime trade. I didn't think the young man would object to a haircut, but he did. Politely but firmly, he turned me down. If I met him today, I would apologize for my error in judgment and lack of awareness. My only excuse is that I was still thinking like a suburban store manager and so concerned about the appearance of the restaurant that I failed to recognize his Afro as an expression of personal pride and pride in our race.

Getting the restaurant in shape was my focus at that moment, and I have no doubt that it was the right approach. We began cleaning and reorganizing almost from the day I took over the store. We washed inside and out. I got repairs done. As the sense of teamwork increased, the other employees joined with me to push the maintenance person—a competent worker called "Smiley," who was very good at his job when he showed up for work. I told him that I valued his skills but needed someone whose attendance I could count on. Once he saw that I was serious, Smiley almost always met my expectations, but there were times when he tried everyone's patience. I implemented a strict "no show, no call, no job" policy; any employee who didn't come to work and didn't call to let a manager or assistant manager know was subject to immediate dismissal. But my employees requested that I bend the rule a little for Smiley, to give him a chance to commit to the team. He was so good at his work that I tolerated his occasional unannounced day off. As Ralph Waldo Emerson said, "A foolish consistency is the hobgoblin of little minds …. " Everybody consistently reminded Smiley of the importance of calling if he couldn't come in, but I wasn't foolish enough to let an exceptional, though eccentric, worker go. I did, however, ask Carl Osborne to transfer one of my assistant managers to another location—after I went looking for Smiley one day and discovered him and the assistant manager drinking beers together.

Three of my new hires were men in their sixties. One of them was an odd duck; he rarely talked except to ask a question, which was okay since his station was French fries and not counter service. He was a careful and dependable worker, just uncommonly quiet. I noticed that each day, he would come to the site early, but he didn't come inside. He would sit on the street curb, waiting by himself until his shift began. From that vantage point, he got a good idea of how much litter there was around the store. The problem with litter is that people tend to drop things when an area is already littered. The McDonald's operations manual recommended that store personnel pick up litter for one block in all directions of a store, but so far none of my employees was taking the initiative. I needed someone to be a good example. At the time, I was still arranging for reliable maintenance, but until I could get it, I had to improvise. Since my silent employee was on the street anyway, I asked him to police the block, for extra pay, and he did a fine job. I also had to set the tone, so I picked up litter wherever I saw it, often stopping my car on the way to work to collect trash along the road, and I encouraged all my employees to do the same.

Turning a Sub-standard Store into a Standout

My reason for concentrating on upgrading the physical environment was straightforward. I was going on my grandmother Totcy's admonition: "Stand out. Don't blend in." For a long time, the McDonald's at 1164 Bladensburg Road had just blended in. The store was not dilapidated; it was uncared for, like a house with "good bones" hidden behind peeling paint, cracked windows, and an overgrown yard. I believe that physical appearance affects not only the impression outsiders have of a person or a business, but also the way that the person or business functions. The environment influences how people think, and it is very difficult to maintain enthusiasm for a job when the work environment is drab, dirty, and disorganized. When managers exhibit a "Who cares?" attitude, employees become equally indifferent in a multitude of ways. Morale suffers, workers slack off, and problems like poor quality control, waste, and employee theft increase. I was sure that a spruced-up, shiny clean, and well-ordered restaurant would impress our customers, but more importantly, I was convinced that the improvements would bring out the best in my employees and assistant managers and encourage uniform observance of McDonald's standards. I talked with them about *the full meaning of service*, and they started *thinking* of an impressive physical environment as part of our service to customers. What they thought about, they brought about.

Employee dress standards were another issue that contributed to the overall appearance of the restaurant. The McDonald's uniform then consisted of a white cotton shirt with logos on the sleeves, a black string tie, dark pants, and a paper cap. The company supplied the shirts, ties, and caps. Unlike the kids who worked in suburban stores and had easy access to washing machines (or moms who washed and ironed), inner city employees often had difficulty laundering their shirts on a daily basis. Some would show up in stained or wrinkled McDonald's shirts; some would wear nonstandard white shirts; and some would appear in their street clothes. I couldn't tolerate dirty clothes, but I understood when employees wore their own clean clothes rather than a messy uniform shirt.

The problem was that when a worker was out of uniform, he was indistinguishable from the customers. He could be anybody—not a proud and efficient McDonald's employee. One of the basics of McDonald's success is consistency in product and service. The uniform, like those golden arches, is a visual symbol of the consistency that customers rely on. Uniforms also have the practical effect of discouraging robberies. When employees' clothing is no different from customers, it's easier for robbers get into a store and blend in, until they pull guns and demand money.

So I worked on bringing personal appearance up to standard. I explained why the uniform was important, and I also stocked up on clean, pressed shirts so that an employee who didn't have his own could change into one at the store. I got everyone to stop the bad habits of using aprons to clean up spills and wearing aprons when they were on counter duty. I had everyone write their names in their caps, making it harder to claim that a cap was lost or misplaced.

Small details? Maybe, but if a manager isn't paying attention, they can consume his bottom line. For example, I couldn't understand why we were using up so much linen. Aprons, towels, and cleaning cloths were washed daily, but they were wearing out at an unacceptable rate. When I had the employees investigate, they discovered that we were adding too much bleach to the wash, and the excess bleach was breaking down the fabrics too quickly. The fix was easy; with the correct amount of bleach, our linens lasted longer and replacement costs were significantly reduced. It seems like a little thing, but when lots of minor details go unattended, they add up to big problems. Instead of dousing a little flame, you wind up trying to put out a bonfire.

Attending to the operational details also raised the employees' standards, so I began adding details at the service level of their jobs. Here's an example: I'd get whoever was mopping the floors to focus on cleaning out the corners, getting down on his knees to hand-scrub. (As a child, I had seen how scrupulously the women in my family cleaned, and much later, I did my share during my Army training.) The purpose was not merely to get clean corners or, in another example, to wash the edges as well as the tops of our counters. My larger objective was to get my workers to *see* details—like dirt in corners and on the baseboards, dried ketchup drips on counter edges, and fingerprints on stainless steel equipment—for themselves. I wanted them to take the initiative and feel empowered to handle such problematic details without specific directions. But first, they had to become aware that the problems existed.

I knew that my younger employees were less likely to be responsive if I just ordered them to scrub and scrape. So I would conduct mini-training sessions, ten minutes or so, before the start of a shift. I would ask questions designed to promote discussion: "Why are clean uniforms important?" "What does a customer think when she sees ketchup crusted on the edge of a counter?" I guided the discussion and kept it on track, yet the ideas came from the employees. I would observe their facial expressions and other nonverbal cues; if someone rolled his eyes or shrugged his shoulders, I'd draw him into the conversation, encouraging him to share his thinking with me and really listening to him. We also worked on specifics of customer service, including the speed of service and the basic courtesies of greetings and filling orders. Unlike the average suburban teenager, many of my Bladensburg Road workers had never been taught or exposed to the fundamentals of everyday etiquette. On a number of occasions, I caught employees being rude to customers without realizing that they were being rude. We talked about good manners and how an employee's behavior affects the customer's impression of the worker himself, his teammates, and the entire restaurant.

Through our give-and-take sessions, the team was evolving from "I, me, mine" thinking to a "we, us, our" mindset, strengthening the sense that *we* were all one team. I was the captain, but everybody was important, and the team functioned at its best when everyone's ideas were respected. Those mini-sessions often started some lively debates, and after a while, my employees began asking their own questions based on their observations of details that could improve our overall service and customer image. The emphasis on seemingly small details had a cumulative effect. From clean corners and counter edges, our discussions progressed to larger issues, like speeding up service to reduce customers' waiting time.

By the end of my first month, the store was looking great, and so were the employees. We kept the area free of litter. The Golden Arches were gold again, and the red and white trash cans sparkled and no longer overflowed. Internally, we had restored order to our storage system and brought inventory under control, which helped reduce the wastage. I emphasized the rational use of materials, especially paper products, linens, and soap, and careful adherence to McDonald's standards of portion control and food holding times. There had been a lot of sloppiness in food production—too many condiments on some burgers, too little on others; failure to calibrate the cold drinks equipment to get the right syrup-to-water ratio; and so on. With close supervision and experience, my crews became consistent and accurate.

McDonald's has strict quality and safety standards for holding times—the amount of time every cooked item can be held between preparation and being served. When the time limit is reached, unsold food is discarded. Over-production means that food has to be tossed out, and the store eats the costs. Under-production causes delays in food delivery that annoy customers. I took the time to give the team extra instruction in the methods for estimating the amount of food to be prepared at different times of day and controlling food production. This included keeping a sharp eye on the parking lot to see how many vehicles pulled in and the number of passengers in each, as well as the volume of walk-up trade. I explained clearly why portion control was important—emphasizing that our customers counted on us for consistency. My employees asked good questions, understood the answers, and caught on fast.

I continued to see reductions in operating expenditures. Controlling variable costs, enhancing the store's already high volume, and leveraging our new emphasis on superior service into higher per-ticket sales all led to increases in profits. (Shortly before my departure late in 1968, I was informed that the store's profits were exceeding $6,000 a month, after the owner's draw—a very high level at that time.) The more I talked with the team about the importance of details, the more I tried to praise employees for taking initiative. My praise encouraged them to attend to the small things that, a month earlier, they would have ignored. For the staff, the focus on the environment and the operational basics had the effect of raising standards. Everyone saw the daily improvements as the reward for their hard work, and they earned all my praise.

Our Customers, Our Community

I guess people might wonder why the appearance of the store seemed so urgent. After all, the Bladensburg Road restaurant was already doing a relatively high volume of business. I could probably have reduced overhead and maintained the volume without expending so much energy on the cleanup. But my experience at Good Hope Road and then at 3510 Duke Street had taught me the value of putting one's high standards on display. This is especially important in poor and working-class areas, where businesses don't usually go out of their way to look their best. People without a lot to spend deserve to get their money's worth, just like everybody else. When we gave value, we created long-lasting, positive impressions.

To my way of thinking, standing out by creating a clean, attractive physical environment is *a tangible expression of respect* for customers and the entire community. Think of all the TV commercials these days in which companies proclaim, "We care." Well, it's easy to say, but the test lies in the doing. McDonald's was one of the few restaurant options that people in our area had, and I wanted to make our restaurant outstanding in every respect, so it would always be our neighbors' first choice. Adequate food and service wasn't sufficient to achieve this goal. We had to identify with our customers, understand their needs, and honor their decision to do business with us by offering superior service and facilities at all times.

Shortly after the April riots, I heard a powerful story about the consequences of positive community relations from my cousin Ken Jones. When the rioting began, Kenny was on duty as an assistant manager at my old Good Hope Road restaurant. A group of looters broke off from the main action, crossed the 11th Street Bridge, and were heading for the store. They got as far as the parking lot. Before

Kenny and the other employees could react, a number of young men from the neighborhood confronted the looters and drove them away with shouts of "You're not gonna burn down *our* McDonald's!" What an incredible moment that must have been—to be defended by neighbors who had nothing to gain for themselves but wanted to protect *their* store. I can't imagine a better example of the strong bonds of loyalty and respect that can be forged between a business and the community of people it serves.

When we cleaned that Bladensburg Road site from top to bottom and kept it clean day in and day out, we were sending a message: "We have confidence in this community. We're proud to be a part of it, and we're doing our best to make you proud of us." It's a message that, to this day, people in low-income circumstances don't hear very often. Back in the late 1960s, big cities tended to regard their low-income areas and citizens as problems without a solution, ignoring basic needs and keeping services to the bare minimum. D.C. had the additional handicap of being governed directly by the President and the Congress of the United States. In the great scheme of national politics, the city was a very low priority, and without home rule, its citizens, particularly its poor, had no one to turn to for help. It had taken a Constitutional amendment, ratified in 1961, to give the people of the District the right to vote for President. Not until 1974 did they get the power to elect their city mayor and council members.

In 1968, municipal services were erratic or non-existent in areas like Trinidad, where the store was located. Just blocks away from the restaurant, the public spaces, historic buildings, and monuments frequented by tourists were kept pristine. But on Bladensburg Road, it was rare for us to see a street cleaner. There were no trash receptacles on the streets, and garbage collection was erratic. If we wanted to keep our surroundings clean, we had to do the city's work as well as our own.

More seriously, policing was minimal. There were no beat cops walking the streets, and the police didn't appear until *after* a crime was committed. The lack of consistent police presence contributed in a major way to the high rate of armed robberies at inner-city stores. Night shifts were especially dangerous, and managers and assistant managers who closed their stores in the wee hours of the morning were always at risk. In the past, whoever cashed out had taken that day's receipts directly to the bank for night deposit, but that practice was scrapped when the rate of physical attacks soared. Every store had a safe, so managers started locking up the daily receipts overnight and then taking their deposits to the bank in broad daylight. That helped, but it didn't stop the muggers and thieves, and eventually, the company turned to armored car services. In the tense weeks and months after the riots, some restaurant managers began carrying guns, though this was against company policy. One of my assistant managers bought a gun. I didn't like it, and I never armed myself. But I had a hard time arguing with a man's right to protect himself and his workers when official law enforcement wasn't around to do its duty.

I figured that the best defense was a good offense. It's a tactic familiar to students of self-defense—and military veterans. Walk with confidence; hold your head up; look people in the eye; don't show fear. Fear signals weakness and vulnerability. So I had more than aesthetics and community relations on my mind when I tackled the store's physical environment. We were in one of D.C.'s most dangerous areas. The restaurant's rundown, uncared-for appearance— plus having the equivalent of a modern-day crack house next door— made it look vulnerable. There were white folks who worked in the neighborhood, but they didn't hang around after dark. Most of the crime in Trinidad was black against black, and there is no bond of color between thieves and their intended victims. Cleaning up and maintaining the store and its surroundings was a demonstration of our determination to control our environment. We didn't hide behind our glass windows; we were out on the lot and in the streets. We kept the lights on; the lights of our gold arches were turned off when we closed, but the parking lot was brightly lit throughout the night. We made our presence felt.

It didn't take long for people in the community to begin thinking of the McDonald's at 1164 Bladensburg Road as a safe harbor. In those troubled days, security became a serious component of the service we offered. Today, when people in the retail trades talk about "the dining experience" or "the shopping experience," they are referring primarily to the ambiance—the furnishings, color scheme, decorations, lighting, sounds, smells, etc. that evoke certain feelings and contribute to a customer's enjoyment of doing business. But in light of the terrible events of September 11, 2001, safety has resurfaced as a key component of the customer's "experience." In the late 60s, people had similar feelings; they didn't fear terrorists, but the lawlessness in big cities was equally unnerving. In our part of D.C., the riots had compounded these fears, even though the vast majority of people who lived and worked in the area were honest and law-abiding citizens.

I stayed at the Bladensburg Road restaurant for nine months, and in that time, we didn't have a single robbery. There was one incidence of vandalism—a broken plate-glass window, which was replaced immediately. (Boarding it over would have conveyed indifference.) Shortly after I left, however, the store was held up and an employee was shot and wounded. So I have to credit some of our success to pure luck, but I also believe that our efforts made the store a lot less attractive to criminals. Trustworthy and self-confident employees in their neat uniforms, a clean store and clean surroundings, managers and workers who looked customers in the eye and paid attention to details—all the changes that made us stand out in a positive way also made anyone with criminal intentions stand out in the negative. Intruders felt like obvious misfits when they entered our space, and they often avoided us.

As I said, almost all of my employees were black, but one notable exception was a white teenager named Lindsey Reed, who had worked for me at 3510 Duke Street. He was smart, and he had helped me a lot with reducing costs. When I left Alexandria, he and a couple other young men from Duke Street insisted on coming to work for me at Bladensburg Road. I couldn't talk them out of it, so I hired them on an as-needed basis. Maybe some of the other crew members were stand-offish at first, but not for long. Lindsey got on well, and he was a real asset. But considering the dangers outside the store, I made a point to watch his back. I knew that his color made him a target, so I would walk him to his car after work and make sure he left safely. When I was getting ready to move to Chicago at Christmas time in 1968, Lindsey presented me a gold Cross pen engraved with my name. I knew how expensive the gift was, but Lindsey said, "You need this. You're an executive now." That pen was his way of letting me know how proud he felt about my promotion and how much he valued our friendship. Our colors and the difference in our ages and positions didn't matter; we were friends, and we looked out for each other. I kept up with Lindsey until I learned that he had been killed in a traffic accident. I have never forgotten his generous and genuine friendship, and his spirit is alive for me today.

Almost a decade after his death, I got another unexpected gift from Lindsey Reed. A McDonald's executive came back to headquarters after a business trip and sought me out. On his airplane flight, he explained, he'd gotten to talking with one of the flight attendants. When the executive said he worked for McDonald's, she told him about her late brother, who had worked for McDonald's in Washington. She said her brother had a manager whom he admired greatly. Her brother had spoken so highly of this manager that she remembered the name: Roland Jones.

SOME THOUGHTS ON LEADERSHIP

Beyond praising a young man whose life was tragically brief, my point in writing about Lindsey Reed is to illustrate the kind of employer-employee relations that can be fostered when each party approaches the other with respect. There are many ways to manage people successfully, and styles of management are inevitably individual. I can't say that my personal style is the best, but I know what does *not* work. When an employer or manager fails to respect his or her employees, the relationship is doomed. There are very few workers who will strive for perfection if they feel disrespected. An employee might work well enough, but he or she won't go the extra mile for leaders who never praise or are so indulgent with praise that it becomes meaningless, who are hyper-critical, who bully or manipulate, and who demand more effort from their employees than they expect of themselves. Employees know the differences between the work they do and the work their managers do. Resentment festers and grows when workers see that higher-ups are not making much of an effort or are pushing their responsibilities off on others.

There are a small number of people who are born leaders, but for most of us, leadership skills have to be developed. The first step is to establish trust with the people one leads. A leader seeks opportunities to establish dialog because communication establishes that nature of the relationship. It's not a matter of personality. I'm outgoing; I like to get to know people, and I continue to enjoy many good friendships that grew out of employer-employee relationships. Those attributes have been extremely valuable to me in the service industry, but in leadership roles, I've also had to define the appropriate limits. No matter how personable a manager is, the first responsibility is to lead. On the other hand, I have worked successfully for and with people who are as reserved as I am gregarious. A few have been downright cold fish. But when they conveyed respect for their subordinates, I respected their leadership. I knew that we would probably never be buddies, but because I trusted them as leaders, I gave them my best efforts.

I believe that managers or employers who fail to respect their workers are wasting the most important resource at their disposal— the human resource. No person has an exclusive on good ideas. To be in the superior position doesn't necessarily mean that one has superior knowledge or ideas or creativity. Maybe my attitudes go back to my father and mother, but to me, the most effective blueprint for a business leader in relating to employees is the teacher-student model. Good teachers convey knowledge to their students; great teachers are also open to learning from their students. Great teachers understand that they *share* the classroom with their students. A great leader encourages a good balance of positive give-and-take and promotes collaborative efforts, with the goal of achieving mutually beneficial outcomes.

I think a lot of well-meaning managers are afraid of undercutting their authority if they ever solicit suggestions and advice from the people they supervise. They ignore the fact that, especially in retail, the best ideas often come from the employees who are closest to the customer contact level. Instead of establishing rational lines of demarcation, these managers erect insurmountable walls between themselves and their workers. To me, that's cutting off your nose to spite your face. A manager who never listens to the people he leads or disregards what he does hear is not leading. For my part, I remain sincerely grateful to employees like Lindsey Reed, who, at every step of my career, have taught me invaluable lessons that contributed to my becoming a better manager and a more effective leader.

These observations are leading to my next move up the McDonald's ladder. I was about to take on a management role that, just months before, would have been inconceivable for a black man. And once again, Carl Osborne would open the way by showcasing my achievements.

A CALL FROM CHICAGO

Carl was the second African American hired into management by Gee Gee Distributing. Just like me a few years later, Carl had no ambition to make his career in the restaurant trade. He had attended Florida A&M, been drafted and served in an integrated Army unit in Germany, and then finished college on the GI Bill. In Jacksonville, Florida, he had worked as a postal clerk and successfully led a protest that ended unlawfully segregated facilities—restrooms, drinking fountains, lunchrooms—in the post office building. With his wife, Doris, he'd moved to Washington with the objective of earning a law degree. In August 1963, Carl was hired as a McDonald's management trainee by Oscar Goldstein, one of Gee Gee's two owners. Carl initially saw the job as a way to fund law school, but in his interview, he learned that Mr. Goldstein was serious about employing blacks to expand Gee Gee's franchise inside D.C. By the time Carl completed his training, he was converted to the restaurant business.

Carl was as committed as any man I ever knew to creating opportunities in management for other black people. He was smart; he worked incredibly hard; he could be cautious, but he wasn't afraid to stand up to white managers and supervisors when he knew he was in the right. I think Carl brought some of his own racial prejudices up with him from the South, but he changed when he began working with his mixed crews of employees and socializing with some of the white managers. He said that his first good relationship with a white person in McDonald's was with his supervisor, Paul Rinhard. (Paul, a terrific guy, was also the supervisor who provided me with the 3510 Duke Street opportunity.) Their friendship opened Carl's eyes to the positive benefits, personally and in business, of real communication between the races.

But in his crusade to get more blacks into management positions, Carl never mellowed. He used to say that as a black man in a white company, you give the business your loyalty, your time, and your hard work, "but you never give up your black soul." Lose your black soul, he said, and you have given away your self-esteem.

What galled Carl, who was managing a store on New York Avenue when I first met him, was this: The expansion of Gee Gee's stores inside D.C. was progressing rapidly, and the new stores were full of black employees, but there were just two black managers—Carl himself and Matt Mitchell. When Paul Rinhard was named director of operations (managing all the regional supervisors), Carl took over as supervisor of the D.C. restaurants—the first black supervisor in the entire McDonald's system. He was already scouting for capable black assistant managers to promote when the opportunity presented itself. His first chance came when a corrupt white store manager in a Maryland suburb was fired by senior management. Carl recommended Bob Beavers, whom he had trained and mentored. Bob got the job.

But it was the D.C. riots that gave Carl his real breakthrough, and he changed the color of inner-city management. As he explained when he offered me the Bladensburg Road restaurant, it was no longer possible to assure the safety of white managers in the riot areas. The city restaurants he supervised had been increased from five—the normal load—to twelve. McDonald's Corporation had purchased all of Gee Gee's stores, and corporate executives, who had no experience dealing with this kind of crisis, turned to Carl. The most experienced black men in the old Gee Gee system were brought in as inner-city restaurant managers. A few, like me, were already managing stores, but most were talented assistants primed to move up.

Carl set high standards because he knew that if one person failed, it would reflect on everyone. That was a fact of life not unique to McDonald's. For blacks, members of other minorities, and women to succeed in corporate America, they had to work twice as hard and do twice as well as white men. Carl could not allow any weak links to break down the chain of black managers he was assembling in D.C. As our immediate supervisor, he followed every move made by his black managers. He wanted results, and he got them. What we accomplished in D.C. clearly impressed some key executives in corporate headquarters, and over the next few years, the black-managed McDonald's stores in Washington became the primary farm team for the major league of corporate management.

The first corporate opening came in the fall of 1968. McDonald's decided to hire an African American as a regional field consultant in Chicago, a position somewhat similar to a supervisor's but with a constituency of store owners rather than managers. Outside of Washington, there were no black supervisors in the system and never had been. But the winds of change were picking up strength. In the inner sanctums at McDonald's corporate headquarters on LaSalle Street in downtown Chicago and in the regional headquarters in the Chicago suburb of Oak Brook, white executives were making decisions that were, in the context of most of corporate America at the time, radical. If McDonald's was to move forward with its expansion into urban centers, the company needed the expertise of people who understood urban markets—racially and ethnically complex populations that were entirely unlike the homogeneous white suburbs where the company had flourished since Ray Kroc founded McDonald's System Inc. in 1955. It wasn't altruism that integrated the company. It was a hard-nosed business decision.

Carl was asked to recommend someone for the field position in Chicago's Midwest regional office. At a meeting of his D.C. managers, Carl asked if anyone might want the job. Several of us expressed interest, so two corporate executives—Ed Schmitt and Frank Phalen—came to D.C. to interview us. After these meetings, as Carl drove the execs back to the airport, they asked him if he had a favorite candidate. Carl said that I was his choice. Later, he told me the reasons he gave. He cited my teaching and radio experience— strong training and communications skills. He praised my people, sales, and management skills. He told them how I had taken the Bladensburg Road store to "a level that others had only dreamed of!" (his words, not mine). Carl also believed that I was the best able to work with and lead black restaurant owners. That was very important, because the company was making its first move to actively seek black men to take over franchises in problem areas. The field consultant would be the key link between black franchisees and what was then an all-white corporate management.

As the result of my interview and Carl's "pitch," I was invited to Chicago for more meetings in October of 1968. I learned that the field had been narrowed to two candidates—me and another African American, who was a manager in the Eastern region. I was confident that I could handle the job, but I wasn't sure about how or where I would fit into the white mindset and conservative structure of the company. When I was first taken to the headquarters building and given the standard tour and round of introductions, I couldn't help looking for people like me. I saw only two black faces in a sea of white ones—a woman who may have been a secretary and a man who seemed to be a butler.

I loved the work I was doing in D.C. With my bonuses, the income was great, and I had very real opportunities for further advancement. I had made a home in Washington. I was married now, and my wife had a secure teaching position in the District's public schools. My thirtieth birthday was just a few months away. The prospect of uprooting was more daunting than it had been when I'd headed off to D.C. in my dad's new Chevy and bunked in with my cousin John while I was job-hunting.

Yet every position I had held so far seemed to be building to this point. During three and a half years in Washington, I'd gone from trainee to manager and worked in a variety of socio-economic environments—the middle-class Alexandria store where I trained, the Maryland suburbs, the "in transition" city neighborhood of Good Hope Road, 3510 Duke Street with its white working-class clientele, and finally the riot-torn, all-black Bladensburg Road community. These were experiences that few, if any, managers in white suburbia could equal. I had proved to myself that I could not only handle change but also create it. But what would I be getting into in Chicago?

The situation in Washington was an anomaly within the

company—a unique cluster of black men in management who understood and supported one another. In Chicago, I would be on my own. I was well aware that there were individuals in Chicago who wouldn't welcome a black man into the heart of the corporation, and I wondered how much support I'd get if they offered me the consultant job and I took it. I thrived on challenges and hard work, but I didn't want to be brought in as window dressing—the "token black."

As I walked into the comfortable Oak Brook regional headquarters to be interviewed by men who could alter the future for me, I had a lot of questions but little idea of what to expect. A bit of an Old Testament verse from my Sunday school days flashed into my head. I was indeed "a stranger in a strange land."

Chapter 6

Moving Up the Ladder

Management is doing things right; leadership is doing the right things.

PETER DRUCKER, ECONOMIST AND MANAGEMENT GURU

Probably the most meaningful part of my October trip to Chicago was the people. I had interviews long conversations really with Ed Schmitt, vice president and Midwest regional manager, and Frank Phalen, both of whom I'd already met back in D.C., and with Mike Quinlan, who was Ed's administrative assistant. If I got the job, Ed would be my boss and Frank my department head.

Frank, a field service manager for McDonald's Midwest region, had picked me up at the airport and taken me on a tour of nine of the restaurants that I would be responsible for if I accepted the job. The last store we saw, located at 6560 South Stoney Island Avenue on Chicago's South Side, was considered the most troubled in the territory. In every respect, it was in worse condition than any McDonald's I had ever seen, including the Bladensburg Road store when I first went there. The Stoney Island restaurant looked shabby and dilapidated; many of the tiles on the exterior were broken or gone, the lighted arches and road signs were broken, and the lot and side streets were filthy. Other businesses and buildings in the area were generally well kept, and there was a nice park across the street, so the store stood out like a sore thumb. Inside, much of the equipment either wasn't working or functioned poorly. I saw buckets everywhere, some catching water that leaked from the ceiling and others catching grease dripping from the obsolete frying vats. No one was really supervising the employees, and the food was terrible—served up dry, hard, and cold.

None of the employees was dressed in the McDonald's uniform, and everybody's white apron, including the manager's, was dirty and covered with grease and ketchup stains. This store had basically been taken over by one of Chicago's most notorious street gangs, the Blackstone Rangers, whose 'headquarters' was a nearby community center. Some of the Rangers worked in the restaurant, and others hung out there. This created the ideal environment for a lot of unauthorized food giveaways; I could imagine how many meals were not paid for and how much cash was disappearing from the till.

I appreciated being shown the stores, especially the one on Stoney Island Avenue. Right off the bat, I gained a much clearer understanding of the challenges I would be facing. In the meetings that followed, Ed and Frank didn't try to gloss over the problems. Chicago's inner city wasn't so different from D.C. Neighborhoods had already changed or were in the process of transitioning from working-class white to lower-income black populations. In the aftermath of Dr. King's assassination, black anger and resentment were running high, and it wasn't safe for white owners and managers, who were perceived as exploiting the community. Some of the white owners—men I'd be working with directly—feared for their lives and had basically abandoned their stores. When a white field consultant was shot at on the parking lot of the Stoney Island store, their worst fears had been confirmed. As far as I knew, McDonald's had never given up on a store, but the company had little idea about how to rescue locations like Stoney Island Avenue.

When the formal job offer was made to me, I didn't immediately jump at it. I had doubts, especially when I was told that the salary was substantially lower than my expectations. I needed time to evaluate the pros and cons of the move. I would be giving up the kind of bonuses I received as a store manager in D.C., although perks, like a company car, that came with the new job might compensate for much of the decrease in pay. Ed and Frank made it clear that they weren't asking for miracles, but I would be expected to show some notable progress by the end of a year. A six-month job review was general practice, and if things were going well, I would be considered for a salary increase.

I wanted the job. My experience in D.C. told me that even a store like the one on Stoney Island Avenue could be an opportunity. In spite of less money, the position in Chicago was definitely a move up the ladder. But I had another concern. I wondered how much support a black man would get from inside the McDonald's Corporation and if I would be accepted by the white owner-operators.

Ed Schmitt had a tremendous impact on my decision. He was a straight shooter, and he didn't pull any punches. He told me that the company needed me but a lot of people didn't know that they needed me. He said that a number of people in the corporation weren't ready for me—or any blacks—in positions higher than local store management. Ed didn't try to hide the truth; he wanted to prepare me for the kinds of racism I was likely to encounter as the only black man in a white, Midwestern, conservative corporate environment. He said that some people might not even talk to me and that almost everybody would talk about me. With embarrassment, he admitted that irrational racist stereotypes still prevailed in some people's minds, like the fear that a black man might try to date the white secretaries in the office. Ed clearly wanted me to come on board, but only if I knew exactly what I was getting into.

The irony is that Ed's frankness and his genuine concern for my welfare impressed me so much that I wanted to work for him. He reminded me of my father and my Grandpa Jimmy Jones. As Ed talked, I thought about one of my dad's sayings: "Sometimes it's good to get in over your head; it makes you look up."

I had to choose. I could stay in Washington, where managers were the best compensated in the McDonald's system, and hope that changes would bring opportunities for future advancement. Or I could step up now and, maybe, open opportunities for others like me. I knew that I had Ed Schmitt, Frank Phalen, and Mike Quinlan on my side, and the other execs I'd met had been friendly. Besides, I was the first black man ever to be offered the chance to advance from local management into McDonald's corporate structure—the first black empowered to speak to and for corporate management. What message would I be sending to my people if I turned it down?

I decided that the opportunities in Chicago outweighed the obstacles, and I said "yes." Honestly, I was confident that I could do the job, but returning to D.C., I still wondered how I would handle the prejudice that Ed Schmitt had warned me about. I had done well so far, dealing with individual bigotry at the store level. But as the lone black man in the regional office, under the nose of corporate headquarters, was I getting in over my head? Only time would tell.

I returned to D.C. to wrap up business there and begin packing. At Thanksgiving, I flew back to Chicago for several days to find a place to live and organize the move. Frank Phalen, who was helping me look for housing, introduced me to Guy Roderick, one of the inner-city store owners. Guy was great; he gave me the lowdown on life in the city and different residential options. Thanks in part to his advice, I chose an apartment on the South Side that put me near the stores I would be serving. I wanted to be in the community and close to the action.

Before I left D.C. for good in December, my McDonald's friends in Washington gave me a going-away party. It was an emotional gathering for all of us, and I could see in their faces how much hope they were investing in me. So much was riding on my success. If I made it, others would follow. But if I failed, it would justify the thinking of those who wanted to keep the corporation lily white. I could either pave the way for more African Americans in the company and help elevate the status of McDonald's urban operations, or I could create new roadblocks. The burden was on my back, and it was a heavy load.

REPORTING FOR WORK

January 6, 1969: It was a cold Monday morning when I reported to McDonald's regional headquarters to start my new job. Typical weather for Chicago was bone chilling to a Southerner like me. I wasn't a stranger to the snow and cold, but the wind …. In Chicago, they call the wind off the lakes "the hawk," but I thought it was more like an icy knife, capable of cutting through the heaviest overcoats. I hurried toward the warmth of the office building on 22nd Street in Oak Brook.

I went up to the fifth floor and entered a large space filled with offices, secretaries' desks, and a small area of office cubicles. I soon learned that the cubicles were reserved for the field consultants and the McOpCo store supervisors. (McOpCo is the acronym for

109

McDonald's Operating Companies, the corporate division that manages stores owned by the corporation.) Regional field consultants and McOpCo supervisors spent so much time out in the stores that we didn't really need regular offices.

The receptionist wasn't at her desk yet, so I wandered in, looking for a familiar face. There was a break room down the hall, and several white men were gathered around the coffee maker. As a black man in a business suit, I immediately attracted curious looks.

Mike Quinlan came to meet me. Mike, a quiet guy in his mid-twenties, was Ed Schmitt's administrative assistant, and he was also in charge of franchising. When he was a college student, Mike had begun his McDonald's career working in the mail room, and eventually he went on to be chief executive officer and chairman of the corporation. From my first day on the job, Mike was very supportive; he was a great resource for me and always made himself available when I needed his assistance. I soon considered him a friend. Mike, who had grown up in one of Chicago's West Side bedroom communities, had never known many African Americans, and like most white people his age, he was naïve about black culture. He wanted to learn, and I enjoyed teaching him about our black folkways. In the meantime, he taught me about franchising, purchasing, and corporate culture. It was a profitable exchange.

Frank Phalen was there too, and he began introducing me to my new co-workers. Ed Schmitt made a special point of coming out of his office and greeting me. It was a thoughtful gesture. I knew Ed was glad to see me, and his personal welcome set the tone for everyone else in the region—whatever their private feelings about having a black colleague might be.

Frank showed me to my cubicle, then took me to his office where we reviewed my schedule. My first several weeks were to be

110

an intense orientation. I spent most of that time meeting with department heads and managers in the corporate and regional offices, getting acquainted with what they did in fine detail. I also spent a lot of time with other field consultants. There was much for me to learn. As a former store manager, I knew the ins and outs of running a restaurant. But as a consultant, I would be the point man between the company and the owners of all the stores assigned to me. I had to be fully informed about every aspect of the business, from real estate to marketing. I had to know how the system worked, who did what, and where to go for answers to my questions.

At that time, there were six regions in the McDonald's system: Midwest, Mideast, West, South, East, and the newly designated Mid-Atlantic region, which was formed after McDonald's purchased Gee Gee's forty-plus stores in D.C., Maryland, and Virginia. The Midwest region, under Ed Schmitt, comprised Illinois, Minnesota, Wisconsin, North Dakota, South Dakota, Nebraska, Iowa, Kansas, Missouri, and Indiana. This region had a special significance because it was the corporation's home base. Ray Kroc was born in Chicago, the son of Bohemian immigrants. Except for a brief time in Florida in the 1920s, it had always been his base. He had built his first McDonald's restaurant in the suburb of Des Plaines, and he'd set up his company in a downtown Chicago office building. Unlike a lot of corporate chiefs, Mr. Kroc never lost contact with the ground level of his operation—the stores. And Chicago was right under his eyes.

In 1969, there were two field service managers in the Midwest region; Frank had the Chicago metropolitan area and northern Indiana, and I reported to him. I was assigned fourteen stores. The usual load for a field consultant was around thirty stores (and by the end of my first year, my own territory would grow to thirty-one). But nine of my first restaurants were the most troubled in the region, so I wasn't being given an easy assignment.

111

As it turned out, I wasn't the only one breaking down barriers at that time. One night during my orientation, Frank took me to a dinner meeting of the Chicago-area McDonald's owners association. This group included the men with whom I'd be working, and I was pleased to have the chance to meet them. It was a nice evening at a historic Italian restaurant, the Como Inn. As I'd expected, everyone was white, but I was welcomed by most of the owners. Then, toward the end of the event, I met a black man whom Frank had already told me about. His name was Herman Petty, and he had just become the first and only black owner-operator (with two white partners) in the McDonald's system. His restaurant was located at 6560 South Stoney Island Avenue—the store I mentioned earlier as the worst one I had visited back when I interviewed in October. Herman and I only had time for a very brief chat, so we agreed to get together again soon. I had no way of knowing how much time I would be spending with Herman.

INSIDE THE MCDONALD'S SYSTEM

Field consultants were the heavy-lifters in the McDonald's system. Our "customers"—which is how I thought of my clients—were the restaurant owners, or franchisees; in McDonald's, they were later referred to as "licensees." Most owners operated their stores; in partnerships, McDonald's required that the operating partner own at least fifty-one percent of his restaurant. This rule reflected Ray Kroc's basic work ethic; owners should stay close to their customers and be directly involved at the store level. There were plenty of "silent partners," but the owner-operator had to be the majority owner, with his feet firmly planted in daily management.

Field consultants didn't supervise owner-operators; our

responsibility was to work *with* them and to see that the company's responsibilities to its franchisees were fulfilled. The ideal relationship between owner-operators and field consultants was collaborative. We worked together, as a team, with the goal of maximizing each owner's benefits through efficient implementation of the McDonald's system. Field consultants monitored the stores (this function was completely open and owner-operators knew that we were exercising oversight), graded current performance, and also helped owners anticipate future obstacles and opportunities. A good consultant spent ninety percent of his time in the field, working with the owner-operators in their stores and helping them adhere to McDonald's standards in order to consistently get the most out of the company's nationwide system and resources.

What distinguished McDonald's in the fast-food industry was its *comprehensive system*. When Ray Kroc started the company in 1955, other food franchising corporations had little contact with their local owners. National companies like Tastee-Freeze and Dairy Queen, the leaders in those days, sold regional franchises, so a single franchisee would hold the rights to a very large territory or an entire state. The regional franchisees then licensed sub-franchisees, who were responsible for their individual units. The franchiser at the top of the pyramid had almost no control (and often didn't want it) over the stores that carried his company's name, and standards varied wildly from place to place. But as long as the franchise company collected its royalties, everyone seemed to be okay with this highly decentralized and often haphazard structure.

Mr. Kroc had a very different approach. Although he licensed a few large territories to owners like Gee Gee Distributing, McDonald's did not have sub-franchisees. Mr. Kroc and his first employees developed a true, top-to-bottom system with clearly defined lines of communication between the corporation and store owners. Each part of the system was designed to support each other part and to assure the standardization that was, to Ray Kroc, the key to quality products and service, growth, and profitability. By standardizing stores, facilities, and every phase of operations—including suppliers—the McDonald's concept could be easily cloned in virtually any location. Standardization simplified training of managers and employees. Standardized operational procedures (contained in McDonald's voluminous operations manual) accommodated easy execution, consistent quality control and customer service, and monitoring of stores. With the standards and procedures clearly spelled out, often in excruciating detail, standardization promoted daily adherence at the store level to the corporation's goals of quality product, speedy service, and cleanliness.

The system wasn't monolithic. It could be adapted when a change was likely to produce improvements. Ray Kroc always encouraged new thinking, whether it came from an executive or a store manager, that could lead to better ways to do things. He was the role model because he had started McDonald's by looking at fast-food service with a fresh eye, and he revolutionized the whole industry by doing something different. His McDonald's didn't just license a name and provide a few typed pages of operations guidelines. McDonald's licensed its *System,* in which no detail was left to chance. Although individual owners had a great deal of freedom in the management of their stores, the ultimate control was always focused at the top of the company. Over time, through trial and error, Mr. Kroc and his key executives evolved a business model that became the gold standard for the industry.

The history of the McDonald's Corporation has been well

documented elsewhere, so I'm not going to repeat it. But for my story, it is important to explain how much authority and responsibility resided in McDonald's corporate and regional offices. The first field consultant (before the title existed) was Fred Turner—an intense, driven man who basically created the McDonald's operating system. Fred, an Army vet and college dropout, had been hired by Mr. Kroc in 1956. He worked with new franchisees, helping them get their stores open, educating them in the principles of QSC—quality, service, cleanliness—and monitoring their performance. While Mr. Kroc was on the road selling franchises, Fred Turner was using what he learned from his early clients (and from his own experience working in a couple of McDonald's restaurants in Chicago) to map out the system that would make consistency the hallmark of everything McDonald's does. He put the rules, the methods, and the rationales on paper, developing not just a manual but the bible of operations.

By the time I started in Chicago, Fred Turner was the president and chief administrative officer of the company. Ray Kroc was chairman of the Board and chief executive officer. I eventually got to know them both and to see how they complemented each other. Mr. Kroc (I always called him that) was a visionary thinker, focused on the big picture, and a natural leader; he demanded perfection, but he lacked the temperament to attend to details on a regular basis. He was not a micro-manager. Like most entrepreneurs, he wasn't really a manager. However, his genius was that he recognized the talents of people like Fred Turner, with his laser-eye for details, and Harry Sonneborn, the financial brain behind McDonald's profitability—men who were highly effective managers and shared his loyalty to the company and the system.

Mr. Kroc was over fifty when he founded the company. For most of his working life, he had been a top salesman of other people's products, and he had a reasonable success with his own company, marketing Multimixer milk shake mixing equipment to soda fountain and fast food operations in the 1940s. But at an age when most men begin to contemplate a comfortable retirement, Mr. Kroc was still searching for his pot of gold. He found it in the long lines of customers he observed at the most popular drive-in hamburger stand in San Bernadino, California. The two brothers who owned the stand, Maurice and Richard McDonald, were doing something unlike anything Mr. Kroc had seen in all his years of selling Multimixers to burger joints across the country. As he wrote in his autobiography, *Grinding It Out*, "It was a restaurant stripped down to the minimum in service and menu, the prototype of legions of fast-food units that later would spread across the land. Hamburgers, fries, and beverages were prepared on an assembly line basis …. Of course, the procedure allowed the [McDonald brothers] to concentrate on quality in every step, and that was the trick."

Mr. Kroc spent a year convincing the McDonald brothers that *he* was the right person to introduce the McDonald's name and the McDonald's system to the nation beyond San Bernadino. His original motive was to expand his Multimixer business, not to become the king of fast food, and he thought he could sell his McDonald's franchises in his spare time! But he saw how American society was changing in the post-World War II boom years. He could envision the role that speedy food service would play in the brave new world of nuclear families, suburban houses with two-car garages, shopping malls, and restaurant customers whose dining priorities were reliably good food, convenient locations, fast service, and value for their money. I remember him saying, "We have to know what our customers want before our customers know what they want."

From everything Mr. Kroc later said and wrote about the

history of his corporation (which was first named McDonald's System Inc.), it's clear that at the start, he was in over his head. But he always looked up, not down. He had the extraordinary ability to inspire absolute loyalty to his vision. About a month after Mr. Kroc opened his first company-owned store, he hired Harry Sonneborn, a finance guy who had just quit his job at Tastee-Freeze and was determined to sign on with McDonald's. Sonneborn, like Mr. Kroc's secretary June Martino, worked for little take-home pay but showed his faith by taking stock. The next year, Fred Turner came on board for wages of $475 a month, according to *Grinding It Out*. Most of those early employees and many of the first owners and investors became mega-millionaires—a reward for years of hard work and devotion to Ray Kroc's vision.

When I started work in Chicago, I was too preoccupied with my new responsibilities to think much about senior management or my own long-range prospects. After my orientation, I hit the ground running and began meeting with the owners of the fourteen stores in my portfolio. At first, I did a lot of looking, listening, and tasting. The stores all had similar problems, but in different degrees. Guy Roderick's store on South Cottage Grove, for instance, was in good shape, but Guy was looking to sell and relocate to Florida. He needed my help to facilitate a rapid sale and a smooth transition to a new owner. I worked with his store manager to refine some aspects of operations and get the restaurant in top form—like sprucing up a house before putting it on the market. (Early in the company's history, McDonald's developed a real estate system by which the company owned both the land and the buildings, leasing the locations to owners. When a restaurant was sold, the owner set the price and negotiated the sale, but the company had to approve the transfer of ownership and leasing contracts.)

117

McDonald's graded stores on an A-to-F scale, like in school. On that scale, Guy's city restaurant and three others were probably at B- or C+. The Stoney Island Avenue McDonald's and several other stores were Fs.

The inner-city restaurants were largely staffed and sometimes managed by blacks but owned by whites. For a variety of reasons—including poverty and lack of employment, populations that were rapidly shifting from predominately white to black or ethnically mixed, and the growing militancy of young blacks who seemed to gain nothing from the end of legal discrimination—it had become nearly impossible for white owners to control their operations. There were exceptions; a couple of my client stores in middle-class black neighborhoods functioned well. But the general atmosphere was so tense that a number of white owners rarely made an appearance inside their restaurants. They weren't getting much help from the higher-ups because, frankly, corporate McDonald's was as bewildered as the owners. The inner-city shift from white to black happened so quickly—Mike Quinlan recalls that the change occurred in a five-or-six year period beginning in the early 60s—that the company was taken unawares. The first signs were declining sales, followed by more management problems, high employee turnover, and increases in crime and vandalism. Mr. Kroc's vision of post-World War II America hadn't included decaying inner cities. The customers that the company cherished were suburban families—mom, dad, and their kids—and suburbanites in the late 1960s were white.

McDonald's Urban Problem

There were already some McDonald's stores in cities, but this was more a matter of chance than choice. It typically happened when a successful suburban owner wanted to open an urban location (as Gee Gee Distributing had expanded into inner-city D.C.) or when stores on the fringes of cities were swallowed up by metropolitan expansion. The McDonald's corporate mindset remained firmly suburban, although stores inside large cities were often among the most profitable in the system, due primarily to higher sales volumes. Whether inner-city communities were rich, poor, or in-between, residential or commercial, their populations were large and concentrated. For the fast-food industry, more people generally meant more customers and higher sales, although there were some notable exceptions.

Ray Kroc had understood that the real key to sales was speed of service, combined with a limited menu of quality products and low prices. Back in those days, fast-food companies were operating in a seller's market; people would buy what they produced. McDonald's sold burgers, fries, shakes, and cold drinks—no Value Meals, no Happy Meals, no breakfast menu, and for sure, no salads. A double hamburger and double cheeseburger had been introduced in 1963, the Filet O' Fish sandwich a year later. The Big Mac wasn't added until 1968.

A short menu with few variations—customized orders were strongly discouraged—and assembly-line production meant that food orders could be prepared, assembled, bagged, and handed to the customer in less than a minute. The McDonald's system also accommodated consistent control over the quality of the food. The burger and fries a customer bought today would look and taste the same as the burger and fries he bought yesterday or last week or six months ago. The McDonald's product and speed of service was perfectly suited to big-city business districts. For low-end, white-collar city workers in the 1960s—secretaries, office clerks, sales clerks and the like, who got no more than thirty minutes for lunch and didn't have expense accounts to cover their meals—*fast* food was quickly replacing the traditional deli, cafeteria, or brown-bag-from-home lunch. McDonald's provided filling meals quickly and at prices working people could afford every day.

Out in suburbia, fast-food meals were still regarded as a convenient alternative to mom's cooking. In the 1970s, one of the company's most memorable advertising campaigns—"You Deserve a Break"—would capitalize brilliantly on the image of busy suburban women who turned to McDonald's as a reliable, family-pleasing treat on those occasions when it just wasn't possible to get a home-cooked meal on the family table.

In poor city neighborhoods, however, the catchy "You Deserve a Break" jingle fell flat. Poor working people don't get breaks; the challenge of feeding themselves and their families was a struggle. Then, as now, grocery prices were often exorbitantly high in hardcore urban centers. Most city dwellers didn't have easy and regular access to suburban supermarkets and their lower prices. Weekly grocery shopping was nearly impossible for people who relied on buses, subways, and their own, tired feet. In addition to the high cost of groceries, meal preparation could be difficult for people who were holding down several jobs and working at backbreaking tasks, often for earnings at or below minimum wage. So for poor and working-class city folks, cheap and tasty fast food wasn't just a convenient option; it was like the answer to a prayer. A typical inner-city family could eat well at a McDonald's for a good deal less money than they would spend on groceries for a comparable meal.

The sales opportunities stimulated McDonald's interest in the cities. Fred Turner recognized the bottom-line significance of inner-city stores. After the April 1968 riots—which occurred in a number of cities where McDonald's already had stores—he also saw that the company's suburban model couldn't simply be imposed on urban operations. He and his corporate executives didn't know how to proceed. But they wanted the problem fixed, especially after their experience in Cleveland, Ohio.

In the fall of 1969, when I had been in Chicago for less than a year, the whole country was treated to headlines about a dramatic boycott of four white-owned, inner-city McDonald's restaurants by black activists in Cleveland. Led by David Hill, a self-anointed "rabbi," angry residents set up picket lines at the stores on the city's predominately black East Side. They were demanding that McDonald's remove the white franchisees and replace them with black owners from the community. The protests turned violent, and McDonald's responded by temporarily taking over the four restaurants. (What the protestors didn't know, or didn't want to hear, was that McDonald's had already approved the sale of one store to a black man, Chuck Johnson, and was actively seeking other black owner-operations. The irony is that the boycott *delayed* the finalizing of Chuck's deal for several months and slowed down the company's recruiting efforts.)

Desperate for a peaceful resolution, the company sent in some of my friends from D.C.—including Carl Osborne, Roscoe Coleman, who had become the manager of my old Bladensburg Road store, and Bob Beavers, a D.C. alumnus who had been promoted to a corporate position six months after I started my job. There was some discussion about me joining this team in Cleveland, but because I was already establishing good relationships with a couple of black owners in Chicago, I decided to stay out of the fray. If I went to Cleveland, there was a good chance I might be perceived as a corporate "Uncle Tom" by the black owners, managers, and employees in the Chicago communities. I didn't want to risk damaging the trust I was building with our new black owners and potential owners.

Carl Osborne told me how he arrived in Cleveland wearing his blue McDonald's blazer and tie. At the airport, he was confronted by a restroom attendant, who was black and very angry. In a barrage of four-letter words, the attendant made it plain that the McDonald's boycott was deadly serious. Carl remembered hurrying to another restroom and changing his clothes before going to see the restaurants that were under siege. The situation at the stores was so volatile that a white police sergeant gave Bob Beavers a gun and told him how to use it.

Based on what they saw, Bob and the D.C. guys gave their recommendations to corporate, and the company—represented by Ed Bood, the vice president of franchising and a lawyer; Don Devitt, the Mideast regional manager; and Bob Beavers—entered negotiations. The company agreed to re-franchise the Cleveland stores to black owners, but Bood balked at "Rabbi" Hill's demands that he and the other activists receive a hefty "commission" to "supervise" the choice of black owners. When these terms were publicly revealed by a local black physician and political leader, the steam went out of the boycott. David Hill was shown up as a con artist. He was later convicted of blackmail in another incident and fled the country.

The whole mess settled down, but it (and McDonald's first serious and potentially negative experience in the spotlight of national press coverage) accelerated the sense of urgency at corporate headquarters in Chicago. The company *had* to pursue a more aggressive minority franchising program. The question was whom to recruit and how to go about it, and the company was looking to Bob Beavers and me for leadership in its recruitment effort.

SALT AND PEPPER

As I mentioned, the Cleveland boycott happened before the end of my first year as a field consultant. In the meantime, we had begun to make progress in Chicago, but I was learning how hard it was to find black men to be owner-operators. The cost of a franchise was one big obstacle. The black middle class then was still small, so the pool of potential owner-operators was limited. The average cost of a new, turnkey McDonald's franchise was around $150,000. Purchase prices were more varied for existing stores, and those with a history of strong sales could be very expensive. But either way, few banks were anxious to lend money for what they considered "ghetto" enterprises.

In 1968, two white Chicago businessmen—I'll just call them Mr. X and Mr. Y—pitched an idea to McDonald's that must have seemed like a godsend. The plan was to put black and white investors together in what became known as "salt and pepper," or "zebra," ownership packages. The black partner in these arrangements would be the owner-operator and the visible face in his store, without having to come up with the full cost of the franchise. The white partners would bring business savvy to the table; provide a substantial part of the capital for a turnkey operation, including training, labor, and adequate working capital; and share the profits, but they would stay in the background. To the men in the corner offices, it must have sounded like the logical way to expedite black ownership and fix their urban problem. In practice, it was often a disaster, especially for the black partners.

I didn't know too much about "salt and pepper" partnerships when I started work in Chicago, although Frank Phalen had mentioned Herman Petty's deal to me. The basic idea was to get the black owners into the communities first, improve the stores, and

123

eventually enable black owners to use their profits to buy out their white partners, which seemed like a positive objective to me. McDonald's goal—to get black owners into black neighborhoods as quickly as possible—was well-intentioned but incredibly naïve. In reality, it was more a hope than a plan, because no one knew how these partnerships would work in the real world. What mattered was that Fred Turner thought it was a good solution, and he stuck by the "salt and pepper" concept even after it proved to be unworkable.

I learned about the reality from Herman Petty—the first black owner in the system and the first *victim* (my word, not his) of the "salt and pepper" plan. Herman owned a barbershop up the street from the Stoney Island Avenue store, and he also drove a city bus at night. By the standards of the time, he was solidly in the black middle class, but he certainly didn't have the funds on hand to buy a McDonald's franchise.

Herman later told me how his ownership came about. He had attended a franchise trade show and met Mr. X and Mr. Y, who were interested in finding a black partner for a McDonald's franchise. Herman knew nothing about fast food or franchising himself, but he trusted Mr. X, an experienced CPA, and Mr. Y, who was a sales manager for an international office equipment company. After a number of months of planning, the three approached McDonald's and bought the Stoney Island franchise for $125,000 (over-priced considering the state of the store's physical facilities, rapidly declining sales, and poor image in the community). After-tax profits were to be divided equally—a third to each partner—an arrangement that effectively assured that the sole black partner would never get control of the business while the partnership was in effect. Herman would operate the store, and his partners would train him in the business. At least, that was how it was supposed to work. By the time

I met Herman again in February 1969, he already knew that his store was in serious trouble. He had no experience in this kind of operation, and he had few funds to make the necessary improvements.

Herman's training to be an owner-operator consisted of an advanced operations training course at Hamburger University. To get the maximum benefit from Hamburger U's in-depth operational and basic business curricula, which are rigorous and thorough, a student must come to school with background in McDonald's restaurant operations—the kind of on-the-job experience a person gets as a junior or senior store manager. But Herman had never been in a McDonald's in his life. He didn't know food service and had no franchising experience, and his own background didn't prepare him for the complexities of operating a multifaceted business. His partners, who were essentially hustlers, were no help. When Herman completed his training and walked out of Hamburger U, he was more bewildered than when he began. He is a smart guy, but sending him to Hamburger U was like dropping a fifth grader into a college calculus class. There was no way he could catch up in a matter of a couple of weeks.

When Herman finished his Hamburger U course, he went to one of his partners' offices and met with both partners. As Herman remembers, they drove in separate cars to the Stoney Island store, and after a quick look around, his partners handed him the keys and said, "It's your store, Herman. Go run it." He was expected to take over operations and begin managing the restaurant immediately. He met a few afternoon workers and the nightside shift and wound up staying overnight, going through the inventory. The next morning, he met his dayside employees as they drifted in for work.

He didn't see his partners for a few weeks; Mr. X and Mr. Y were too busy putting together similar "salt and pepper" deals in other cities. Herman was working on salary, and he didn't have the accounting expertise to analyze profit-and-loss statements or the value of management services or accounting fees. So he didn't know that Mr. X and Mr. Y were also charging huge administrative and management fees, based on percentage of sales, against the store—a scheme that I wasn't aware of until almost a year later. Not knowing what his partners were up to, Herman was working day and night, trying to learn the business while he struggled to run the store.

When I began visiting regularly with Herman, he had been on the job for less than two months. I could see that he felt embarrassed because he knew so little about operations. But he wasn't afraid to ask for my help. He told me that he didn't know whether or not the store was an opportunity for him, but he wanted to make it work. Herman had three very important things going for him. First, he understood the community because he was a part of it and was respected by his neighbors—a critical advantage when he dealt with the members of the Blackstone Rangers, the gang which had basically taken over the store under the previous ownership. Second, he was absolutely determined to make the first black-operated restaurant in the McDonald's system into a shining example to everyone. Herman had the positive "one for all and all for one" attitude that positioned him to become an excellent owner. Despite the depressing condition of his store, he knew that someday it could be successful.

Third, Herman was a hard worker, and he set high expectations for himself. He also had a real hunger to learn everything about the business. Right from the start, he made smart business decisions, setting up an account at Hyde Park Bank (which three years later financed his buyout of his partners) and arranging for armored car security service to make daily deposits. His wife, Shirley, who worked a day job, took over the store's administrative responsibilities, and she was a hardworking, dependable, committed team player.

During my first six months in the Midwest region, I initially spent more of my time with Herman than the other owners in my territory. I could do this because a number of the stores were awaiting or in the process of changing ownership; therefore, I could justify relatively limited involvement until new owners came in. Still, I worked one-on-one with all the owners and their store managers to determine the source of whatever difficulties they had and to develop solutions together. In some cases, the trouble was instantly obvious— like a middle-class, suburban type of store that had a true "teen problem," white teenagers swarming the lot in such numbers that it was often impossible for customers to get on the lot at night.

More common were operational difficulties. I often rolled up my sleeves and went back to work in a store—the best way I know to identify and thoroughly understand the magnitude of production obstacles and personnel problems, gauge customer reactions, and evaluate the extent of inefficiencies in customer service. Working alongside a store's employees, I was teaching them by example, demonstrating the company's standards and the benefits of doing things in a set way, and modeling problem solving. By working with store crews, I was showing them that *my* standards were McDonald's standards. I was raising the bar, and good workers rose to the challenge, meeting higher standards and claiming ownership in them. This is the kind of hands-on and interactive instruction that had been so beneficial to me in Mr. Jordan's woodworking classes back at Booker T. Washington High School in Memphis. I knew, from my D.C. experiences, that teaching in this way was almost always the best approach for young workers who are inclined to resent lectures and overreact to criticism they perceive as negative, and it generally worked even better with more mature employees.

Just as important, I was directly and indirectly modeling effective training methods and demonstrating the value of bottom-up communication for the store's owner and managers. This proved to be especially helpful to new owner-operators who had little or no experience in operational management or employee training. The owner-operators were my clients, and my first obligation was to them. However, I quickly came to regard the owners, their managers and employees, and their customers as *my customers*. I was there to communicate at all levels that everybody must serve the customer or serve someone who is serving the customer.

All the stores had some troubles, and about half of them were serious, but in every instance, the owners wanted to make improvements. Still, I hadn't been so sure about how much cooperation I would get when I started. After my first meetings with the individual owners, I planned a get-together with all the owners of stores in black and transitional areas. It seemed like a good idea. These owners had issues in common—particularly related to the changing demographics in the communities they served and their stores' negative image with new and existing customers. Also, several of the owners were preparing their stores for sale (McDonald's was already encouraging white owners to sell and relocate outside black inner-city areas), and I was certain they could benefit from sharing information and supporting each other. I've always had great faith in opening lines of communication and promoting collaborative efforts among people with mutual interests, and I had high hopes for that meeting.

So I arranged for us all to gather one evening in late February in a classroom at Hamburger U. I believe that Herman, the only black owner, couldn't attend that night, so other than me, it was an all-white gathering. I spoke first to get the ball rolling, but I hadn't talked long before I saw the blank looks. No one was paying attention; they just weren't interested in what I had to say. I wasn't sure why they even came to the meeting—curiosity or maybe as a courtesy. Whatever their motives, I was certain my meeting had turned into a fiasco.

Then a man named Norm Rothenberg asked to shake my hand. Norm was one of the owners of the advertising agency for the Chicago-area stores, and I had asked him to attend in order to participate in the discussion of marketing issues. I didn't know what he had in mind, but I wasn't getting anywhere on my own. Norm stepped forward. He held my hand firmly as he addressed the owners. "I understand what Roland is saying," he began. "Look at our hands. You can't tell from my hand that I'm Jewish. But from Roland's hand, you can see that he's black. He knows what he's taking about. He's lived it. He feels it. And we should listen to him."

Norm saved the meeting. The men in the room began talking to me and to each other. I'm still not completely sure why the owners initially gave me the cold shoulder, but I doubt racism had much to do with it. It seems more likely that, when I stood to address the room, I represented the company, not my race. These owners had been given a lot of promises in the past, but they had seen little action. Some of them felt they were being driven out of their stores. In their eyes, I was just another company "suit"—somebody offering up more promises that wouldn't be fulfilled. And they'd heard it all before.

Norm Rothenberg reminded them that I was different. For the first time, McDonald's had sent in a black man to help them, a black man with experience in the kinds of urban neighborhoods their restaurants served. Norm's handshake and his words cracked the dam of resentment and indifference the owners had built up. It was a productive meeting after all, and from that time on, I got the kind of cooperation that was essential for me to establish trust and do my job.

129

Herman Petty also differed from the white owners in the inner city. Obviously, he was black, but the real distinction was that Herman was staying on, not moving out. Both of us knew that our success was critical to the future of black ownership in McDonald's.

One of the things I worked hardest on with all the owners in my territory was setting priorities. Even in stores with relatively minor problems, it was important to decide what to tackle first. In stores with a multitude of difficulties, an owner-operator could be overwhelmed, not knowing where to begin. Should he try to repair broken or worn-out equipment first? (I knew that raising the subject of large financial outlays was a turn-off; many owners didn't have the money to replace major equipment, and white owners who were selling their stores often didn't want to re-invest in new equipment.) Or should the owner get his employees better trained in order to upgrade quality and product appearance? Should he focus on cleaning up his store, or should he try to solve his wastage and pilferage problems? What often happened was that the owner would attempt to do everything at once, spraying out fixes like room deodorant. The fixes were inadequate and temporary, and they soon fell apart. Lacking focus, the owner would naturally become frustrated, and his enthusiasm for making improvements would fade. Paralysis oftentimes follows frustration.

I immediately concentrated on replacing this unproductive mindset and establishing an attitude of persistence—sticking with a problem until it was resolved. I wanted the owners and their managers to begin thinking from the *customer's point of view*. I would ask an owner-operator what problem most affected his customers' experience at the restaurant and their perception of it. Was it the look of the store and its environment? Was it inconsistency in the quality and appearance of the food? Was it slow service, or was it the quality of the service? Once an owner adjusted his own perspective, he could usually see what he needed to do first. If old equipment was affecting quality or slowing down service, then focus on repairing the equipment and maybe upgrading when it was financially feasible. But if employee training was the main source of the problem, concentrate on upgrading training. I always saw effective, detail-focused training as a major opportunity to make long-term improvements.

Setting priorities didn't mean ignoring other problems, but thinking like a customer enabled an owner to work toward lasting solutions and to see the results in positive customer responses and increased sales.

To establish my own credibility with the owners, I also looked out for their wallets by pointing out simple and easy-to-implement cost-saving opportunities. In D.C. and particularly at the Bladensburg Road store, I had seen the improvements that came from paying attention to seemingly small details that had been taken for granted. Working with owners, I had to raise their consciousness of the cumulative effects of attending to details—how getting control over a multitude of small things spreads success from the customer contact level throughout operations and creates bottom-line profits.

Scraping all the ketchup out of the cans, calibrating the beverage equipment and condiment dispensers every day, and being strict about portion control in food preparation are quick and easy ways to improve consistency while minimizing waste. Here are two more examples of small details that can produce widespread benefits. Breaking down and flattening cardboard boxes so that no product goes outside in boxes without authorization lessens opportunities for employee theft. By flattening boxes and stamping down trash in cans, employees make fewer trips to the dumpster. The lot is cleaner. The owner might be able to reduce the frequency of trash pickups and associated costs. Employees have time for more productive work, labor costs may actually be reduced, and as a bonus, customers get a better impression of the store's physical environment. These simple procedures also cut down on excessive use of plastic can liners, which, unlike that July day in 1965 when I started as a manager trainee, had become standard inventory items.

Attention to cost saving had even broader effects. It changed the way operators, managers, and employees thought about the details of their jobs, and it boosted their self-confidence. The owners often felt better prepared to train their managers and give effective advice.

So my approach was fourfold: improving customer perceptions; helping owner-operators and managers think like customers; empowering them to set priorities; and saving money. Focusing on operational details that could easily be improved opened the way for reducing costs and having more cash available almost immediately—a source of something close to "instant gratification" for owners. Seeing savings in small details often prompted frustrated or discouraged owners to take on larger tasks, even ones they'd avoided in the past. Most began to see that what they'd thought of as their best could continuously get better.

Getting back to Herman Petty, his situation was unique among the urban store owners. Herman had problems that encompassed literally every aspect of his operations: quality, service, cleanliness, and facility maintenance. Not one piece of equipment in his store was in proper working order—if it worked at all. There was no air-conditioning. There was no freezer. He had inherited untrained employees, all gang members, whose work ethic was basically to wing it. Waste and pilferage were rampant. Inside and outside, the store looked like it was ready for the wrecking ball. I imagined what Ray Kroc would do if he ever saw the place, and I thanked our lucky

132

stars that Herman's store was not on the founder's commute route.

How does one set priorities in a situation where everything is a priority? That's what Herman had to decide, and I would help him. As I've said, he had already made some smart business decisions. He had also begun addressing his employee problem, which was enormous. Herman realized at the start that everybody was stealing—lifting money from the cash register or taking food and supplies out the back door. He could have fired them all on the spot, but that would have literally shut down the store. Herman decided to use his advantage—his position as a respected, well-liked, and lifelong member of the local community—to weed out the inherited workers and change the basic makeup of his staff, including his managers. He had a good idea of the type of employees he wanted, and they weren't gang members.

In addition to being smart and a quick learner, Herman has a great personality and gets along well with just about everybody he meets. As the local barber, he already knew many of the young men in the Blackstone Rangers. He had cut their hair since they were little kids. They liked him, and he was black—two very good reasons not to treat Herman as they had the previous white owners. Some of his store workers tried to do better (or at least to stop their stealing) out of respect for Herman and their sense of allegiance to an African American businessman. Herman also cultivated a positive relationship with the leaders of the Rangers, and they helped him whenever one of the gang members in his employ needed to go. The head Rangers would inform the person that he should find other employment, and that was that.

It was always Ray Kroc's preference that McDonald's store employees be male; his suburban vision included clean-cut, smiling, and friendly teenage boys behind the counter of every store. Mr. Kroc believed that mixed-gender crews, especially when the workers were young, invited sexual tensions that slowed productivity and adversely affected the company's All-American family image. That was his personal prejudice, and for a long time, it prevailed. But legally, the corporation couldn't dictate any owner's hiring decisions, and even before Herman came into McDonald's, owner-operators were seriously discussing the hiring of women. So within a few weeks and mostly through attrition, Herman replaced the employees he had inherited—recruiting mainly women, who were generally respected by gang members in those pre-rap music days. He also began hiring returned military veterans as managers. For Herman, hiring women was initially a matter of necessity, since the gang members had proved to be unreliable and non-gang members would have been unacceptable to the Rangers. Women and older vets were more disciplined, more dependable, more willing to learn, and more inclined to work as a team.

A more immediate concern was the sorry state of his store's physical environment and equipment, even though the previous owner had done some superficial cleanup before turning over the store. I worked with Herman to train his employees in the importance of cleanliness. We got them into uniforms, set expectations and taught them how to clean, emphasized attention to details, and made it clear that the exterior appearance of the store was just as important as the interior—everything I had done at Bladensburg Road in D.C. While we were training the employees, I was also teaching Herman how to train others, which he had never done before. Again, he learned fast, and the training got easier as new employees came in.

As for the equipment, well, Herman had no cash available for major repairs, so we decided to fix what we could by ourselves. It was a stopgap solution, but the goal was to get as much as possible in acceptable working condition, and as the store's cash flow improved, to re-invest in professional repairs and replacements. The process of upgrading the crews, cleaning up the store, and making repairs went slowly at first. To my amazement, though, Herman never let down. He practically lived in that store, learning, working, and improving. He even taught himself how to repair major equipment. In addition, he took steps to improve the store's image in the neighborhood, meeting with business, church, and community leaders and telling them about the changes he was making to upgrade the store. When local congregations held church suppers, Herman would donate free burgers, and folks repaid his generosity by patronizing his McDonald's. It was sharp marketing, but for Herman, it was just the right thing to do for people he had known all his life.

By the summer of 1969, sales were going up (and as the cash flow improved, Herman's partners became more interested in trying to divvy up the money). By the end of the year, sales had increased by 75 percent, and Herman was able to take over a second store, located at 7601 South Vincennes Avenue. Though he was still burdened by the "salt" in his "salt and pepper" partnership, Herman didn't have to go through another rocky start at the new restaurant. The second store was newer than his original store but had similar problems— including an untrained, inefficient staff. This time, Herman simply fired them all. He had hired new employees and trained them at Stoney Island prior to the takeover. When the "Under New Management" sign went up on South Vincennes Avenue, its owner-operator and his staff were prepared to tackle the new challenges.

I was spending less time with Herman by then, though we continued to work together on upgrading his restaurants. My own load was growing; I had stores in Kansas City and St. Louis and was preparing for a thirty-one store territory, more than double my original

135

assignment. My clients included all new black owner-operators who had come into the region during the year or were preparing to purchase stores. From the corporation's point of view, good progress on their urban problem was being made, and at review time, I got my pay raise.

But something Herman said on a beautiful spring day in 1970 began to nag at me. We'd just had a one-on-one training session at his Stoney Island store, and we were standing outside, looking in the windows. Herman was rightly proud of what he'd accomplished so far, and he was grateful to me. But he didn't see how I could give the same amount of time, focused attention, and training to each of the new black owner-operators that I had with him. Being assigned all the black-owned stores in the entire Midwest region, at my own request, meant more work and a lot more travel, and Herman knew that I was worried about how I would get everything done.

"Hey, Roland," Herman said, "we don't know anything. We don't even have trained managers. You're the only one who knows the business. But you're frustrated—beating your head against a wall because you're trying to work with everybody like you've done with me. There's no way you can train us all individually. Why don't you get us together and train us as a group?"

Herman was right about my frustration. The new black owners coming into the McDonald's system were no more ready to run their stores than Herman had been. The specifics varied from owner to owner, but they all had to deal with a unique set of concerns, unlike anything their white suburban counterparts faced. Their markets, their employment pools, the kind of training they needed for themselves, the training they provided for their employees, their financing, their security issues, the maintenance and repair of their physical facilities—so much that operators in the hardcore inner cities had to handle was different from the classic McDonald's suburban model.

As the number of black-owned-and-operated stores increased, I found myself struggling to help each of these new and inexperienced owners get their stores up to standard and also to train them to the level where they could really benefit from their required Hamburger U course and the company's supplemental training. In the meantime, I had my other, white-owned stores to help and to monitor. My time was being stretched thinner and thinner, and if I didn't come up with a solution, I didn't see how I could continue to be effective.

Why don't you get us together and train us as a group? I kept turning Herman's question over in my mind. I always encouraged collaboration in the stores and between me and my client operators, but was it possible among owner-operators themselves? Would they be interested in training together and maybe helping each other? I thought that we could make it work, but there was another question: How would the corporation react to the formation of a collaborative, self-help group among its African American owner-operators? I knew that Fred Turner referred to all such efforts within the company as "splinter groups," and I wondered if the corporation would make its resources available to support a black owners' group. Or would they be divisive in a way that would convert a viable solution into a multitude of additional problems? I didn't know, but I found myself increasingly curious to find out.

My grandfather Jimmy Jones taught me the value of money and the meaning of generosity.

My grandmother Totcy Pete Jones always told me to stand out and not blend in.

My grandmother Hattie Porter Williamson started her own business and passed on the entrepreneurial spirit.

My grandfather Gentle Yerger Williamson taught me the value of loving what you do and doing what you love.

My mother, Mary Elizabeth, with my baby brother Carl on
her lap, my daddy, Lewis Charlton Jones, and me in a
1942 family portrait.

That's me, having fun in a 1940 picture taken in the
church yard in my hometown,
Mason, Tennessee.

Fifty-three years later, I'm still enjoying myself, here
with mom, who was 72 when this photo was taken
in Nashville.

Specialist Roland Jones in Korea in 1962. Above,I posed, in
Class A dress uniform, in front of the
barracks, called a hooch, where I lived. Below, I'm
in my khaki uniform, ready for another day at work. Serving in
Korea was a great experience,
teaching me about personal discipline and the
value of diversity.

When I was promoted to field service manager in
McDonald's, Fred Turner, left and Ray Kroc gave me this
personally autographed photo.

Ed Schmitt, my mentor and friend, was the best
business strategist and people manager I ever worked for and was
a tireless champion of diversity at every level in McDonald's.

When times were toughest, Gerry Newman's innovative
financial strategies saved many minority McDonald's
owners from failure.

Mike Quinlan, who rose from the mail room to the chairman's office, was my first friend at McDonald's in Chicago. We sometimes disagreed, but he always supported me and my efforts to achieve diversity.

Tom Burrell, an advertising genius and the father of black consumer advertising in McDonald's, changed the way American companies market to all their customers.

I got to know Ed Rensi many years before he became president of McDonald's. Always a straight-shooter, Ed never hesitated to tell it like he saw it and to switch directions when he was convinced that he had called it wrong.

Chuck Johnson, shown here in his restaurant, became the first black McDonald's franchisee in Cleveland, Ohio, after the 1969 boycott.

This is a 2003 picture of my friend Lee Dunham, left and me with Ruby Stroman. At the 1971 McDonald's international convention, Mrs. Stroman showed us all what it means to stand up and speak truth to people in power.

"Brothers standing on the shoulders of brothers"

Almost from the beginning, African American owner-operators were determined to help each other succeed in the McDonald's system. With my help, their commitment to work collaboratively led to the founding and expansion of the National Black McDonald's Owners Association (NBMOA). Some of the key players in the early days were (top row, left to right) Walter Pitchford of Chicago; Ed Wimp, Chicago; Lee Dunham, New York; and Ralph Kelly, Detroit. (Second row, left to right) Carl Osborne, the first black McDonald's multi-store supervisor and later a franchisee in Columbus, Ohio; Herman Petty, Chicago, the first black McDonald's franchisee; and me.

Walter Pitchford and his wife, Elizabeth, at a National Black McDonald's Operators Association convention.

In 1975, entertainer *par excellence* Sammy Davis, Jr., joined me and others on the Big Mac Bus for a McDonald's grand opening in Reno, Nevada.

Carl Osborne, left, with Mayor Tom Bradley of Los Angeles, who attended the 1979 National Black McDonald's Operators Association convention held in his city.

Carl Osborne took this picture of me holding the first dollar we made in my first McDonald's restaurant in Nashville. Our opening day was memorable for many reasons, including our first robbery.

The "Better Boys' store" in Chicago, a recycled-franchise in 1970, was the first A-rated hardcore urban store. It's also an example of McDonald's original, walk-up-service-only building design.

In 1972, the first convention of the National Black McDonald's® Operators Association barely filled a hotel room.

This congratulatory photo ran in *Ebony* and *Jet* magazines a few years ago to commemorate our first Midwest regional black owners' convention in 1972. That's me, bottom left.

At the 1982 NBMOA convention in New York City, franchisee Al Joyner (standing) got everyone's attention when he spoke to us about the difficulties he was facing in Mobile, Alabama.

My beautiful bride, Susan, and I celebrate our wedding
day in 1987 with our friends Benjamin and Francis Hooks,
plus 400 other reception guests in Nashville. Ben
officiated at the ceremony.

When I turned fifty, Susan threw a surprise birthday party.
Carl Osborne, right, came down from Ohio; the evening
wouldn't have been complete without him.

One of my Nashville buddies, Dr. Bob Mallard (No. 513) and I pass mile 16 of the 1984 Chicago marathon. Only 10.2 miles more to go!

Runners make great friends. In the 1988 Jones-A-Thon, my friend David Wilds, right, and I run the last mile with Al Moore, center, a Nashville lawyer and recent heart transplant recipient.

Susan and I with our friend Mickey Ely, right, prepare to start the 1989 Jones-A-Thon, a January tradition in Nashville.

Roland Parrish, left, a Dallas franchisee, volunteered his staff to help Kurt and Gloria Holloway (center) and other New Orleans McDonald's owners re-open after Hurricane Katrina. He asked me along to give encouragement. With support from individuals, NBMOA, and McDonald's Corporation, owners are feeling confident they can rebound and rebuild.

Chapter 7

Turning New Corners

The difficulty lies not so much in developing new ideas as in escaping from the old ones.

JOHN MAYNARD KEYNES, ECONOMIST

I had gotten through my first year as a field consultant. An anniversary is always a good time to look back and take stock, but I was working too hard to have much time for personal introspection. It was later that I realized how many changes had been set in motion during 1969.

By the end of the year, McDonald's had twelve black-owned-and-operated stores, and more deals were moving through the pipeline. The first *new* black-owned store had been opened in Detroit. The first African American professor, John French, was soon to join the Hamburger University faculty. More black men were beginning to move up in the company, starting with Bob Beavers, who had come from D.C. in July 1969 to serve as director of McDonald's new, corporate Community Action and Development program—a forerunner of the company's Urban Operations department, which I would later direct. Over the winter, the number of black field consultants increased to five, and McDonald's was committed to having at least one black field consultant in every region. The company had survived the Cleveland boycott and was living up to its end of the bargain by installing black owner-operators as rapidly as possible. In the fall of 1969, for the first time in the company's history, black owners and black executives attended McDonald's national convention as full members of the McDonald's family.

Judged by numbers alone, it might not seem that the progress was particularly impressive. But numbers never tell the whole story. McDonald's had walked into what some white executives still considered to be a minefield, and they hadn't backed off. Not everybody in key executive positions was like Ed Schmitt, who welcomed diversity, was actively pursuing integration, and gave me his full support from day one. Ray Kroc didn't have much direct involvement in integrating McDonald's; his focus was on other things, including his recent marriage to his third wife, Joan, and his interest in exploring new directions for his company. (Despite the progress we were making, some people firmly believed that Mr. Kroc was racist, because of several incidents that may or may not have been within his control. I'll discuss those issues in Chapter 8.)

Fred Turner was no gung-ho activist in the cause of diversity either, but he recognized the value of urban markets to McDonald's and the necessity of finding qualified owner-operators who looked and thought like the people of the communities they served. He supported the "salt and pepper" packages, probably because they seemed like a simple and straightforward solution to the problem of finding black owners for stores in urban areas. Fred was a straight-line thinker; if he wanted to get to point D, he would find the most direct route through points A, B, and C. His logical mind had been just what was needed to develop the McDonald's system and to balance Mr. Kroc's visionary leadership. I'm sure Fred believed that the company's diversity problems could be resolved by the same linear A-to-B-to-C methods that he thought worked so well in other business situations.

A lot of the country's white corporate leaders at that time chose to ignore racial, ethnic, and gender issues. I suppose they hoped that the whole "black activist thing" would die down on its own. I credit Mr. Kroc and Fred Turner for addressing the problems—however clumsy the company's initial efforts were.

During my first year in Chicago, I came to understand that neither the company's founder not its president wanted to be directly involved, yet they were willing to give their executives a surprising degree of discretion and latitude in order to get the problems fixed. When I first met Fred Turner, during my orientation in January 1969, he told me that there were two markets he was concerned about—Chicago and Miami. I was there to help with Chicago. Having just come from inner-city, post-riot Washington D.C., I wondered why he defined the company's problems so narrowly. It seemed like focusing on a couple of trees when the forest was on fire. I can't say how his thinking evolved, but six months later, Fred sent out a memo directing his corporate executives, regional managers, field service managers, field consultants, and franchise managers to go the extra mile to assist McDonald's new black owners, wherever they were located. His memo was a landmark. Everyone now knew that integration was a priority with the president of the company. Given the close relationship between the two men at the top of McDonald's, it could be inferred that Fred Turner was also speaking for Ray Kroc.

Shortly before his memo was sent out, I and a few others were meeting with Fred when he said something I've never forgotten. He said, "The time for the white businessman in black areas is over." I knew at the moment that he was totally serious about bringing black owners into McDonald's. He wanted it done.

Except for his support of the "salt and pepper" partnerships, however, Fred didn't personally engage in the push for black ownership. A couple of years later, his concept of company loyalty would lead people around him to try to sidetrack the plans of black owners to organize themselves for mutual support and self-help. But Fred wasn't against black groups; he was against *all* special-interest groups inside the company. To Fred, McDonald's was the group, and any kind of independently organized group inside the company was a betrayal of the whole.

I don't believe that Mr. Kroc, Fred, or the majority of their white executives ever truly understood the cultural differences between the races. As a business problem, yes, they got it on an intellectual level. But in their guts, no. This fact made Fred's dedication some years later to the promotion of women in McDonald's (which, in the long run, was even more threatening to the male power structure than racial inclusion) all the more surprising. It turns out that Fred's zealous support of women was probably inspired by his administrative assistant, Marge Cooke, and by the difficulties his own daughters experienced in the world of work in the early 1980s. It's human nature; a parent's love of his or her children will spark a powerful emotional response to their problems. In Fred's case, seeing the troubles facing young women he cared about seems to have generated a broad awareness and understanding of the sexist treatment of women in the workplace and prompted another, later change in the face of the McDonald's Corporation.

In my first year, I'd experienced my share of the racism Ed Schmitt had warned me about. There was just one man in the regional office who didn't try to hide his prejudice; he never said one word to me in that entire year. He even refused to respond when I greeted him

157

as we passed each other in the office. Once I had him pegged, however, his behavior didn't bother me too much. I knew where he stood, and I dealt with him by making it easy for him to avoid me. Why waste energy on a hardcore bigot who wasn't interested in changing?

There were subtle actions that were more difficult to read. Was it always racism? I thought so at the time, but now I'm not sure. Like most people of my race in those days, I tended to be sensitive to slights. Many were real—like the rudeness of an openly hostile couple I once encountered at a company party. But sometimes I misjudged.

One day, I was walking through the office and saw a group of my co-workers clustered together, whispering. A guy who I knew didn't like my presence in the office looked my way and said something to the other men; the group instantly broke up and everyone went back to whatever they were supposed to be doing. I think I can be forgiven for assuming they were talking about me. But in fact, I was wrong. As I later learned, they were talking about a gay man who had been fired for inappropriate behavior (today we would call it harassment) toward a store employee. My co-workers didn't know my attitudes well enough to feel comfortable sharing the gossip with me. The truth of that situation reminded me of my father's teachings: Withhold judgment and refrain from forming opinions and conclusions until you know the other person's circumstances.

There were other incidents, but long ago and particularly in my Army days, I'd learned that most prejudice is grounded in ignorance. People fear what they don't know. Getting angry at ignorant people would only bring me down to their level and feed their prejudices. I had too much to do to use up my energy on pointless confrontations, so I had to pick my battles. I wasn't always successful, but what annoyed me most was not the flagrant displays of racism. It was the persistent presumption among some people that I should be happy to be the sole black in the office. For a long time, I would smile agreeably and brush off well-meaning but thoughtless comments like, "Aren't you proud to be the only black field consultant?" Then one day, when yet another person asked if I didn't feel happy about my unique position in the company, I'd had enough. "No," I retorted. "I'm not happy being the only black man in this office. I'm embarrassed that there aren't a lot more of us!" I didn't lose my temper, but I came close. And I think I made my point. Sure, I was glad to be the first black person in McDonald's middle management, but I didn't want to be the only one.

Mostly, I kept my cool and did my job. I knew I had the full support of my bosses, Ed Schmitt and Frank Phalen, and allies in Mike Quinlan, George Sensor, the regional office manager, and Bill Coates, the senior field consultant. Maybe more important at that time, I'd established relationships of mutual respect with the store owners who were my clients. I don't know how I might have been treated if I had been sent into white suburbia instead of the inner city. But almost from the start, the white Chicago owners-operators had welcomed me without any apparent regard to my race. They knew that they were in a sink-or-swim situation—whether they were trying to sell their stores or hang onto their urban locations—and I was the guy tossing them the life preserver.

MORE BLACK OWNERS ON BOARD

The second black owners in Chicago were a group of seven African American men who purchased four restaurants in July 1969—creating the first 100 percent black, multi-store ownership in the McDonald's system. The group was led by Edward W. Wimp, a successful accountant who had gone into real estate; his son Edward L. Wimp; Ted Jones, a high-profile Chicago CPA whose clients included the boxer Joe Louis; and Cirilo McSween, an insurance executive and well-known civil rights activist. Although the Wimps didn't have the same exact names, everybody called them "Ed Senior" and "Ed Junior." At age twenty-seven and with no experience in restaurant management (he had been working in real estate with his dad), Ed Junior was designated as the operator of the four stores.

The group's restaurants were located on East 35th Street, East Pershing (39th Street), South Park Way (now Martin Luther King Drive), and East 79th Street. The East 79th store was in a white middle-class neighborhood transitioning to black. The other locations were predominately black. All four stores were in bad condition—F or worse. They were a few years newer than Herman Petty's store, but like Herman and his partners, the Wimp group had seriously overpaid—more than twice the actual value of the stores by McDonald's general guidelines. As I began to understand how sales of stores were structured, I could see how unfair deals like these were, and I questioned why McDonald's allowed such over-priced store purchases to take place. A portion of the blame lay with buyers who jumped into the deals without doing their homework. But few of the first black owners had experience in large and complex corporations, from which blacks were excluded until the late 1960s. Ed Senior and Ted Jones were exceptions; they were very successful in other business fields, though the realities of food service operations were unknown to them. Just like a lot of white owners, they were dazzled by the potential for mining gold under the McDonald's arches, but they didn't yet understand the arduous process of operating their properties.

McDonald's could have helped, but it seems clear now that the company followed a hands-off policy in those early days of white-to-black store transfers mostly because it didn't occur to anybody in the company to provide assistance. The corporate execs were so focused on getting black owner-operators on board that they didn't pay adequate attention to the actual terms of the sales. (The sale prices of stores were negotiated between the current owner and the new owner, though McDonald's had to approve the new owner and the licensing and leasing transfers.) It was a kind of corporate benign neglect that hurt both the company and many of the first wave of black owners, who put their capital into the purchase and often had little or nothing left to invest in essential improvements and to take full advantage of their stores' earning potential.

The Wimp group's restaurant on 35th Street at Wabash Avenue should have been a magnet for business. It was near the main campus of the Illinois Institute of Technology, and there was a Catholic school, De LaSalle High School, across the street. The immediate area, near the Dan Ryan Expressway, included the White Sox stadium, two large public housing projects, and an El railway station. The residents of the neighborhood were predominately black, but there was also a consistent flow of suburban traffic coming in and out of the area. Even at its worst under the previous owners, the 35th Street store had a high sales volume.

Physically and operationally, however, this store was a disaster almost on a par with Herman Petty's Stoney Island restaurant. Its image with the local residents was abysmal. To get the store upgraded to McDonald's QSC standards, I had to help the owners do virtually everything that Herman and I had done at South Stoney Island. Plus, we had to find ways to re-connect the store to its community. I was ready to get to work, but I soon realized that the situation with the Wimp group presented a set of problems and

161

personalities that were very different from Herman Petty.

Ed Junior—young, good-looking, very personable, a college graduate, and completely inexperienced as an operator or manager—had pretty much of a laid-back, "it will come out all right in the end" attitude. His father and the other senior partners in the group saw their four stores as an investment rather than day-to-day businesses that had to run efficiently if they were to produce and maintain the kind of profits they wanted. At the outset, the older partners were what Mr. Kroc called "money chasers"—people who are eager to reap the rewards of ownership but have little or no interest in the business itself. This money-chasing attitude wasn't unusual. Beginning in the late 1960s, a franchising frenzy was sweeping America, inspired largely by the phenomenal success of McDonald's and Kentucky Fried Chicken. It seemed that every Tom, Dick, and Harry with some dollars to invest was getting into fast-food franchises, especially start-up companies that were attached to a celebrity name, like Minnie Pearl Fried Chicken, Roy Rogers Roast Beef, and others. It was a bubble similar to the dot.com bubble of the 1990s, and it burst soon enough. A few of the "money chasers" made big money, but many more lost their shirts. The reputation of the franchise industry generally took a black eye, but well-established and well-run companies—McDonald's above all—were able to stay above the fray and probably benefited in the long run from the shakeout.

As for the Wimp group, I found myself pushing Ed Junior to get his stores up to McDonald's standard while coping with the unrealistic financial expectations of his elder partners. Ed Junior was often stuck in a limbo of mixed messages—between my emphasis on improving the stores (which required spending money where necessary) and the other owners' single-minded focus on the bottom line. Ted Jones especially put pressure on Ed Junior to produce financial results. I had a number of clashes with Ted, who had a leader's mentality and didn't like to take advice or direction from anyone. It was a long time before Ted and I were able to get along and become friends, though I began to see that I could have been more effective if I had been more patient with him and tried to understand his issues. I was too busy trying to force him to understand my concerns. I should have remembered what my grandparents taught me: Frustration stops where understanding begins. Cirilio McSween, on the other hand, got interested in the day-to-day business after a while and became very helpful to Ed Junior. Cirilio eventually sold his interest to Ed Junior and went on to open several successful Chicago McDonald's restaurants of his own.

Despite the problems, I really had fun working with Ed Junior. He had literally everything to learn about operating restaurants. I knew that upgrading would be a gradual process, given his inexperience and the fact that he had to divide his time among four troubled stores. Fortunately, Ed possessed genuine people skills and a real knack for working with young people. His outgoing personality, his sharp appearance, and the fact that he rode a motorcycle made him something like a rock star to young employees, and he was able to parlay their respect into better on-the-job performance. Ed also made friends in the areas where his stores were located, and because of his good nature, he was like a walking public relations campaign for his restaurants. When he learned that the Catholic high school across the street from his 35th Street store had banned students from going to the restaurant when it was under previous ownership, Ed visited with the school's officials. He introduced himself as the new owner and told the worried educators how the restaurant was being changed and improved. He also began making generous donations to the school. As the store started to look better and safer, students began showing up for burgers and fries. The donations doubtless influenced the school officials' decision to ease up on the ban, but I give a lot of the credit to Ed's people skills.

Our immediate focus was on "clean up, paint up, fix up" of the four stores and on instilling what Mr. Kroc termed RMA—right mental attitude—in Ed's managers and employees. Ed had inherited a number of young employees who, with good training, were capable of advancement. Initially, we had to show them how taking pride in themselves and the restaurants and tending to details improved their jobs. We concentrated on improvements that the employees could see with their own eyes. Once a change was real to them, they understood how it saved them time and made their jobs easier and more enjoyable.

Ed was also learning as we worked in his stores. He had to be prepared to train employees, particularly his managers, by himself. His easy-going attitude could be frustrating for a hard driver like me, but it probably helped him cope with the responsibilities of having four stores (one of the larger multi-store ownerships in Chicago at that time) dumped in his inexperienced lap by his older and supposedly wiser partners.

Throughout 1970 and 1971, other inner-city store transfers were being negotiated and finalized in the Windy City. My friend Guy Roderick, for instance, sold his South Cottage Grove restaurant to Noel White and Lester Hairston in early 1970. We were also getting more black managers into urban stores that were still white-owned. In the fall of 1969, I was one of the men whom Ed Schmitt sent to Washington to interview candidates for another Midwest regional field consultant position. Joe Brown was hired, becoming McDonald's second black consultant in January 1970. Within a couple of months, three more of my colleagues from D.C. were hired as regional consultants: Pat O'Brien in the Mideast, Floyd Corsey in the East, and Ralph Torrain in the West. I had input in all these decisions. The Southern region in Atlanta, however, didn't want my advice and instead, recruited their first black consultant, Jim Boyd, from inside the region. (Jim was later told to stay away from me because I was a "bad influence.")

One of the most extraordinary success stories in McDonald's came about when the company acquired and immediately transferred ownership of a Chicago store at 5220 West Madison to two, predominately African American, community service groups, the Better Boys Foundation and the West Side Organization. Better Boys had begun as an athletic club for street kids, but had expanded into a variety of community-based activities. For the organizations, the West Madison McDonald's served several goals: It offered opportunities for employment in a very poor area. It enabled employees, especially young people, to develop fundamental job skills and the work ethic essential for personal success. Because the store was owned and operated by blacks, it served as a living model of successful black capitalism. It also became a source of funding for the nonprofit community outreach programs of the Better Boys Foundation and West Side Organization.

The West Madison store was an F- when the two organizations took over, and the need to upgrade was urgent. I had met a thirty-seven-year-old Chicagoan named Walter Pitchford when he was training to manage another group of stores. The sale of those stores had fallen through, and Walter returned to his job at Inland Steel, but he had impressed me with his intelligence, leadership qualities, and street smarts—just the combination that would be critical if the West Madison store was to succeed. I contacted him about applying for the manager's position at West Madison, and he got the job. As manager,

Walter would report to the executive directors of the two organizations, but basically he would function as the store operator. His previous training, however, hadn't prepared him for all the immediate problems he faced. His owners were supportive, but they had no experience to offer. Walter needed our help.

With my increased responsibilities in the Midwest region, I no longer had the time for the intense, on-site training and hands-on work I had done with Herman Petty and was still doing, to an extent, with Ed Wimp and his managers. When Ed Schmitt suggested we bring in someone from Washington to work with Walter, I recommended Jim Cobham, a friend and colleague from my D.C. days. Jim had succeeded me as manager of the Duke Street store in Alexandria, and then he had taken over managing the Bladensburg Road store when I left for Chicago at the end of 1968. He was a great QSC man and had a real gift for customer service. McDonald's paid all the expenses necessary to stabilize the West Madison store until Walter was ready to take over.

What Jim accomplished was a near-miracle. In fifteen days, he and Walter had the store on track and headed upward on a straight path out of the operations cellar. Sales rose by 100 percent in that brief time. Quality standards in production and service were put in place; employees were in neat McDonald's uniforms; the store and the lot were cleaned; and customers were walking away happy. Jim continued to work with Walter, his assistant managers, and the employees for four months. Then Walter took control, and he never looked back. The "Better Boys' store," as people called it, continued to get better and better under his management. McDonald's first experiment in community-ownership was a source of pride for all of us—particularly when it became the first rehabilitated urban McDonald's store to receive an A rating from the company.

McDonald's no longer rates restaurant performance on the old-school A-to-F scale, but back then, an A grade was extremely hard to earn, and even harder to maintain, especially in hardcore urban areas, where regional politics occasionally influenced grading.

When McDonald's made a company-wide promotional and training film about what was involved in the achievement of an A rating, the Better Boys' store was heavily featured. As far as I know, that film was the first time everyone in the McDonald's system was exposed to a superior black-owned and black-operated franchise. It was certainly one of the best and most amazing operations I had ever seen, and it consistently exemplified Ray Kroc's QSC standards.

THE DECLINE AND FALL OF "SALT AND PEPPER"

I don't want to create the impression that black men, once we got our foot in the door, were universally successful. Those first black owner-operators in urban areas faced high odds against success, and a number of them, including most of the "salt and pepper" partnerships, failed. I'm not making excuses for the failures, but there were factors that were common to almost all black owner-operators in those early days—unique factors of race and history that made succeeding all the more difficult for them.

In the first place, very few black Americans in the 1960s and 1970s had any experience in corporate business entities. For three centuries, during and after slavery, blacks had been deliberately and relentlessly denied access to the avenues of legal, political, commercial, and social power. A strong black professional class—primarily doctors, educators, ministers, and a sprinkling of lawyers—arose after the Civil War, but its purpose was to serve the black population exclusively. Black businesses thrived, but only within their

167

black communities. Out of these groups, a small black middle class emerged, but again, these achievers were kept out of the mainstream. Blacks were also excluded from the national business and professional associations, such as the Chamber of Commerce and the American Medical Association, that are so important for updating knowledge and networking. Blacks responded by establishing their own associations, but they were limited in scope. From sea to shining sea, black Americans (and nearly all women) had been locked out of the institutions and the business and social networks that provide the education and training, the human contacts, and the financial connections that are fundamental to doing business in the world's largest capitalist economy. There's a business saying that the real deals are made on the golf course, which means the kinds of country club settings where white businessmen play together. The only blacks who entered this cozy world were caddies and waiters.

Groundless stereotypes—all variations on the theme of black inferiority, which had been used to justify slavery—persisted. Because of segregation, white Americans had little or no exposure to successful black entrepreneurs and businesspeople, though by the late 60s, white America was used to black entertainers and athletes. Negative stereotypes—that blacks are lazy, shiftless, slow, temperamentally volatile, dishonest, and so on—were so firmly implanted in the white psyche that black efforts to enter and function within the white business community were generally met with mistrust and condescension. For example, it was nearly impossible for an African American entrepreneur to secure a large loan from white banks for a new business venture. It didn't matter how good a black loan applicant's record in business was, how impressive his *bona fides* were, or how solid his business plan was. White loan officers and loan committees would listen, promise to consider his application seriously, and almost always turn him down. It was done with business-like courtesy, but the implication was clear: We can't depend on black people to be responsible. (This situation, though much improved today, still exists for minority and female borrowers.)

In the late 1960s and 1970s, there was also a lot of resentment in the white power structure that change was being forced on the private sector by the new civil rights laws and pressure from the government. The status quo was being overturned, and the business community generally didn't adapt easily or graciously. The usual tendency was to blame the beneficiaries of the shift from segregation and discrimination to integration and diversity. The reaction could be as gross as an Atlanta restaurant owner named Lester Maddox wielding an axe handle to keep his Pickrick Cafeteria segregated. More often, it was subtle. As the first disenfranchised minority to demand and receive access to and equality under the American system, blacks bore the brunt of white resentment.

It's my belief that from Ray Kroc down, the majority of McDonald's corporate executives were sincere in their efforts to make the company more diverse in the 1970s. I can't say that everybody's motives were altruistic. In fact, it's clear to me that the first impulse to integrate was driven by a sense of crisis—the threat to the company's urban markets after the riots of 1968 and the Cleveland boycott of 1969. The company's initial attempts to "fix" their urban problem were naïve and sometimes heavy-handed, but to McDonald's credit, it learned from its mistakes. And one of its biggest mistakes was the "salt and pepper" partnerships.

The fate of the "salt and pepper" deals is like a business-class case study of good intentions gone wrong. After Mr. X and Mr. Y brought Herman Petty into McDonald's at the end of 1968, the two white men immediately took their "salt and pepper" show on the road, finding more black partners. In a very short time, they had seven urban "salt and pepper" restaurants: two with Herman in Chicago, one in Kansas City, one in St. Louis, and three in the Los Angeles area. Without their black partners, they were also using their "salt and pepper" stores to leverage purchases of other business interests. For a short while, X and Y were regarded as golden inside McDonald's, supported by Fred Turner, Ed Schmitt, and others.

Working so closely with Herman, I started seeing problems that couldn't be chalked up to his or his partners' inexperience (neither Mr. X nor Mr. Y had any franchising experience before McDonald's). The white partners were never around and apparently had no interest in the operation of their stores. There were no funds for making essential physical improvements that good businessmen would have known about *before* they signed a licensing agreement. Herman wasn't the type to complain, but the more he told me about his partners, the more uneasy I became.

It was nearly a year, however, before I discovered credible evidence. I hadn't seen any of the monthly profit-and-loss statements from Herman's Stoney Island store until one day in the fall of 1969 when Bob Beavers shared the latest statement with me. I'm not an accountant, but I had seen a lot of P&L statements, and I could tell that the numbers were off. Herman's white partners were charging accounting and administrative fees as a percentage of store's sales, and though Bob thought the fees were probably in line, I was sure the charges were much higher than normal. I had never before seen accounting fees based on sales performance. And why would Mr. X and Mr. Y be collecting management fees for their own store (which I knew they did nothing to manage anyway)? What were they up to? It looked like double-dipping to me. I took my concerns to my field service manager and Ed Schmitt. Ed got on the case immediately.

After investigating further on his own, he took his findings to corporate, while simultaneously initiating action to terminate the "salt and pepper" deals in his region.

Ed recently confirmed to me that in 1968, he had initially presented Mr. X and Mr. Y's "salt and pepper" proposal to his corporate superiors, including Fred Turner. Nobody can remember now whether this happened before or after Herman Petty was brought into the picture, but three facts are clear. First, no one had reason to question X and Y's business credentials at the start. Second, Herman was never privy to his partners' scheme. Third, the concept of black and white partnerships seemed like a safe way to attract black owner-operators and secure adequate financing (arranged by the white partners) for the purchase of existing franchises. Like everyone else, I thought "salt and pepper" packages were a good idea when I first heard about them. Even in retrospect, I and others who saw what happened still believe that such partnerships could have worked, especially in the very early days of white-to-black store ownership transfers. It was two unscrupulous individuals, not the concept, that failed.

At any rate, McDonald's near-sacred rules of ownership—notably that a store's operator must hold a majority position of at least 51 percent and that owners must be actively involved in the day-to-day operation of the business—had been relaxed to accommodate the speedy transfer of urban stores from white to black hands. This bending of the rules, however, complicated the process of uncovering exactly what Mr. X and Mr. Y were doing and how much money they were milking from their "salt and pepper" stores and from the company. The two white partners continued their ride on the gravy train for almost three years, until the hard proof was in and Fred Turner became convinced they had to go.

I personally became frustrated at what seemed like foot-dragging by corporate. In 1970, I was field consultant to the three black operators who were partnered with X and Y in Chicago, St. Louis, and Kansas City. I was also keeping in touch with Ralph Torrain, the consultant who had the "salt and pepper" restaurants in California. We saw how the black operators were struggling to keep their heads above water—and how near they were to going under. The situation eventually degenerated to the point at which suppliers to the "salt and pepper" stores were going unpaid for months, and X and Y were sending hired bag men into the stores to rifle the tills. I wondered why Fred didn't act sooner, and every time I had the opportunity, I told him how bad the problems were. He would hear me out, but I knew he was annoyed by my persistence. He didn't like being pushed into decisions that were contrary to his opinion. As I got to know him better, I understood why. Fred Turner's personal sense of loyalty to the company was so unshakable that it was difficult for him to comprehend people like X and Y who had no sense of loyalty at all. He was inclined to give others in the system another chance to redeem themselves—until the evidence was overwhelming.

In the end, after Mr. X and Mr. Y were forced out (no legal action was taken), only two of the black owners were able to survive—Jim Heard in Los Angeles and Herman Petty in Chicago. Herman had established a positive relationship with Hyde Park Bank, and through the bank's new minority business development department, he negotiated a substantial loan in 1972 that enabled him to buy out his white partners and become sole owner of the South Stoney Island and South Vincennes Avenue stores. The loan was amortized in such a way that it was adequate to cover debts created by X and Y's shenanigans, plus high priority, long-delayed improvements to Herman's restaurants.

Other "salt and pepper" owners weren't so fortunate. McDonald's helped the black franchisees to the extent of working with banks to arrange re-financing for the stores and with suppliers to set new payment schedules for unpaid bills. Even with more advantageous financing, however, the black owner-operators were held entirely responsible for the debts that Mr. X and Mr. Y had run up against their stores. I suppose the owners could have gone after their former partners in court, but the costs of law suits would have been greater than any money they might have recovered. From the very start of the corporation, McDonald's operated under the policy that the company would not assume any debt for a store. When a troubled store was sold, its debts were passed on to the new owner. McDonald's made no exceptions. Though the black franchisees in the seven "salt and pepper" deals managed to retain ownership of their restaurants after the departure of X and Y, all but Herman Petty and Jim Heard were sooner or later crushed by the debt load and had to sell their stores. Herman and Jim both stayed with McDonald's and became very successful owner-operators. After Jim's death in 1981, his widow, Lonear, took over the operation and expanded the Heard family's ownership in Los Angeles.

It has been reported that the cost to McDonald's Corporation was around $500,000 on the deals, and there's no knowing the full scope of the failed owners' losses. The upside was that "salt and pepper" packages were at last abandoned. By the time Mr. X and Mr. Y vanished from the radar, McDonald's had enough experience with integration to know that it was not necessary to compromise its ownership criteria to 'help' potential black owners by partnering them with whites. It was an expensive lesson, but the company had learned that failures were not related to skin color.

On a personal level, the end of the "salt and pepper" deals also brought a mending of my relationship with Fred Turner. I never doubted that I was right to badger him about the urgency of the black operators' situation—though I knew he perceived my frequent approaches as troublemaking—but I wasn't tempted to say "I told you so" when the whole thing blew up. Fred never said anything directly to me, but his attitude changed from that point forward. I had always respected him, even when I couldn't understand his actions. Now, I could see that the feeling had become mutual.

There were other failures unrelated to the "salt and pepper" deals. Several resulted from poor selection on the company's part; in the initial rush to put black owner-operators into urban stores, unsuitable matches were made. Just being black didn't automatically qualify an owner to run a store in a black community. A middle-class black businessman, for example, could be just as unschooled in the culture of a low-income, predominately black, inner-city neighborhood as a middle-class white businessman. The black owner's color was no guarantee that he had the street smarts to make a hardcore urban store viable.

Also, black owners were being recruited for restaurants that were among the worst in the system. Because the company was not giving close attention to the pricing of the stores, the owners often overpaid and then lacked the financial resources to bring sub-par operations up to standard. In part, this happened because some black owners didn't know how to exercise due diligence when they were negotiating to buy a store. But there was also an excessively confident and enthusiastic attitude among some senior McDonald's executives that led them to oversell the potential of black ownership and underestimate the difficulties. This corporate optimism was genuine and infectious. But it was often unrealistic, leading some blacks to buy into ownership without understanding the day-to-day demands of rehabilitating low-rated, hardcore urban stores. In a few situations, especially on the West Coast, novice black owners were drawn into an extravagant life style that they couldn't support. An expensive home and expensive cars can be suitable rewards for an owner with well-established and profitable restaurants; for a newcomer, such extravagances can be a trap, draining cash flow and preventing the kind of re-investment required to improve his business.

For all the difficulties, however, more and more black owners were coming into the system. I found myself traveling throughout the Middle West to tend to my newly assigned stores outside of my Chicago territory. I was in communication with the black field consultants in other regions. Pretty quickly, I was getting a clear picture of the particular problems facing black owner-operators. The list of obstacles began with the low standards of the staff and physical facilities they inherited and their less than favorable financial arrangements, combined with the lack of business experience and inadequate operational background. The owners were frustrated by their limitations, and I was frustrated because on an individual level, I did not have the time to help each owner-operator overcome these primary difficulties.

Herman Petty's question—"Why don't you get us together and train us as a group?"—seemed to me to provide a solution. I began to think that I *could* get the Chicago owners together, right there on the South Side.

FORMING A UNITED FRONT

When I began sounding out the black Chicago owner-operators about working together, I was surprised at how positive the responses were. I had expected some objections because I knew how little time these guys had for meetings outside their stores. I'd also wondered how willing they would be to work in unison and share information. But when I made my proposal, everybody was ready to jump on board.

I organized our first get-together in late May or early June of 1970. It was a pleasant spring evening, as I recall, and we met at the Holiday Inn on Halsted Street. I put the meeting room on my expense account. There were six of us—Herman Petty, Ed Wimp (Junior), Noel White, Lester Hairston, Walter Pitchford, and me. I don't think I mentioned my plans to anyone in the regional office; there was no reason to. What emerged from that meeting was what I hoped for— consensus—and we began training sessions immediately. I suggested that our sessions be a blend of hands-on instruction and group discussion. The goal was to get the operators to the point where they could comfortably train their own managers. Until we reached that goal, I would instruct their managers. We also discussed training of employees, especially bright young workers with management potential. The owners' group wouldn't be limited in number; every new black owner-operator, plus any manager-operators like Walter in the Chicago area, was welcomed.

We agreed to meet weekly on Monday evening. Our meetings would prove to be a test of the operators' commitment because of Monday night football on television; they were all football fans. But over the next three years and with new operators coming into the group, we never lost a man—not even the biggest Bears fan—to football.

We continued to gather at the Holiday Inn for several weeks; then we switched our meetings to the Swinger's Lounge, a South Side bar and grill that had a private room, or to Ed Junior's house. The owners had decided that they should shoulder all the costs of the group's activities independently. They were truly committed to *self-help*, so no longer was anything expensed to the company. We also had numerous in-store sessions, gathering at the owners' stores for training in the nitty-gritty of every aspect of operations. Training in different stores, in different neighborhoods, gave the owners experience in a wide range of restaurants in various stages of upgrading. I also observed that working side by side created a sense of cohesion and a strong desire to collaborate on problem solving.

Not long after our first meeting, as our training sessions progressed, the owners began talking about formalizing the group. They decided on a name—McDonald's Black Operators Association. The owners lived with that name for a few weeks, until someone said that they needed to put "Black" first. This name change would have a significance that, at the time, we probably didn't fully appreciate. Initially, the change was a way of defining the group more precisely and showing solidarity. What set the new Black McDonald's Operators Association—BMOA—apart within McDonald's was the focus on sharing and self-help by a group of owners and operators whose issues and problems were unique among the thousands of McDonald's owners in the system.

Ed Wimp was BMOA's first president. His election was part of a strategy of anticipating possible consequences. I was concerned that there might be a backlash from the company, and I discussed it with the owners. We decided that the president should be the person least likely to be subject to any pressure from corporate, and that was Ed Junior. Of the founding BMOA members, he had the most stores and was paying more rent to McDonald's than anyone else. Also, his four restaurants were the least desirable for purchase. He and his partners had bought the stores for well above actual value, and they would want to recoup their investment. Yet the stores were still in need of so much upgrading that finding new buyers willing to pay the price was unlikely. McDonald's had a strong interest in seeing the

Wimp group succeed, and that fact made Ed almost bulletproof.

I didn't hide what we were doing, but throughout the summer and fall of 1970, when we were getting BMOA on its feet, I didn't go out of my way to discuss our training sessions or the formation of BMOA with anyone in the regional or corporate offices. I felt sure that Ed Schmitt knew about the training sessions early on and that he approved. But I didn't want him to be caught between his own commitment to support the black owner-operators in his region and the company's (meaning Ray Kroc and Fred Turner) tradition of responding negatively to any self-generated organizations that senior executives perceived as "splinter groups." I believed that by keeping a low profile at the outset, BMOA would have a better chance of bucking corporate tradition. I was already getting a reputation, especially with Fred Turner, as something of a rebel. As the only corporate representative involved with BMOA, I might pay a price sooner or later for flying under the company's radar while the group coalesced. But the benefits were worth the risk.

By November 1970, we were ready to make our presence known within the company. The members of BMOA decided to give a crew recognition party at a South Side supper club on Thanksgiving evening, so the employees could spend the day at home with their families. The club was closed for business on the holiday, and we had the place to ourselves. It was a fun event. Crews from nine black-owned, inner-city McDonald's restaurants filled the club. We had food, music, dancing, entertainment staged by some of the young workers, door prizes of Ronald McDonald dolls, free turkeys, and a presentation of awards to the high-performing crew members and management team.

A month later, I submitted some photos from the party and a brief and carefully worded memo to the editor of the company's national, internal newsletter. I didn't mention BMOA—just that a group of Chicagoland owners had formed a "mini co-op" to host the crew recognition event and that the members of the little "co-op" had decided to continue meeting with the goals of increasing sales, improving operations, and to "combine efforts in developing young black businessmen and contribute to the solution of sociological and economical problems in the black community."

Stores from across the country sent items to the newsletter, so getting in was not easy. I didn't really expect that my memo would make the cut. To my surprise, one of the photos and a short report appeared in the February 1971 newsletter. The copy had been reworked but was pretty close to my memo. It read:

> Faced with similar sociological and community relations problems, several Chicago operators formed a "mini co-op". The crew members, managers and operators of the stores involved in the co-op hold meetings ranging from parties—with entertainment and outstanding crew award presentations—to more serious problem solving sessions. Especially because of the variety of the meetings and the crew members' intense interest, the success of the mini co-op seems assured.

Without being named, BMOA now had its first official recognition. The photograph from the Thanksgiving party featured eleven, earnest, young black crew members and managers, male and female, under a balloon-draped McDonald's banner—a picture to warm the hearts of every executive involved in the company's serious, often difficult, and sometimes misguided efforts to expand black ownership. The announcement wasn't likely to alarm anyone. But a

179

close reading by a perceptive person might have picked up something more interesting than social news. There was now a "mini co-op" of black owners in Chicago who were meeting regularly and engaging in "serious problem solving."

The word was out. This first notice caused barely a ripple, although the members of BMOA were pleased by the inclusion of their crew recognition party and so many young black faces in the usually all-white company publication. That, in itself, was a breakthrough. But ripples have a way of widening and becoming waves. Inside McDonald's, the wave was building, and it would break about six months later—at another, much larger party near the white sand beaches of Waikiki.

Chapter 8

Keeping Good Company

White people, like black ones, are victims of a racist society.
They are products of their time and place.

SHIRLEY CHISHOLM, U.S. CONGRESSWOMAN

In October 1971, McDonald's hosted its first international business convention, drawing several thousand attendees from the United States, Canada, Western Europe, and Japan to meet and mingle with the corporate leaders and managers under the tropical sun in Honolulu, Hawaii. I had attended one previous national convention, so I knew that Ray Kroc could throw a great party. I expected the Honolulu convention to be even better. As the big jet flew me across the Pacific, I recalled the last time I'd traveled this route—when I was on my way home from Korea and about to become a civilian again. That time, I was a serviceman, unsure what to do with my life. Now, I was a business traveler for one of America's largest and most successful corporations. I couldn't help thinking about how far I had traveled and how much the nation had changed for black people over the past eight years. When we landed at Honolulu International, beautiful young women in hula skirts greeted us with the traditional "Aloha" and draped sweet-smelling flower leis around our necks. I was in a great mood—feeling optimistic about the convention, the company, and the country, even with its many unresolved racial issues.

Despite the lure of the beaches and blue water, a lot of business was conducted during our three days at the Hawaii convention. The owner-operators were shown the latest innovations in building construction, restaurant equipment, food production, and packaging. At the top of the agenda was the introduction of McDonald's newest menu items—the Quarter Pounder and Quarter Pounder with cheese—and the marketing that would sell the big burgers as a "meal on a bun." There were seminars constantly underway on hot-button topics ranging from financing to advertising. Vendors from McDonald's vast network of suppliers were also on hand to display their products and services.

There were plenty of formal and informal opportunities for operators to talk with senior management. I remember particularly a management forum at which Fred Turner and his executive team answered questions about any issues of concern to operators. During the forum, the new ranks of black owner-operators got their chance to put the senior executives to the test. My friend Noel White, a Chicago owner and the current president of BMOA, stood up and asked about the problem of cash register repairs. Normally, when an operator reported that his cash register was acting up, a representative of the equipment company went immediately to the store to make the repair on site. But white repair reps were refusing to go into black neighborhoods in Chicago, and black operators had no option but to take their equipment to the supplier and leave it until the repair was made. This caused delays and serious inconvenience until the register could be retrieved and re-installed. The members of the Hawaii panel heard Noel out and promised to find a solution. Whether anything would actually be done remained to be seen. But something was done. McDonald's immediately pressured its equipment suppliers to hire and train black reps, and it wasn't long before a call about a broken register from a black, inner-city operator got the same prompt attention that suburban store owners took for granted. The company made good on its promise, and I know that black owner-operators felt more confidence in corporate management as a result. (That was also the first concrete example of the ripple effect BMOA would have. White-run supply companies' hiring and training of black repair specialists to serve black customers in McDonald's created more employment opportunities for blacks.)

A McDonald's convention was a working convention, but there was no shortage of fun. Mr. Kroc believed in fun; he often said that he'd never worked a day in his life because he enjoyed whatever job he was doing. He knew that the owner-operators were the backbone of the McDonald's system. He wanted the convention to be a treat for these hard-working operators and their spouses, for many of whom the trip to Hawaii was the only vacation they would allow themselves. The balance of serious business and pure fun was carefully planned as a well-deserved break for the people whose "blood, sweat, and tears," to quote Winston Churchill, and commitment to the McDonald's standards were the foundation of the company's continuing success.

For the operators and their spouses, the real star of the convention was Ray Kroc himself. Within the McDonald's culture, Mr. Kroc was a legend, and everybody wanted to shake his hand. A small, dapper man approaching his seventieth birthday with a young man's zest for life, Mr. Kroc didn't hold himself aloof; he loved talking about McDonald's with people at all levels of the company. With his McDonald's "family" gathered around him in Hawaii, he was in top form—happy, energetic, down-to-earth, and generous with his time.

Nearly everyone I know who remembers the 1971 convention agrees that it was going beautifully, until the next-to-last day. We gathered in the afternoon in a massive hotel ballroom that had been converted into a theater. The program included a lavish Broadway-style song and dance production praising the accomplishments of the company and the franchisees, followed by a special guest speaker. I remember that the mood in the room was mellow. We'd had two great days already, meeting new people, renewing old acquaintances, doing some productive business but also enjoying ourselves. Then everything changed. The good time was suddenly overshadowed by the afternoon's headline speaker—broadcast commentator, newspaper columnist, and public speaker Paul ("The Rest of the Story") Harvey.

Harvey was like the Rush Limbaugh of that time—a hardcore conservative and rabid anti-communist whose blend of political, patriotic, and religious rhetoric was extremely popular, especially in Middle America. There's still some debate about who actually invited him to address the Hawaii convention, but it's generally agreed that the invitation came from Ray Kroc. Mr. Kroc enjoyed treating his convention guests to speechmakers who were famous and entertaining. At the 1969 national convention—the first I attended—the main banquet speaker had been black comedian Nipsy Russell. Only a handful of blacks attended that event, held in Miami, and I'm sure our presence had nothing to do with the choice of an African American speaker. I'm equally certain that Mr. Kroc, who was conservative but not politically active, selected Paul Harvey as someone who would please a large gathering of small business owners and their wives. After all, Harvey was much in demand as a speaker for such business occasions, and highly compensated for his appearances. It was natural to assume that he would be popular with a McDonald's audience.

Harvey had barely started speaking before it became clear that a serious miscalculation had been made. I think his subject was supposed to be the virtues of free enterprise, but the speech was so riddled with self-righteous clichés and negative stereotyping that it was impossible to find any virtues in it. Basically, Harvey said that people who couldn't make their way in America's free market were just lazy freeloaders and that they deserved poverty. He didn't specifically single out black people, but he condemned welfare recipients and condoned the recent police brutality during the Attica prison uprising in upstate New York. The whole speech seemed to be about race. When he equated laziness and failure with rioting, you had to be really dense not to know to whom he was referring.

There were plenty of people who applauded at the end of Harvey's presentation, but many in the audience were clearly disturbed and remained silent. Quite a few had walked out during the speech, including Fred Turner and his wife. I was sitting in Fred's row, and when he passed me on his way to the door, I said, "Hey, Fred. How you doing?" He wasn't smiling when he replied, "I was fine until that son of a bitch started speaking," and hurried on. I had seen Fred angry on other occasions, and I knew he was furious. Uncharacteristically, Ray Kroc didn't stay around to chat when the program was over. Some who saw him leave recall him dashing away so fast that he forgot the cane he used because of his arthritis. It was Fred who came back and talked with troubled guests, doing his best to distance McDonald's from the speech.

Today, Paul Harvey's speech might be called a "buzz killer." His words had sapped the convention of its spirit and left behind a very bitter taste. Lots of the white folks in that room were shocked by the speech and embarrassed for the company. The couple of dozen black attendees were stunned. We were proud of the progress that we and the company were making, and some owners wondered if all their hard work was for nothing. I honestly couldn't understand what had happened. I knew little about Paul Harvey, whose national popularity didn't extend into African American circles, so I was totally unprepared for his speech. Yet my instinct and my knowledge of the corporation and Mr. Kroc told me that the choice of Harvey was a bad error of judgment but it hadn't been done deliberately. I believed then and I believe now that Harvey had spoken his own mind—not the company's. If Harvey had been considerate and shared the topic and basic content of his speech with Mr. Kroc or Fred Turner in advance, I doubt he would have been on the podium.

Others disagreed. They blamed Mr. Kroc, Fred, and corporate management in general, and they wanted to protest. A number of the black owners got together and talked about what had occurred and what to do about it. Ruby Stroman, the wife of a World War II Tuskegee Airman (black fighter pilots) who was the first African American McDonald's owner in the state of New York, decided to take action. Mrs. Stroman was in the process of deciding whether to leave her current employment with Head Start (the federal program for pre-kindergarten education of poor and at-risk children) in order to join her husband, Roosevelt, in his business. She had accompanied Roosevelt to Hawaii in order to better evaluate the company and its top management. Until Paul Harvey's speech, her impression had been positive.

Feisty and articulate, Mrs. Stroman wanted to make a statement. On behalf of the other black owners, she wrote a one-page letter titled "Minority Report: McDonald's Theory vs Practice" and had it delivered to Fred Turner and other senior executives. I don't

186

know if Mr. Kroc received a copy, but if not, I'm sure he saw one soon enough. In her letter, Mrs. Stroman asked the questions that all the black attendees were asking: "Living in a fast changing world that's undergoing many social changes for survival, what can be the impact of the kind of address presented by a PAUL HARVEY for a McDONALD'S Corporation?... What kind of people are we interested in when we profess [to be a] 'People Business'?... Are we as interested citizens concerned about having respect for human dignity no matter what the pigmentation of [a] person's skin or origin might be?" She took the company to task for "preaching double standards"— promoting the concept of team-building and then allowing Harvey to insult not just the blacks in the room that day but a significant segment of its employees and customers as well. The letter accused McDonald's of being blind to the realities of life for minorities in America. From start to finish, the ideas were both angry and well-reasoned. I don't know who saw the letter before it was delivered, but it captured the sense of bewilderment and betrayal that so many of the black owners felt at that moment.

There was not, as far as I know, a formal response from the company, though I think there must have been a good deal of one-on-one fence-mending. The company's top public relations agent at the time, Al Golin, recalls that Mr. Kroc did make an apology during his remarks at the convention's closing event, which I and most of the black operators didn't attend. Al, who stayed on in Hawaii with Fred Turner and his wife for a week after the convention, affirmed Fred's genuine anger and frustration at the Harvey speech and its impact on the company.

Most of the people who heard the speech came to the same conclusion I had reached—McDonald's was responsible for giving Paul Harvey a platform, but corporate management had been taken unawares by what he said and genuinely regretted the incident and the pain it caused. However, some, including Ruby Stroman, remain convinced that the Harvey speech was an expression of Ray Kroc's and, by extension, the company's thinking. Mrs. Stroman, for one, decided not to involve herself with McDonald's and remained with Head Start until she retired.

The story didn't make the national press, and the general fallout was relatively short-lived, but McDonald's didn't hold another international convention until 1976. Since then, I've wondered how the international owners reacted to the Harvey speech, particularly the Europeans. Anti-American sentiment related to the American presence in Vietnam was strong in Western Europe in the early 70s. (Several years later, when the number of owners made a company-wide, national gathering impractical, the company went to conventions by management zones, a four-zone structure that encompassed multiple geographical regions.)

A year after the Hawaii convention, Ray Kroc ran into a much more public buzz saw when it was reported in the press that he had donated $250,000 to the re-election campaign of President Richard Nixon. The donation, which was among the largest individual contributions to the Republican campaign, brought Mr. Kroc an invitation to dine at the White House. But the gift was soon being characterized by McDonald's critics as an attempt to buy favors from the Nixon administration, especially in relation to the company's petition to the federal Wage and Price Control Board to reverse an earlier decision and allow McDonald's to raise the prices of its new Quarter Pounder sandwiches. (The country was in an economic recession throughout the 1970s, and Nixon had instituted certain price controls as a means to hold down inflation.) Critics also linked Mr. Kroc's huge contribution to a proposed exemption of part-time student workers from the federal minimum wage standard, a piece of legislation that was nicknamed "the McDonald's bill" in the press. Before long, Mr. Kroc and McDonald's were being associated with the growing Watergate scandal as an example of the kind of campaign financing excesses that were corrupting the political system.

It was a public relations nightmare. The company was deluged with scathing calls and mail. When we heard that a letter bomb had been sent to Fred Turner and fortunately caught by security before it was opened, there was little doubt about how serious the situation was. The company's squeaky-clean image took a major hit, even after McDonald's was cleared of any impropriety in the Quarter Pounder pricing decision by two Watergate committees in Congress, the General Accounting Office, and the Department of Justice.

I saw the negative impact at another level—among the black consumers and workers in the restaurants. The vast majority of African Americans were anti-Nixon and anti-Republican; they didn't appreciate the apparent fact that the wealthy founder of a company they supported with their patronage seemed to be so cozy with the President. A quarter of a million dollars to "Tricky Dicky" Nixon? That struck a lot of black folks as an outrage when the national economy was in recession; jobs, particularly blue collar and menial positions, were disappearing; young black men were dying at a higher rate than their white comrades in Vietnam; and the poor were bearing the brunt of the suffering. Young McDonald's employees were especially upset about the minimum wage exemption for student workers (which was enacted in a less drastic form than the original bill); many of the black kids in urban stores were helping to support their families, and they feared that worse was to come. In fact, McDonald's never paid less than minimum wage, but that didn't lessen the anxiety. To most black people in those difficult days, backing Richard Nixon was clear evidence of racism.

The truth, as Mr. Kroc himself admitted in his 1977 autobiography, *Grinding It Out*, was that the donation was an uncalculated blunder. He had intended to donate only $25,000 to the Nixon campaign—at that time, a reasonable sum for a multimillionaire businessman—because he wanted to see Senator George McGovern defeated in the '72 presidential election. Mr. Kroc's fundamental belief in the free market made him distrust the anti-war and socially liberal Democratic candidate who might drag the country's businesses further into government regulation and bureaucratic red tape. But Mr. Kroc attended a Republican fundraising event and was inspired by Maurice Stans, Nixon's Secretary of Commerce. Impulsively, Mr. Kroc pledged $250,000, increasing his intended donation by a factor of ten. People who knew Mr. Kroc best say that impulse was about as deep as Ray Kroc's political involvement went. He had never made any large political contributions before 1972. He wasn't a party man; he didn't have much interest in politics and its intrigues. He based his voting on whoever he thought would be best for his business. Once, during a speaking event attended by Mr. Kroc and Fred Turner, a college student asked Mr. Kroc if he dictated the politics of his executives. Fred answered for his chairman, telling the audience that "Kroc voted for Nixon and I voted for McGovern." Mr. Kroc got the laugh when he added, "That's right, and we were both wrong."

Maybe the best evidence that his contribution wasn't intended to buy influence is that it was made openly. A politically savvy man would have done it in secret and covered his tracks. Mr. Kroc compounded the problem by reacting angrily to his critics—effectively stirring the hornet's nest—and it was awhile before he understood his mistake. As he wrote in his book, "[It] wasn't until later that I realized I had made the contribution for the wrong reason. My attitude was not so much pro-Nixon as it was anti-George McGovern. I should have known at the time that this went against my rule of not trying to make a positive out of a negative action."

The damage was done, however, and the company had to deal with the negative backlash. Eventually, it became back page news as the Watergate cover-up scandal mushroomed. President Nixon was re-elected in November 1972. A little less than two years after his landslide victory, Nixon resigned before he could be impeached. Over the traumatic months leading to the President's final disgrace, most people forgot about Ray Kroc's campaign contribution.

Was Ray Kroc a Racist?

I have never believed that Ray Kroc was a racist. I believe that in his absolute devotion to the welfare of his company, he was often naïve and could be less than sensitive to the broad social issues of racism, sexism, and other forms of prejudice. As I have said before, I don't think Mr. Kroc and most of the corporate executives at McDonald's back then could ever fully grasp the depth and breadth of the cultural and economic disparity between white male Americans and the rest of us. I also understand that Mr. Kroc was a man of his times—he was born in 1902—and his belief system was formed in a period few of us today can comprehend. His conservatism was grounded in "can do" optimism and unwavering faith in his country's limitless capacity for individual and national greatness. The opening sentence of his autobiography reads: "I have always believed that each man makes his own happiness and is responsible for his own problems." He was proud of his own immigrant heritage and happily identified himself as a "Bohunk"—the street epithet for someone of Bohemian descent. I

191

doubt it occurred to him or to many others of his generation that whatever their ethnic origins, the first door to individual success was open to them because they were white and male. With a very few remarkable exceptions (men like the scientist George Washington Carver and diplomat and Nobel Peace Prize laureate Ralph Bunche), the heights of power were inaccessible to everybody else because that door at the bottom of the ladder was locked against them.

When Ray Kroc launched McDonald's in the mid-1950s, his employment practices were, in the context of American business, egalitarian. He hired white males into key positions, but they were a diverse lot in terms of ethnicity, religion, and education. He didn't care where someone worshipped or what schools they had attended. He hadn't gone to college and didn't see a diploma as a particular advantage in business, though he placed the highest premium on professional and personal integrity.

People who were around in those days pretty much agree that Mr. Kroc's personal prejudices were much more eccentric than race. He didn't have much respect for "yes men" and valued people who disagreed with him. But he favored lean, clean-shaven executives who kept their weight down, their hair short, and their fingernails and business attire spotless. He was known to fire people for trivial offenses, like a cluttered desk, but his famous hot temper was a lot more bark than bite, and he usually forgot the whole thing within a few hours. (Mr. Kroc couldn't fire owner-operators, but he was notorious for dressing down, loudly and colorfully, operators and restaurant managers whenever he found littered parking lots or out-of-uniform workers during his frequent unannounced visits to McDonald's stores wherever he went.)

Some of his critics accused him of being a male chauvinist, but it's more accurate to describe him as a traditionalist. He admired and respected women and married three of them. The death of his daughter, Marilyn, from complications of diabetes, was the great tragedy of his life. In the office, however, he saw women's roles as limited to adjunct positions—secretaries and clerks. This was an attitude he shared with millions and millions of men born and raised before World War II. But he made exceptions. The best known is his secretary, June Martino. For her loyalty in the company's start-up days, when money for wages was very tight, he compensated her with ten-percent ownership in the company. (Her husband, Lou, was an electrical engineer. He started the company's first research and development laboratory. Working with a food technologist named Ken Strong, Lou Martino perfected the computerized cooking process that made McDonald's French fries the company's crowning glory and developed much of the automated equipment that improved standardization and speeded up McDonald's production line.)

Mrs. Martino, a very capable accountant and administrator, was soon named secretary-treasurer of the company, and after her retirement, she became an honorary member of the Board of Directors. The people who worked with her valued her even more for her personal skills. She could manage Mr. Kroc's temper and calm the boiling waters he often left in his wake. Kind and considerate of others, she was also extremely good at spotting potential management material. It was she who got Mike Quinlan his first job at corporate McDonald's, in the mail room.

I came to know Mr. Kroc pretty well when I was in Chicago, and I will always regard him as a friend. I was a little awed by him, too, and I regret that I didn't take full advantage of the opportunities he offered me to spend more time with him. I know that he was interested in me and followed my progress in the company. Mr. Kroc had an open door policy for his employees, and it wasn't a stunt;

whenever I wanted to see him, all I had to do was ask. I found him invariably patient with my questions and genuinely interested in my ideas. And he wasn't all business either; just like me, he had loved baseball since he was a boy, and we could always talk about the game and his favorite team, the Chicago Cubs. In 1972 Mr. Kroc tried unsuccessfully to buy the Cubs from owner Phil Wrigley. A couple of years later, he did purchase the San Diego Padres and transferred his allegiance to his California team. But I don't think he ever gave up his hopes that the Cubs would someday repeat the glory days of his childhood.

Was he a racist? I never saw it. Although others in the company attempted to block the expansion of the Black McDonald's Operators Association, Mr. Kroc never interfered. He wasn't active in the recruiting of black owners for urban stores and black field consultants, but I know that he approved of the company's integration. His public statements were positive and supportive of diversity. After he made his personal fortune, he established the nonprofit Kroc Foundation to contribute to worthy causes, from medical and scientific research to art museums to social welfare programs. The Kroc Foundation was color-blind. To celebrate his seventieth birthday in 1972, Mr. Kroc and the Foundation donated $7.5 million to charities, primarily in the Chicago area, and one of the major recipients was the PACE Institute, which provided rehabilitation and education services for prisoners—the majority black and poor—in Chicago and Cook County.

I said that Mr. Kroc wasn't involved in recruiting black owner-operators, but I know personally of at least one occasion that demonstrated his inherent fairness. Willie Wilson, an inner-city Chicagoan with a seventh grade education, was working as a crew chief in a South Side suburban McDonald's in 1970, when all the white managers walked out in a conflict with the owner. Willie stepped up and ran the store, single-handedly, until the dispute was finally resolved. But when the white managers came back, the store owner, who was flagrantly racist, demoted Willie back to crew chief—until Joe Brown, the field consultant, and I intervened on Willie's behalf. Willie was a smart young man, and he had proved his management skills in a crisis, but the owner wouldn't promote him above assistant manager or increase his pay and eventually fired Willie when he asked for a raise. Willie then went to work for Herman Petty and began nursing his dream to be an owner.

Ray Kroc didn't know about any of this until 1979, when Willie took advantage of the open-door policy and called Mr. Kroc about applying for a franchise. Mr. Kroc was tied up preparing for the annual spring stockholders' meeting, so he asked Willie to call him back as soon as the big meeting was over. Willie wasn't taking any chances; on the morning of the stockholders' meeting, he went to the site and waited around until he could introduce himself to Mr. Kroc. They got together in Mr. Kroc's office that same day, and hearing Willie' story, the chairman of McDonald's called the corporate franchising department. Franchising apparently said that Willie couldn't qualify for ownership, but Mr. Kroc wouldn't take "no" for an answer. He told his franchising executives to figure out how to make it happen. Seven months later, Willie Wilson was the new owner-operator of a McDonald's restaurant on West 79th Street in Chicago. Willie ran that store successfully and went on to acquire several more McDonald's locations. When he sold his stores in 2003, he became a vendor and now provides operating supplies to McDonald's stores.

The point of this story is that Ray Kroc looked at Willie Wilson's abilities and enthusiasm, not his skin color. Willie wasn't well-educated in the traditional sense, but he was thoroughly schooled in the McDonald's system, had a strong record in operations, possessed good "walking around" street smarts, and wanted the responsibility of ownership. Plus, Willie was persistent—a quality he shared with Mr. Kroc. Though McDonald's had tightened its ownership requirements over the years, it was still relatively easy for someone with a lot of money to get a franchise. Mr. Kroc, however, was looking for something more important than net worth. He saw a good McDonald's man in Willie Wilson, and Willie lived up to his judgment. Race was never an issue—not in Willie's case nor in similar situations when Mr. Kroc sponsored other unconventional ownership agreements.

Bottom line, I don't think Mr. Kroc thought much about race. That, and his early twentieth century upbringing, best accounts for blunders like the Paul Harvey speech and the Nixon campaign contribution, which showed his ignorance of racial sensitivities. But it also goes to the heart of the man I knew. His "race" was his business. He loved McDonald's and all the people who were part of it. Whatever position a person held in the company, Mr. Kroc expected him or her to work hard, perform with competence, put the customer first, and most important, be loyal to McDonald's mission and standards—just what he expected of himself.

Yes, he could be insensitive and temperamental. But racist? All my life, I have dealt with racial prejudice in its many forms. I believe that racism is a conscious decision. For an adult to act on the assumption that his own group is superior to any other group is a deliberate choice. The Ray Kroc I knew had his share of flaws, as we all do, but racism wasn't one of them.

MUTUAL TRUST AND COLLABORATION

Viewed in retrospect, the Paul Harvey speech in Hawaii in 1971 did have one positive outcome: It sparked a sense of unity among the black operators who attended the convention. Because BMOA then included only Chicago operators, we had planned to get together with other black owner-operators while we were in Honolulu. Noel White worked on an agenda, with some help from me, and Noel invited all the black conventioneers—operators and their wives—to a meet-and-greet gathering in his hotel room. I didn't attend because we thought that the presence of a company representative might stifle the kind of open conversation we hoped for. The objective was for the owner-operators to get to know one another in a no-pressure social setting and start sharing problems and goals. In other words, to network. I think the gathering took place before the Harvey speech, but it provided the framework for the operators to vent their feelings openly after the speech and cement the bonds of mutual interest. We didn't realize it then, but that Hawaii "caucus" of maybe a couple dozen black owners from different parts of the country was a small but crucial step in the creation of a national organization.

Returning to Chicago, I continued my training sessions with the black owner-operators and managers. The owners now began conducting some of the training for managers and crew. In selecting store employees for our joint training program, we focused on crew chiefs, male and female, who showed management potential; our objective was to develop a pool of well-qualified and qualifiable managers. The operators and managers would meet at the South Shore YMCA. When training for crew members was added, we needed a bigger space and rented a large meeting room at a Holiday Inn, though much of the actual hands-on training still took place in members' stores.

We instituted store operational "blitzes"—unannounced visits to BMOA members' stores. We would get together for a training session and go to every BMOA member's stores. The objective was to experience each store's food and service from the customer's perspective. We saw it all, literally inspecting the store from every possible angle and looking for problems customers might encounter, even before they entered the parking lot. We would check everything, and these visits often resulted in on-the-spot training sessions with a store's manager and staff, as well as generating topics for our formal group training sessions.

The purpose of these blitzes was multi-fold: 1) to provide demonstrations of operational methods in different store environments and problem solving under typical daily conditions; 2) to evaluate the effectiveness of individual solutions to problems; and 3) to provide constructive criticism based on observing physical facilities, tasting product, gauging customer reactions, and seeing a store at work—employee appearance, attitudes, and overall customer service.

The blitz concept wasn't new in McDonald's. Ray Kroc's unscheduled visits to stores were infamous, and everyone pitied the hapless operator or manager who suddenly found the chairman in his parking lot, picking up litter and ranting about grease stains on the pavement or a light bulb that had gone out. Mr. Kroc's habit may have inspired the company to implement unannounced visits as part of a program of evaluation, focused on specific markets. As a field consultant, I had participated in market blitzes in St. Louis and Detroit, and I introduced the concept to the Chicago BMOA owners. We adapted the blitz by making our evaluations more in-depth and applying the results to our overall training program.

BMOA blitzes were unique in that the participants were peers evaluating peers. Members knew that their fellow operators' critiques would not be all positive and that reacting defensively to negative comments would be counterproductive. The blitz program succeeded because the operators were able to set their egos aside. Through our training sessions, they had come to share a common set of standards—McDonald's standards of quality, service, and cleanliness—and were now prepared to make evaluations based on those standards. They also understood that it wasn't enough for their restaurants to become as good as the average white-operated suburban store; they had to be better. It had become obvious within the BMOA membership that improvements came faster when operators worked as a team. I organized and led blitzes for about a year and continued to participate later; however, the operators themselves were the prime movers. Once they got their standards and evaluation criteria synchronized, they extended the blitz concept to include store management and crew participation.

As BMOA's commitment to self-help evolved, the members' interaction grew to include shared authority. The operators decided that they would visit one another's restaurants often, seldom passing another member's store without critiquing and providing feedback. If a visiting operator spotted anything that needed management attention, his responsibility was to consult with his fellow owner-operator or the manager on duty. In effect, each BMOA member had the discretion to initiate discussion and advise on corrective action with other members' managers and employees in any problematic area of operations and customer service. I think this policy showed— maybe more than anything else BMOA did in those early days—the truly phenomenal level of trust and respect that the operators had for one another and in the value of their collaborative and team efforts.

Our next step was a big one. As crew training expanded, it

199

became more difficult to hold sessions in stores. So the BMOA operators decided to open a permanent training center and to fund it themselves. We spent the winter of 1971-72 finding a place and equipping it. We leased space in a building on East 103rd Street, across from a McDonald's owned by a BMOA member, my cousin John Perry. The space was adequate for seminars, lectures, discussion groups, regular meetings, and training on the restaurant equipment we had acquired. The equipment training was an important addition to our program; everyone learned how to use and maintain equipment properly in order to achieve maximum efficiency and even how to make minor repairs. Again, the project was funded entirely by BMOA, and it really was a great center—a single location where operators, store managers, and store employees could gather for formal instruction and informal interaction. Much of the training was done by visiting Hamburger U professors, corporate and regional staff members, department heads, and a few outside consultants.

The training center was a major move, and I was concerned that some people might disapprove because the center was created especially by and for black owners and their managers and employees. I also anticipated that some corporate executives might think that a physical facility signaled isolation and could become a challenge to Hamburger University; the company was justifiably proud of Hamburger U and very protective of its educational functions. By bringing in Hamburger U faculty, plus corporate and regional people, I thought we could accomplish two significant goals: First, our members and their managers and employees would be exposed to the resources and expertise available through the corporation. Second, the inclusion of corporate folks, all of whom were glad to be involved, would dissipate any negative concerns that McDonald's executives might be having about BMOA and its activities.

More than a year earlier, Ed Schmitt, my mentor, had moved up from regional manager to executive vice president, a promotion that took him into corporate headquarters. I didn't want Ed's promotion to be complicated by any negative reactions to the BMOA training center, so I informed him of the plan right at the start. As I expected, Ed immediately understood what we were trying to achieve and thought the center was a great idea. I was confident that he would present the news to his corporate executive management peers in the most favorable light and run interference for us if necessary—which he did. By the time the center opened in the spring of 1972, corporate leadership was on board with us. There may have been some behind-the-scenes complaining, but it didn't affect our progress.

Pretty soon, people throughout the McDonald's system were hearing about BMOA, and we began attracting visitors from throughout the country who wanted to see what was happening in Chicago. More important, black owner-operators in other parts of the Midwest region began to participate in BMOA and use our resources. Like the Chicago operators, black owners in St. Louis and Kansas City had been recruited to take over white-owned McDonald's restaurants in predominately black urban locations. They faced similar problems, although their physical facilities were generally in better condition and needed less upgrading. But with the exception of Dr. Benjamin "Doc" Davis—a respected dentist, businessman, and bank owner in St. Louis—the black operators outside Chicago were inexperienced in franchise operations and food service. It made sense to me to bring them into BMOA membership, and the BMOA operators agreed. The pioneer owners in Chicago were more than willing to share their knowledge and experience. It wasn't a one-way street either. Once they got on their feet, the new black owners brought their own strengths into the group. In fact, "Doc" Davis, who was the oldest BMOA member and a skilled businessman, was incredibly generous in helping all the members learn about the business side of running their restaurants.

In Milwaukee, we had a situation unlike the others. NBA (National Basketball Association) player Wayne Embry had joined the Milwaukee Bucks in 1968 and was named the Bucks' general manager in 1972—the first black to reach a top executive position in the league. Wayne had also teamed up with Sherman Claypool, a former service station owner, to become the first black owners to open a new McDonald's restaurant in the Midwest region. When they initially applied for a franchise in the late summer of 1971, however, they had two white partners (not Mr. X and Mr. Y). It looked like another "salt and pepper" deal in the making, and I raised a ruckus and got it stopped almost immediately. So Sherman, the operating partner, and Wayne got the new store on their own, plus substantial positive press coverage because of Wayne's name recognition. Soon, however, Sherman was under business pressure from a black militant group and also receiving extortion threats from local gang members, who demanded protection money. Bob Beavers, who came in from corporate, joined with a former police officer who headed the Milwaukee NAACP and a local minister to help Sherman work out the problems with the militants. But Sherman still had to deal with the gangs. The neighborhood was so tense that at one point, Sherman's food distributor failed to make deliveries, and Sherman had to get his products through Chicago BMOA members. He remembers how grateful he was to the BMOA members who went to Milwaukee daily for several weeks, bringing supplies and assisting with management and crew training. After the supply crisis was settled, the BMOA members continued to be available whenever he needed support and assistance.

As new owners—including Sherman and Wayne in Milwaukee, Andrew Murrell in Kansas City, and "Doc" Davis and Mallory Jones in St. Louis—came into BMOA, the self-help concept spread, and communication between owners intensified. Soon owners were traveling back and forth to consult with their brothers, provide assistance as they had to Sherman Claypool, and on occasion, "lend" skilled managers when another operator needed help.

BMOA's influence was growing, McDonald's Corporation was supportive, and the group was ready to take another step. When I organized BMOA's first convention in May 1972, it didn't raise an eyebrow in corporate headquarters. If there was any gossip, I was too busy with the training program to keep up with it. Besides, the company had much bigger burgers on the grill: The national rollout of the Quarter Pounder, introduced to operators at the Hawaii convention the previous October, was underway. The company was beginning to test a breakfast menu, including an item created by California franchise owner Herb Peterson and named the Egg McMuffin by Fred Turner's wife, Patty. Also in the national arena, the fallout from Ray Kroc's $250,000 contribution to President Nixon's reelection campaign was casting a shadow over the company's reputation for integrity. Internally, the company was in the middle of a major acquisition program; between 1967 and 1976, McDonald's purchased more than 500 stores from its franchisees—an investment of close to $200 million that boosted corporate profits and pleased Wall Street, but caused considerable dissension among franchisees, especially those who had been around for a long time. The threat of unionizing store workers was becoming serious. The company was also trying to get a handle on its international operations and solve the thorny problem of marketing the All-American meal—burger, fries, and beverage—to people who preferred sushi or sauerkraut or fish and chips.

In 1972, the company was in transition. McDonald's was no longer an entrepreneurial venture with potential; it had become a major player with a history of successes. Just a year earlier, a new, eight-story corporate headquarters had been erected in Oak Brook, and people there were still adjusting to its open space design—a cutting-edge concept back then. We had watched the construction from the windows of the regional office across the street. McDonald's Corporation now had a visual symbol—McDonald's Plaza, better known inside the company as the "Ivory Tower"—suitable to its status as the leading food franchiser in the United States. (The "Ivory Tower" nickname referred to the color of the building, but it had an obvious irony for some of us.)

In the context of the corporation as a whole, BMOA was, as yet, small potatoes. Our first convention, a two-day event held at the Playboy Towers, didn't seem to ruffle any feathers. Its primary intent was to improve communication among the black operators throughout the Midwest region and to dialogue with the company reps—including Mike Quinlan, now a field service manager—who attended. I was there as a company man, directing and leading the initiative, yet there was no conflict between my role as field consultant and my involvement with BMOA. But the first hint of other problems had already appeared.

There was a group of black franchisees in the Mideast region—Detroit, Michigan, and Toledo, Dayton, Cleveland, and Columbus, Ohio—who were interested in BMOA and kept in contact with the Chicago operators. They were invited to the convention, and we thought they would attend. But they didn't come. Nor did their black regional field consultants, John French, who had taught at Hamburger U, and Roscoe Coleman, a friend from our D.C. days. I found out that no snub was intended. The Mideast owners had been warned off by someone inside corporate, and I was pretty sure who dropped the hammer and why.

As long as BMOA was localized to the Midwest, confined to one field consultant, and focused on training and self-improvement, it had been accepted as a positive by the executives in the Ivory Tower. But the prospect of black operators unifying across regional lines would have raised a red flag for Fred Turner. Everybody knew how he hated the idea of "splinter groups," with their own agendas, operating inside the company. I don't know whether Fred was actually informed about BMOA's invitation to the Mideast regional owners, but there were people around him who knew. It seems most likely that one or two of those people—"yes-man" types who made an art of sucking up—assumed that Fred would disapprove and acted on their own to head off what they perceived as a potential problem.

The threat, subtly implied, was that the Mideast owners might be putting their expansion hopes in jeopardy if they attended the BMOA convention. Many McDonald's owners achieved success by operating multiple stores in their areas. For the new black owners, expansion would have often necessitated moving beyond the limits of the inner cities and into the metropolitan fringes and traditionally white suburbs, either by acquiring existing stores or getting new ones. But the company controlled the licensing, and without licensing, an owner couldn't expand. The expansion issue would become a major source of frustration for black owners over the next two decades. In 1972, the possibility of being denied opportunities to expand was enough of a threat to make the Mideast owners shy away from the BMOA gathering.

A year later, however, when BMOA hosted its second convention in Chicago, the Mideast owners were in full attendance. The 1973 gathering was called the Midwest-Mideast Convention to signify the growing unity of black owner-operators. The convention agenda didn't deal with expansion that year but continued to focus on enhancing communication among members, using knowledge gained from experience to help new African American owners coming into the system avoid the mistakes of the past, and growing the BMOA membership. What really got everyone fired up in 1973 was a discussion I led and a presentation by Tom Burrell, president of Burrell Advertising, Inc. Most of the convention attendees knew little about Tom before that meeting. But he was about to change the way black people perceived McDonald's and the way McDonald's marketed itself to the significant portion of its customers who were not white.

It Pays to Advertise

In the spring of 2005, I went to Chicago to celebrate Thomas J. Burrell's induction into the American Advertising Federation's Hall of Fame. Inside the advertising business, there's no higher honor, and I wanted to pay my own tribute. Tom and I go back a lot of years. We first met in 1973, when I helped him research black-owned McDonald's stores in Chicago. I can't remember who advised Tom to contact me, but I owe a debt of gratitude to that person. The collaborative relationship between Tom, BMOA, and McDonald's proved to be one of the most mutually beneficial that I have ever experienced in business.

In 1971, Tom founded one of the country's first black-owned ad agencies, with the mission of creating effective advertising specifically addressing African Americans. Up to that time, black consumers received virtually no attention from America's major advertisers, and black employees were as rare as hen's teeth in ad agencies and corporate marketing departments. Tom was one of the first to break barriers, going to work in the mail room at Wade Advertising in Chicago while he was still a college student and impressing the agency's creative director. He had become a copywriter for Wade in 1961, then moved on to Leo Burnett in 1964. He spent a year working in London for Foote Cone & Belding, and in 1968, he returned to Chicago as copy supervisor at Needham Harper & Steers. This background is important, because in the 1960s, Chicago was the Mecca of the advertising industry; it was *the* place to work if you were young, bright, creative, and you wanted to turn conventional marketing wisdom on its head. Tom had worked for the very best; he had risen quickly in a fast-paced and highly competitive business. With his resume, I'm sure Tom could have had his pick of any agency he wanted. But he wanted independence and the opportunity to change the way advertisers thought about black consumers. So he took the big leap and, with a partner, set up his own agency in a small office on North Michigan Avenue. The Burrell office happened to be across the hall from McDonald's public relations firm. With only three employees and no clients, Burrell's agency began as a very small fish in a very large pond.

Needham Harper & Steers had become McDonald's national ad agency in 1969, and a year later McDonald's launched its national "You Deserve a Break" campaign, which shifted away from the earlier marketing focus on tasty food and good value to a more sophisticated emphasis on McDonald's as a total experience—a pleasurable interlude in everyday living, like a mini-vacation. The ads Needham produced were directed squarely at the corporation's favorite customers: white, middle-class, suburban, nuclear families with kids. With its catchy jingle and slickly produced TV and radio spots, the campaign was a smash hit in suburbia. But as I said in an earlier chapter, "You Deserve a Break" had little impact on low-income and working-class folks in inner-city black and ethnic neighborhoods. Most of the people who came into Herman Petty's and Ed Wimp's and The Better Boys' stores in Chicago certainly deserved breaks, like more employment opportunities, higher wages and benefits, improved schools, access to health care, and so forth. For them, McDonald's was a cheap, fast source for filling meals—not a Caribbean cruise.

Although the "You Deserve a Break" campaign produced significant sales increases nationally, it had only a marginal effect in McDonald's growing urban markets. Black owners began to complain that they were getting little, if any, return for the fees they paid out of their gross sales for national advertising. One of the most persistent critics was my dear friend Carl Osborne.

Carl had briefly left McDonald's in 1970 to work with a start-up franchising operation in the Washington, D.C., market. Carl's ambition, however, was to be a McDonald's franchisee, and he had left the company when his first franchise application failed. McDonald's—not to mention all the men like me and Bob Beavers whose careers Carl had nurtured so generously in our D.C. days—wanted him back in the fold. So when a McDonald's store in urban Columbus, Ohio, came up for sale, it was offered to Carl. With help from the Small Business Administration, Carl put together the financing, purchased the Columbus store, and early in 1971, he came back under the Golden Arches.

As an owner-operator, Carl was as determined as ever to create opportunities for blacks in McDonald's and change inequities in the system. True to form, Carl began expressing concerns about the company's current marketing strategy, which hadn't been effective in attracting black customers. I don't know exactly how it came about, but Carl and some other black owners got the company's attention, and Paul Schrage, McDonald's chief marketing officer, arranged a meeting. Carl, Chuck Johnson from Cleveland, and Ralph Kelly from Detroit went to Chicago to sit down with corporate marketing executives and representatives of Needham Harper & Steers. The session included presentations by three or four agencies that specialized in marketing to African American consumers. The owners recommended Tom Burrell as the man with the best grip on the black consumer market.

Subsequent to that meeting, Needham asked Tom, their former copy supervisor, to take on a project, developing a campaign directed at black customers. Tom came up with a new theme—"Get Down With McDonald's"—and print and radio ads featuring black families and urban environments. Needham rejected Tom's work, saying that it was "too black" and risked offending white consumers, and told him that his agency wouldn't be getting any more project assignments. Presumably under instruction from McDonald's, Needham reluctantly ran a "Get Down With McDonald's" print ad once, in *Jet* and *Ebony* magazines where it was not likely to be seen by white readers, but never used the radio spots. This experience, Tom says, made him realize that he could not do effective marketing for McDonald's if he had to report to Needham.

It was obvious to Tom that Needham Harper & Steers was basing its creative strategy on the fundamentally flawed assumption that blacks and whites are basically the same and will therefore respond in similar ways to the same marketing. I imagine that the ad execs at Needham had expected Tom to merely tweak their "You Deserve a Break" creative a bit, maybe substituting black models for whites in print ads and giving the jingle a 'black beat.'

Tom understood what the black owners and a few white

executives, like Ed Schmitt, already knew—that hardcore urban black consumers and middle-class suburban white consumers had radically different perceptions and expectations of McDonald's. For most inner-city blacks, McDonald's wasn't a fun break in the daily routine; it was just a place to eat, a "feeding station" in Tom's words. Eating patterns were very different. Blacks were more likely to eat on their own, when they could get the time, not in family groups and not on a conventional schedule. To black adults, a "break" often meant grabbing a few minutes to wolf down a burger and fries. Black families didn't have the leisure to dine out together, and McDonald's often served as a baby-sitter, a place where inner-city children could safely go for a meal when their elders were at work. It all boiled down to one of Tom's most quoted observations: "Black people are not dark-skinned white people."

When Tom told me about his experience with Needham, I immediately asked him to participate in the '73 BMOA convention. I wanted him to lay it all out for the attendees—what was not working with McDonald's current advertising strategy and what could be done to make it more appealing to African American consumers. His presentation impressed the convention delegates, especially after I made some uncharacteristically emotional remarks reflecting my anger at the way Tom's efforts had been treated by Needham. We stirred up the convention, and the members set up a BMOA task force to explore *effective* ways to reach the black consumer market through marketing and media. It was obvious to everyone that the solutions were not going to come from the people who created the problems in the first place. If McDonald's national advertising was going to increase sales for black owners in black communities, we needed a black ad team in control.

The whole concept of "black consumer marketing" was very

new at that time. Tom and a few other African American ad people in the country were only beginning to get some attention inside the advertising industry. But it wasn't easy to convince highly successful ad agencies and their clients that they were missing the boat with black and ethnic Americans. Advertisers were used to thinking of customers in terms of age, gender, education, and economic class, but the realities of cultural differences—differences that resided deep in peoples' psychology and the history of their racial or ethic group—was not factored in. Without serious, in-depth market research (which didn't begin to have a real impact on advertising until the 1980s), traditional advertisers were guided by their "gut feelings." Guys with great instincts, like Leo Burnett, were the lions of the industry, but they were a rare breed. I would say that Tom Burrell was one of that rare breed.

Faced with facts—the size of the African American market and its collective purchasing power—McDonald's got the message years before many other large corporations. It was shortly after the BMOA convention that McDonald's established a direct reporting relationship with Burrell Advertising. Tom worked with Roy Burgold in the corporate marketing department, who reported to the head of marketing, Paul Schrage. Needham Harper & Steers wasn't always happy with this new arrangement, which basically left them out of the loop. But Tom appreciated McDonald's uncomplicated decision-making process. For instance, when a question came up during the shooting of a commercial, Roy Burgold was empowered to make a decision on the spot. There was no time-wasting or layers of corporate bureaucrats to go through in order to get a simple "yes" or "no" answer.

Tom's first project under the new, direct arrangement was a campaign with the theme "McDonald's Sure Is Good to Have

Around." The TV commercials showed McDonald's as part of everyday life in the black community. In one ad I remember, a black mail carrier walked his route and stopped in at the local McDonald's—a reflection of normal activity in which McDonald's played a regular part. This spoke to people in urban areas with a great deal more force than chipper suburban moms and dads packing their kids in the station wagon and driving to the neighborhood McDonald's. Importantly, especially after Needham's rejection of Tom's "Get Down With McDonald's" concept, the new campaign improved urban sales and didn't offend whites, other than the usual loonies who are always offended. Given the opportunity, Tom had proven the validity of his understanding of the black consumer market and his marketing approach. From that point forward, he would guide McDonald's minority marketing—and he was soon working his magic for Coca-Cola, Ford Motor Company, Procter & Gamble, and a long list of high-profile corporate advertisers.

Pretty much everyone agrees that before 1969, McDonald's was slow to get into national marketing and over-relied on publicity and public relations. But the company did have one early national success, thanks to my first employer in Washington—Gee Gee Distributing. Of the two partners in Gee Gee, Oscar Goldstein was the one who drove the marketing of Gee Gee's multi-store franchise. Mr. Goldstein pushed the company's D.C. ad agency, Kal Erhlich & Merrick, into getting Gee Gee's first television sponsorship—an afternoon children's show called "Bozo's Circus," first aired in 1959 on WRC-TV, the NBC affiliate in Washington. Bozo the clown was played by a young announcer named Willard Scott, who delivered the McDonald's sales pitches. This was back when there weren't any restrictions on television advertising to children, and Bozo's messages were direct calls to action, telling young viewers to get their parents to take them to McDonald's. Kids loved Willard Scott as Bozo. Whenever Bozo did personal appearances—Barry Klein, a copywriter at Kal Erhlich & Merrick, recalls that the first was at the opening of a Gee Gee-owned McDonald's in Rockville, Maryland—the turn-out was always huge, as was the impact on sales. Gee Gee's average per-store sales increased at the rate of 30 percent annually during the Bozo years, well above McDonald's national average for store sales.

When WRC decided to cancel "Bozo's Circus" in 1963, Oscar Goldstein wasn't ready to give up his successful marketing strategy. His agency tried using other local personalities, including a popular disc jockey, as spokespeople, but nothing worked liked Bozo. Then Barry Klein had the idea to create a McDonald's clown, with Willard Scott playing the part, and to produce their own commercials. Local TV commercials were rare in the early 1960s; most local advertisers sponsored programs, and on-air personalities simply read a sponsor's ad copy live during the show, as Scott had done on the Bozo show. Mr. Goldstein, who was a lot like Ray Kroc in his willingness to try new ideas, gave the plan a go.

The clown needed an identity. "Archie McDonald," the name of a cartoon character sometimes used by corporate McDonald's, was rejected because there was already a well-known Arch McDonald, an announcer for the Washington Senators baseball team, in the market. So Willard Scott came up with the rhyming "Ronald McDonald." His clown costume was pretty crude, with a cardboard, four-hole carry-out tray as a hat and a seven-ounce paper drink cup for a nose. But in the commercials, Ronald was presented as a clown who did kid things and acted like a kid, and real kids adored him.

Based on the success in D.C., Mr. Goldstein offered the Ronald character to corporate as a national spokesman for the company. Harry Sonneborn, McDonald's president at that time,

213

rejected the idea—until he reviewed Gee Gee's sales figures. The first national Ronald McDonald commercials began airing in 1965. Unfortunately, Willard Scott hadn't made the cut. For store events and personal appearances across the country, McDonald's needed a look that could be duplicated by actors in multiple markets, and Willard Scott was too physically distinctive to be easily copied.

As Ronald's costuming and makeup were refined into the image we all know today, it became clear that the corporate clown appealed to children of every color and culture. The ethnicity of the actor behind the red hair and painted white face just didn't matter. Kids loved the clown, and Ronald soon became a national celebrity. I remember the first time Ronald McDonald made a personal appearance in one of our hardcore urban Chicago restaurants. It was Herman Petty's Stoney Island Avenue store, and the kids from the area were jam-packed on the lot, waiting for Ronald. Their excitement was like nothing I had ever seen. Celebrities didn't visit "ghetto" neighborhoods, and most of these children had never seen a clown except on television. So when Ronald arrived, the kids erupted. They all wanted to touch him—grabbing at his hair and nose and pulling on his floppy red shoes. We hadn't anticipated this kind of response and had no special crowd control. We managed to get Ronald away without any harm done, but the local ad agency, which had set up the event, decided to cancel further appearances at BMOA stores.

When BMOA raised hell, the regional advertising manager came to see me, assuming I would regard the appearance as a disaster and agree to the cancellations. He was wrong. I made it clear that we had miscalculated the number of children who wanted to see Ronald, and I agreed to coordinate the next few Ronald appearances while establishing standardized procedures. The next event was at Herman's Vincennes Store. We had learned our lesson; we planned it in every detail, and other BMOA members volunteered their services on the day of the appearance. This time, everything went off without a hitch, and Ronald's visits to urban stores were resumed.

Barry Klein had come to Chicago in 1968 as McDonald's national advertising manager, primarily handling the highly successful marketing of Ronald McDonald. After Fred Turner became president, he wanted to change the Ronald marketing strategy, and Barry resigned. Barry recalls that there was nothing personal in his departure; it was a disagreement over strategy. Besides, Barry says now, he was kind of a wild card at McDonald's—a long-haired liberal who could never get into corporate mode. But he respected Fred and had a close relationship with Ray Kroc, though he remembers that Mr. Kroc "never quite understood the Ronald phenomenon. He would leave meetings when Ronald issues were discussed, because he was afraid that he would 'screw things up.' He knew his own limits, what he should be involved in and what he should leave to others."

The development of Ronald McDonald by Gee Gee illustrates a McDonald's tradition that not many people know about. Mr. Kroc never wanted his company to move far away from the store level, and he never lost contact with his owners. As a result, the most creative ideas frequently came from owners. I have often visualized the company as an upside-down pyramid. The owner-operators, who were closest to the customers, were at the top, where their ideas could flow freely down to corporate management. If an owner had an idea, he didn't face an uphill climb to get a hearing from Mr. Kroc and his key executives. Inside the company, innovative owners like Oscar Goldstein were paid their due, but their contributions weren't much heralded to the public. Mr. Kroc didn't hesitate to share credit, but the press was so in love with his charismatic personality and his Horatio Alger success story that little attention was paid to the company's unsung heroes.

How many people know that the fish sandwich was the brain child of Cincinnati operator Lou Groen, who catered to a largely Catholic area and needed an item to appeal to his customers on what were then "meatless Fridays"? That the Big Mac was first put on the menu by Pittsburg owner Jim Delligatti? That Santa Barbara franchisee Herb Peterson developed the Egg McMuffin and other breakfast foods that enabled McDonald's to dominate the breakfast market? That Litton Cochran, a multi-store owner in Knoxville, Tennessee, ended McDonald's long search for a winning dessert item by adding his mother's fried apple pies to his stores' menu?

You have to go deep in the company's history to find the name of Tom Christian of South Bend, Indiana—who in the mid-1960s defied Mr. Kroc's implicit ban on hiring women employees and won. Or Reub Taylor, a New England franchisee who codified the polite greeting-order taking-goodbye language and etiquette that for so long distinguished McDonald's counter service. Or Jim Zien in Minneapolis and Patty Crimmins in St. Paul, who banked their entire advertising budget on radio commercials in 1958 and added television to the mix in 1959—bringing McDonald's into the broadcast age.

And how many people realize that a small group of persistent black owners changed the way McDonald's advertised to blacks, which led to a new, culturally sensitive approach to other minorities, to women, to people with disabilities, and may even have influenced the company's international marketing? McDonald's became a leader in the recognition of American diversity, and I'm proud to say that the members of BMOA were the groundbreakers who made it happen.

REASONS FOR OPTIMISM

When I look back on my first three-and-a half-years in Chicago, I can hardly believe how much was being accomplished then and how hard everyone was working to make our gains permanent. The unity of the black operators in BMOA was extraordinary. Even as they struggled to get their own stores up to standard, they were reaching out to help others. There were some very forceful personalities among those pioneering black owners, but no one tried to dominate and the competition was always friendly. Consensus, collaboration, and teamwork were the unwritten rules.

I was well aware that, despite the progress BMOA was making, we had a long way to go to achieve total business integration and we couldn't let up on our efforts. Being inside McDonald's Corporation had convinced me that the corporation was committed to change and prepared to learn from its mistakes. I didn't kid myself that the company was acting selflessly, although I had come to know a number of individual whites in McDonald's who had genuine moral and ethical motives to promote diversity. When I had arrived in Chicago in1969, corporate leadership had been mostly bewildered and confused by its problems in black, urban markets; they were floundering for solutions. By mid-1973, I felt that, as a business entity, McDonald's had come to recognize the impact of black consumers on the growth of its urban markets. When McDonald's established its direct reporting relationship with Tom Burrell, following the 1973 BMOA convention, the company had to throw off a lot of its old assumptions and stereotypes. McDonald's has been criticized by some for its lack of long-range planning—exemplified by its chaotic growth throughout the 1970s—yet I doubt that a more buttoned-down corporation could have so quickly made the systemic changes necessary to achieve real diversity. Back then, McDonald's was willing to experiment and learn through trial and error. It was an environment that encouraged new ways of thinking.

To make positive change, I was working day and night—tending to my client stores in Chicago, traveling frequently to black-owned stores in the Midwest, conducting training for BMOA and getting the Chicago training center running smoothly, consulting with my colleagues in the other McDonald's regions, working on the first cross-region BMOA convention, still cleaning up the "salt and pepper" partnership mess. And I was loving every minute of it. Maybe if I'd been a decade older, I would have felt more stress, but I was in my early thirties, and for me, the work was an energizing force. I had become a very different person from the young boy whom my dad had nicknamed "Grady" because I was so slow at getting things done that I looked like an old, gray man. Now, it seemed that the more I did, the more I was capable of doing.

My loyalty to my own people had become entwined with my loyalty to McDonald's. I knew my work with the black owners and BMOA would strengthen McDonald's and that a stronger, more diverse McDonald's would create more opportunities for black businesspeople, employees, and customers. The work didn't seem so much like work to me because, from Ray Kroc to the kids we trained, I was keeping good company. Whatever the obstacles ahead (and I knew that we were still on a very rocky road), I felt optimistic about the future of blacks in McDonald's and hopeful about my own opportunities for advancement.

Step Up, Step Back, Step Aside?

*A great many people think they are thinking when they are
merely re-arranging their prejudices.*

WILLIAM JAMES, PHILOSOPHER

By the fall of 1972, I had been a field consultant for almost four years. This made me the second oldest field consultant in the company—not in age, but in years of tenure. McDonald's generally promoted quickly and also fast-tracked promising employees through the ranks leading to executive positions. Mike Quinlan was on the fast track when we first met, and he stayed on it to become one of the youngest chief executive officers in the company's history. The first black to participate fully in the fast track program was Reggie Webb. Starting at entry level in 1973, Reggie rose to vice president in record time, and he earned every promotion. As I observed his career, I saw his progress as a shining example of what blacks and other minorities could achieve in McDonald's and *for* McDonald's.

Based on every objective review of my own performance as a consultant, my competence, and the performance of the stores I was working with, I thought I should be moving up as well. In addition to my assigned stores in Chicago, I had requested and been given all black-owned McDonald's in the region. In the wake of the "salt and

219

pepper" problems, I'd developed and implemented a process and procedures by which potential black franchisees would be selected, evaluated, and trained. In order to avoid risky arrangements, like the "salt and pepper" partnerships, in the future, this pre-ownership program was designed to weed out applicants when there wasn't a good business match or long-range potential for a mutually beneficial franchise partnership. I had continued my own education by taking the advanced operations course at Hamburger University during my second year in Chicago. It had been recommended, but I probably could have skipped it, given my experience in store management, my participation in Gee Gee's training program in Washington, and my field service record. But I thought it was important. On my own, I had taken a couple of Dale Carnegie courses, enhancing my public speaking skills, plus a small business course at a local college and a speed-reading course. But in spite of my best efforts, there I was, still a field consultant while others were moving ahead.

I could understand the company's keeping me in the field position in the early phase of recruiting and training black owners to take over difficult, hardcore urban locations in Chicago. As a field consultant, I was closest to the ground, working directly with black owners, managers, and employees inside black communities. I was also achieving good results for the white, urban owner-operators. It probably made sense to keep me in place in the first couple of years. For my part, I had been so intensely involved in the process of integrating the ownership, getting BMOA and the training center established, and my other responsibilities that I hadn't paid close attention to my own career prospects. But as things started to settle down, it became obvious that something, or someone, was holding me back.

If Ed Schmitt had still been Midwest regional manager, I was sure that I would have been moved up to field service manager (the next rung on the regional ladder) or possibly into the corporate offices. But when Ed became a corporate executive vice president at the start of 1971, he was replaced as Midwest regional manager by Bernie Hall, a fine man and a good administrator but less aggressive than Ed. Bernie was eventually followed by the only truly racist senior manager I encountered in the executive ranks. I'll just call him "Neil."

In 1971, Neil came in as a Midwest field consultant from restaurant management. Initially, we were peers. His territory was outside of Chicago, so we didn't often cross paths, though I heard that some other consultants had a few doubts about the guy. Neil wasn't a field consultant for long, however. When Roland Long, who had taken over from Frank Phalen as a field service manager, moved up, I should have at least been considered for the position. But there was no time. The field service manager's job was filled almost overnight, and—wham, bam—to everyone's surprise, Neil got it.

I wouldn't be human if I hadn't been disappointed at being passed over. Fortunately, I was juggling too many plates to waste time worrying about what might have been. Neil hadn't been a field consultant long enough for any of us to know how he would perform as field service manager, and I had no reason to resent him personally. I just assumed my chance would come soon, and I got on with my job.

As a consequence of the company's explosive growth, there were a lot of organizational changes on the McDonald's drawing board in the early and mid-1970s. The six-region structure was becoming inadequate to accommodate the growth, especially in major urban areas like Chicago and Los Angeles. So the old regions were being divided into geographically smaller regions, often with a large city as the core. The number of regional consultants and department heads was growing, along with the number of franchisees. To my mind, the company's growth and structural changes presented new opportunities for me and for other blacks who were coming into the corporate and regional offices.

As field service manager, Neil became my immediate supervisor. I worked okay with him, mainly, I think, because he knew almost nothing about Chicago or urban operations and he needed those of us with experience in hardcore urban areas to handle what didn't interest him. I don't know if any of the white consultants picked up on it at the time, but it quickly became obvious to me and to the black Chicago owners and operators that Neil was uncomfortable with African Americans. He lacked confidence with experienced owner-operators in general, and as far as the black-owned restaurants and BMOA activities were concerned, he left me alone. He did, however, begin making efforts to undercut me with the white owners who were my clients. Most of the white owners told me what he said to them, and a couple of them were more than ready to give me an earful.

I think what bothered Neil most was the notion of a black person being positioned in any way *above* whites. When I worked with black owners and operators, he didn't have a problem. But when I worked with white owners, it didn't matter to him how collegial and productive our relationships were. I'm sure that when Neil saw me in a superior position, it bugged the heck out of him. I wasn't his specific target as yet. Any situation in which an African American had any degree of authority over whites was a problem for him. It was the old plantation mindset—blacks are fine as long as whites keep them *in their place*—and I had dealt with it plenty of times before I met Neil. There had been the white radio station owner in Mississippi who had forbidden any reporting of civil rights news because it might stir up our black listeners. There had been the manager of the suburban McDonald's in Virginia where I had been a trainee and Stan Jeter, my supervisor when I managed the 3510 Duke Street restaurant in Alexandria; both men had been unhappy with blacks holding traditionally white jobs and interacting with white customers. Unlike Neil, however, these two men were, I believe, more worried about white consumer reactions and the impact on business than about black advancement. I wound up learning from both of them—especially Stan.

Neil was a game-player, and he thought the game was strictly about corporate and office politics. I never saw any sign that he loved the business or cared about the quality of the work for its own sake. Then, as now, a "player" in business can be defined as a user, someone who rides on the genuine achievements of others. Neil's problem was that he wasn't a particularly good player, and a lot of people caught on to his act. His racism wasn't blatant; he was forever doing what he perceived as the 'right thing' in political terms. To advance himself, he played nice to everybody's face. Yet he wasn't sufficiently skilled to hide his real feelings; an incident a couple of years later showed me that his prejudice extended beyond black people.

As I said, I had decided to wait for my chance to advance. In the meantime, I had more important problems to deal with. An unforgettable illustration of the kind of difficulties we ran into was Cabrini-Green. In 1971, the company decided to build a new restaurant across the street from the massive cluster of government housing projects called Cabrini-Green, in the old "Little Italy" section of Chicago. The company had great hopes for the Cabrini-Green venture, which was the first new store constructed in a majority black area in Chicago. The potential market was huge; more than 15,000

223

people lived in the projects. Unemployment was extremely high, but our black McDonald's owners in other low-income Chicago areas were already showing increased sales and earnings, so everyone thought it was do-able in the projects. I was convinced that the Cabrini-Green store would provide employment and the kind of job training that would translate into wider opportunities for project residents. The new store seemed to me an ideal opportunity to act on Ray Kroc's commitment to give back to the community.

The plan went forward in a real spirit of optimism. The flaw was that no one, myself included, dug deeply enough into the situation at Cabrini-Green to really grasp the inherent problems. We badly misjudged the economic viability of the location. Most of the people in the projects lived entirely or partly on welfare or Social Security, and they only had money to spend on the few days after their government checks arrived (or, for the fortunate few, when they received their pay packets). Also, Cabrini-Green was among the worst-maintained and most dangerous housing projects in the whole country, and many of the residents didn't feel safe leaving their apartments, much less visiting the restaurant or sending their kids there. Although situated near some of the city's most affluent areas, Cabrini-Green was like an isolated island. Non-residents rarely came into the projects unless they had to, and they left as soon as they could, so there was very little pass-through traffic to sustain business when the locals stayed away.

The Cabrini-Green projects were often compared to a prison, and prisons breed lawlessness. The first trouble came almost immediately when a local black preacher and so-called "activist," backed up by young men from the projects, began pressuring the owner-operator, Andrew Davis, for jobs and favors in what was basically a shakedown scheme. The situation was similar to what

Sherman Claypool faced in Milwaukee, and there was always the potential that it could flare into a mini-version of the 1969 Cleveland boycott. I was Andy's field consultant, and I supported him when he stood up to the pressure. Frustrated, the troublemakers went around us to corporate, and Pat Flynn, the area manager for McOpCo (the company-owned stores), and Joe Brown, who had been the second black field consultant in the Midwest and was now a McOpCo area supervisor, were drawn in to negotiate some kind of settlement, with help from those of us in the regional office. Both Pat and Joe got death threats, but they also refused to cave. Joe was adept at turning the activists' demands back on themselves: They would call for a jobs program; Joe would ask them to present their plan for the program; then they would back off because, of course, they had no plan. Jobs weren't what they were really after. Joe and Pat eventually did negotiate for landscaping work, and McDonald's helped the group start a landscaping business. But the whole thing petered out when the would-be extortionists lost interest.

Andy Davis was an experienced operator and became a valued member of BMOA—serving as president in 1974. But even he couldn't make the Cabrini-Green restaurant successful. With so little money in the housing projects and no outside traffic, the store could not build volume and was frequently empty. It struggled on for several years but was eventually closed by McDonald's. In financial terms, it was a failure. The company never gave up on any store without a fight, so I'm sure there were also some bruised egos inside the Ivory Tower when the Cabrini-Green store was shut down. Still, we all learned a valuable lesson—the same lesson that Tom Burrell was teaching the corporation about advertising. Don't presume anything. And don't start anything until you *know your market*.

ONE STEP FORWARD

I finally got my opportunity to advance late in 1972, when I was promoted to field service manager. My territory comprised Chicago and South Bend and Gary, Indiana. This had been Neil's territory, but he was switched to the outer market (Wisconsin, Illinois except for Chicago, Iowa, etc.) when I formally stepped into my new position in January 1973.

I managed five or six field consultants at first—including Art Smith, who took over my job as field consultant in Chicago and began running the BMOA training program. My field consultants served roughly 150-180 stores. For a while, I also continued as field consultant to the black owners in Kansas City, Milwaukee, and St. Louis. After St. Louis began to function as a separate region, Pat Flynn soon took over as its regional manager, and my responsibility there came to an end, though I continued to be available for consultation. It was great working with Pat again. He had shown his stuff during the Cabrini-Green situation, and I had great confidence in him. The transition of my St. Louis stores went as smooth as silk.

We were still having ownership difficulties in Kansas City—mainly an all-black partnership that mirrored the "salt and pepper" deals—so I delayed handing over the black-operated stores there until the problem was settled. I stayed on as consultant to the one black-owned store in Milwaukee, even though it was in Neil's territory.

If I was ever tempted to get ahead in business by playing the political game, Neil was a great object lesson in why not to. He was the perfect negative role model. Sadly, that's the best I can say about our relationship. When my promotion to field service manager was announced, my colleagues celebrated at a small dinner meeting. Bernie Hall came, and so did someone from corporate. Neil was there too, and just as pleased as he could be about my new job. At least, that was the impression he tried to create.

I hadn't been as excited about the promotion as might be expected. It had been too long in coming. Although it was another first for me—the first black field service manager in McDonald's—the promotion itself was an anticlimax. I was, however, geared up for the work, and I was glad to be on the same level with Neil again. He brought out my competitive side. I was well aware by now how he worked the system strictly to his own advantage, though I think that most of the time, he didn't know what actually was to his advantage. I was ready to prove that my way was the better way. After my run-ins with Fred Turner and others over the "salt and pepper" partnerships and my growing discontent with the company's advertising, some people had branded me as a hell-raiser. I don't think I was, and I also think that a white man in the same position would have been called "forceful" and "determined." (It's much the same complaint women have: A strong female executive is often labeled as a "pushy bitch" while an equally strong male is an "aggressive leader.") But I wasn't prepared to change my approach. If that meant raising a little hell on occasion, so be it.

One of my primary goals was to continue enhancing and enlarging BMOA and promoting the group's self-help capabilities across regional lines. At the 1973 BMOA convention, the Midwest and Mideast regions were unified. The agenda for the 1974 convention, held in Chicago in June, showed a level of sophistication that demonstrated how far we had come. From a group of inexperienced owners in basic training, the black operators had progressed to a convention dominated by seminar discussions of profit-sharing, pension plans, tax shelters, OPNAD (McDonald's Operators National Advertising Cooperative, of which Carl Osborne became the first elected black member in 1973) and local advertising co-ops, and the National Operators Advisory Board. (Known first as the National Advisory Panel, then as the National Operators Advisory Board—NOAB—the operators' advisory group had been formed to facilitate communication between owner-operators and corporate regarding the company's policies. During the original and short-lived panel phase, the members of the advisory board were appointed by corporate, but under Ed Schmitt's leadership, it was changed to a body elected by the owners themselves. BMOA was naturally interested in being represented.) Burrell Advertising also made a presentation of the new McDonald's advertising approach to the black consumer market—the "McDonald's Sure Is Good to Have Around" campaign.

Something else happened at the '74 convention that shocked us all, in a good way, and signaled that we were on the right track. A black owner from Houston, Texas—Johnny Williams—had heard about BMOA and how black owners in the Midwest and Mideast regions were collaborating to help one another. On his own, Johnny came to the convention and asked if he could take part. He was the only black owner in Texas, and he wasn't getting much assistance, either from other owners there or from his regional office, as he struggled to master the business. It just made sense to him to fly up to Chicago and see if the brothers could give him some help. He was warmly welcomed as an unofficial delegate, and a lot of us still regard that 1974 convention as our first 'national' event—all because Johnny Williams took the bull by the horns and showed up unannounced.

Johnny also attended the next year, when the BMOA convention was held in Kansas City. By 1975, however, he wasn't on his own. BMOA chapters were beginning to be formed around the country, and although the event was still organized by the Chicago chapter, assisted by Art Smith, owners and operators from throughout the country attended. Unofficially, BMOA really became a national group that year.

A STEP BACK

I need to go back to a time near the end of 1973, my first year as a field service manager. As co-workers on equal footing, Neil and I hadn't experienced any real conflicts that year. He went his way; I went mine. But another promotion was on the horizon, and the outcome would shift the balance again.

The position that came open was the top slot in the region. Bernie Hall was moving up to zone manager as part of the organizational restructuring, and the question of who would take his place as regional manager was a big deal to just about everyone in the Midwest. It was obvious that Neil wanted the title; whether he wanted the work was another matter. I think most people expected him to get the promotion, but they weren't happy about it. I also knew I should have been in the running this time, and many of my co-workers and the owners were open about their support for me. I was later told by a manager in Human Resources that his department had gotten comments from a number of people and that within the region, I was the favorite choice. Besides Neil and myself, I never knew who else was being considered.

In terms of seniority, I had been in the regional office longer than Neil, but he had been a field service manager almost a year longer than I, so I guess we evened out on that score. There's no question that I had the superior performance record. Maybe my "hell-raising" reputation was a handicap, but I doubt it. It was Fred Turner himself who encouraged me to make waves. The first time I met him, back during my Chicago orientation in 1969, he gave me an autographed picture of a sailing ship, inscribed with this message: "If you're not making waves, you're standing still."

I think it's more likely that the executives who made the

decision hadn't yet caught on to Neil's insincere schmoozing and game-playing. And they were influenced by a perception that Ed Schmitt supported Neil—based, as far as anyone could figure, solely on the fact that Ed had known Neil outside McDonald's (as I recall, they may have attended the same church) and had apparently suggested him as a possible candidate for McDonald's executive training (fast track) program. Neil never really made the fast track, but the myth persisted that Ed had a special interest in his career. By the end of 1973, it was becoming clear to many people that Ed, whose responsibility covered all McDonald's operations, was probably next in line to run the corporation. So when Neil was named Midwest regional manager, the general assumption was that the decision was an attempt to please the future president.

To put it mildly, Neil's promotion did not go down well inside the department or with many owners. Several of the people I interviewed for this book remembered Neil's appointment as a classic case of *The Peter Principle*—"In a hierarchy, every employee tends to rise to his level of incompetence"—formulated by Dr. Lawrence J. Peter in his very popular 1969 book. At the time, a lot of people thought Neil had reached his level of incompetence much earlier.

Six of the seven Chicago field consultants in my area came to me with serious concerns about their futures now that Neil was running the division. I understood their issues very well, and I did everything possible to find fair solutions for my people that were also good for the company. Some of the consultants already had political cover within the company and were unlikely to have serious problems. Others couldn't or wouldn't stay, so I worked to get them out of the department. One was promoted to the East and another to International. I didn't think that Art Smith, who had taken over for me in Chicago and was now consultant to the inner-city black owners and

BMOA, was in any danger. But I couldn't talk another consultant out of resigning from the company.

Personally, I was very angry, and I thought maybe I had finally encountered an obstacle that couldn't be turned into an opportunity. But I wasn't going to let my emotions drive me to make a bad decision. I was too committed to the future of diversity in the company and to the black owner-operators to cut and run. And I didn't want to leave my McDonald's friends and colleagues; we'd all worked too hard to come so far, and we still had so much to accomplish. The disappointment of being passed over this time was truly painful. But I thought about my father, and I was sure he would tell me that when you are down is when you have to look up. Okay, I was down, but I was a long way from being out.

Following his pattern, Neil didn't often interfere with my ongoing relations with the black operators. There were times, however, when we had conflicts over how to deal with operators' issues. I tried to find solutions; Neil looked for political expedients. Then he would go behind my back, directly to an owner, and with a great show of concern, he would propose some fix that didn't do much more than cover up the problem for a while. His method was to make the problem seem to disappear so that it wouldn't reflect on him. He made promises, then delayed and delayed about fulfilling them. At best, he was disingenuous; at worst, he was dishonest. Most owners didn't fall for his promises more than once.

Still, I was able to function effectively after Neil took over the regional reins, and I was really enjoying my work with the field consultants. They were my "customers" now. Based on my own years as a field consultant, I saw my primary responsibility as doing everything I could to enable my consultants to be in the field, not tied down to their desks. My duties included coordinating training for new consultants and continuing education for the others; working with the heads of the support departments, primarily Real Estate, Construction, and Marketing, to get whatever the consultants needed to maximize service to their assigned stores; amassing corporate input and setting priorities; assisting the local purchasing and advertising co-ops; reviewing all the paperwork, including store performance reviews and financial reports, that came in from the field; and helping with special activities including new store openings. A store opening was a big undertaking and very time-consuming because it usually required months of constant communication and coordination with everyone involved in getting a store completed and fully prepared to serve the public. Every aspect of building, equipping, supplying, hiring and training, and marketing had to be factored in and coordinated when an opening was scheduled. There were also uncertainties, like possible delays in construction or difficulties in getting inexperienced owners and managers up to speed by opening day.

Weather is always unpredictable, so owners and company officials had to be ready with a plan B, and maybe a plan C, just in case. I'd learned that during my first month as a field consultant. Back in D.C., I had never been involved in a new store opening, so as part of my orientation, I was sent with a senior field consultant, Jack Weise, who was overseeing openings in Fargo and Grand Forks, North Dakota. It was January; the thermometer registered -30 degrees; there was more snow than I had ever seen; and I couldn't imagine how they would get the store finished and ready by opening day. I quickly realized that Jack did a lot of handholding and reassuring as well as coordinating. Getting ready for an opening is a kind of organized chaos, and the field consultant has to stay on top of the organizing. Jack did it all just right. When I went back to Fargo in the spring, it was warmer, though not by much, and the grand opening went off without a hitch. I remember another opening, in the far Chicago south suburbs, which Fred Turner attended. At one point during the ceremony, he looked over at our little group of field consultants and gave us the thumbs up. A number of consultants worked on that opening because the store included experimental design and equipment that was very important to the company. Getting the A-okay from the president himself was one of the best rewards we could receive.

The consultants under my direction as field service manager were a terrific group—hard-working, dedicated, and enthusiastic about their jobs. It was also an unusual group for the mid-1970s; though all male, it was racially and ethnically mixed: white, black, and Hispanic. We got along great together, and there was a genuine sense of camaraderie. I cared about them, and we all became friends.

I developed a special friendship with Art Smith. Art is black, but the basis of our bond wasn't color. Art took over from me as field consultant for the inner-city, South Side store owners, including the BMOA members. One of his responsibilities was to run the BMOA training program, which was my pride and joy. Art did it brilliantly. A Chicago native, he was skilled at operations and organizing. He was also street-wise; he understood the hardcore inner-city communities and the particular difficulties facing the black people who worked for McDonald's. Under Art's leadership, the training program expanded far beyond my expectations; it was so successful that BMOA decided to hire a permanent program director and training center manager.

Art also worked with me to extend the BMOA operational blitzes to South Bend and Gary, to include white-owned stores in the blitzes, and to involve all the field consultants. The McDonald's restaurants in Gary and South Bend were in excellent shape—all rated A or B—and the owners and managers in both markets welcomed the chance to show off their stores. We would reserve the Big Mac bus—Ray Kroc had personally purchased a fleet of coaches, one bus per region, and a private, luxury jet plane for company business use—and head off for a full day of store visits and discussions with the owners.

In time, we expanded these road trips to cities outside my territory. I particularly remember a three-day trip to visit the urban stores in Detroit—a city with a long history of racial violence and one of the highest crime rates in the country. Detroit had a strong core group of black owners. All their stores were new, so the Detroit owners hadn't faced the cleanup, repair, and replacement issues that still dogged our black operators in Chicago, Los Angeles, Philadelphia, and other urban centers. Don Forney was the first black owner in Detroit. In 1969 the company had wisely licensed him a store in a fringe area, a good location near an expressway where he didn't encounter the kinds of problems—high crime, substandard facilities, untrained managers and employees inherited from previous owners, poor community relations, and so on—that made it so difficult for most black operators in the hardcore inner city to get on their feet.

On the blitz, I was accompanied by my field consultants and the Chicago BMOA members. We arrived in Detroit late in the afternoon and then had dinner with the Detroit BMOA guys, during which they informed us about the local market and their individual stores. After dinner, we checked into our hotel, and I told everybody to unpack and take an hour to relax. One of my white field consultants—a sharp, aggressive young man—was confused. He asked me why we weren't going straight to see the stores. He was surprised when I told him that we were, but not until later; we would be out well past eleven o'clock that night. I told him to enjoy his free time, because it was the last he would get until we returned to Chicago.

Over the course of the blitz, we visited stores day and night, from early morning, before the stores opened, until late at night, after closing. We met customers and observed their reactions to the service. The diversity of the urban restaurants we saw and our discussions with the black Detroit operators were especially eye-opening for the white field consultants, who were mostly responsible for white-operated stores in predominately white suburban and fringe areas back in Chicago and Indiana. They were impressed, and I think they understood why it was so important for everyone in operations to experience a wide variety of stores and see how McDonald's QSC standards apply in diverse environments and circumstances. I know that the conversation was very lively on our bus ride back to Chicago. I continue to believe that customer-level experiences, like that Detroit urban blitz, develop the instinct for quality that is essential not just in the fast-food industry but for any service business. Even when you're sitting on the top of the corporate ladder, you have to keep your feet planted on the ground, where your customers live. That was Ray Kroc's philosophy, and it had become mine.

Aside from my frustrations with Neil's general incompetence, I got along well enough with my new boss at first. I think my anger about his promotion was dissipated by my enjoyment of the work I was doing with the field consultants. Besides, I'm like my dad in that I can't stay angry for long and I *refuse* to accept or play the role of victim; a person can't be victimized without his permission. Things started to change, however, after a couple of months, and I began to get stronger signals that Neil was deliberately trying to undermine me and my position in the company. The first major incident might have been accidental, but it put me on my guard.

It happened at an annual business retreat that the Midwest regional office staged for all urban and suburban owners in the

Chicago ADI (area of dominant influence, an advertising term for the area beyond the city reached by local commercial television broadcasting—no cable TV back then). Retreats were usually held in January or February, the coldest part of the Chicago winter, when everybody was eager to spend a few days in a warm climate. The business of a retreat generally focused on reviewing the previous year, discussing plans for the upcoming year, and promoting unity among owners, field consultants, and the regional department managers. In my experience, these retreats had always been productive, both in getting things done and in fostering a sense of comradeship.

The 1974 Midwest retreat was held at the La Costa resort in San Diego, California. It was customary for the field service managers to be included on the speakers docket, and I was looking forward to addressing all the owners in the Chicago-area market. Through the BMOA training program, I now knew the benefits that accrued when owners cooperate and collaborate to achieve common goals, and I had an idea of adapting the basic BMOA model to form mini-co-ops throughout Chicago. I'd talked with several white owners about the concept, and the feedback had been positive. So I planned my retreat speech around the future of the market and what the operators could expect from each other and should expect from field services. During my talk, I would introduce the mini-co-op concept and get reactions.

I was having a good time at La Costa, especially on the golf course. I loved golf, but I hadn't played for several months. It felt really good to be outside in the California sun, and I played one of my most memorable rounds. I was also anticipating my speech—right up to the moment I was supposed to be introduced and to step up on the podium. But before my name was called, the session was adjourned, and everyone went on to lunch and their tee times. Trying to figure out what happened, I glanced over the short program handed out at the

236

session. My name wasn't there. Yet I knew that I had been listed on the preliminary and final agendas. My name had been on the agenda when I boarded the plane in Chicago.

Bernie Hall, who had still been regional manager when the La Costa retreat was planned (though Neil completed the arrangements after Bernie left), came up to me and asked why I hadn't spoken. He'd expected me to talk and was disappointed that I hadn't. I told him that I was prepared and that I had no idea why I wasn't included on the program.

I was sure somebody had simply made a mistake. When I mentioned it to Neil after we returned to Chicago, he was appropriately apologetic and characteristically noncommittal. He did say it would not happen again, and I let it go.

On the surface, things seemed all right after La Costa. Maybe that's because there was little more to Neil than surface appearances—and raw ambition. I continued to try to find ways to work with him, but no matter what my approach, I never knew what he was up to or when to believe him. We didn't have open conflicts, because Neil couldn't handle confrontation of any sort. The guy always talked in circles, and conversations with him always ended right where they began, with not much in-between. Like many office politicians, he took a lot of words to say nothing. People who worked with him will know exactly what I mean; my problems communicating with Neil were shared by everyone in the department. Nobody could get a straight word out of him.

Then a second incident occurred that was unquestionably deliberate. McDonald's gave annual awards for Outstanding Performance at the regional and corporate levels. The highest recognition was a President's Award. People were nominated by their department heads. For 1974, I submitted the name of one of my field consultants, Rigo Llamas, to Neil. I recommended Rigo for the regional Outstanding Performance award and requested that he be considered for the President's Award in recognition of the really outstanding quality of his work; he was doing everything well, and I don't think I ever knew a better field consultant. I wrote a memo to Neil, detailing Rigo's accomplishments. In the memo, I *very specifically* requested to be notified *in advance* if Rigo wasn't included among the final nominees for the President's Award because, in that event, I wanted the opportunity to make my case for him in person. I didn't hear back from Neil, so I figured Rigo had been nominated.

I should have known better. When the list of regional outstanding performers was posted on the office bulletin board, Rigo's name wasn't on it. I went to Neil and asked him why I hadn't been contacted before the outstanding performers were chosen, as I had clearly requested in my memo. Once again, Neil gave me his usual rigmarole. I have no memory of what he actually said, just that I didn't get a real response. It was a useless exercise. Neil had cut me out, and it was too late to change things. I can't prove Neil's motives, but I am certain he ignored my strong recommendation because he didn't see anything in it for himself. There may have been an element of racism too. Neil wasn't the type to risk offending senior management by nominating a Hispanic employee for their highest recognition. That was when I realized that Neil was an 'equal opportunity' bigot; he discriminated against everyone who wasn't his color or a member of the 'right' group, whom he perceived as acceptable to the power structure.

While researching this book, I learned for the first time of another situation that happened when I wasn't around. A white owner, who was well-known to us as a racist, complained to Neil about his "damn nigger" consultant, Art Smith. Neil didn't bother to talk to Art or find out if there was any validity to the white owner's claim. He simply decided to get rid of Art to satisfy the white owner. So Neil talked to John Perry, who was then president of BMOA, hoping John would buy into his plan. Instead, John told him in no uncertain terms that Art was doing a great job and that the BMOA members would raise a real stink if he tried to remove Art. I guess Neil weighed the odds—one white owner against all the black owners—because nothing happened to Art. But the incident was typical of Neil's worst flaws: racism, politics, and incompetence. The racism is obvious, and a really competent office politician would never have talked with John Perry, or any black owner, before firing a respected black field consultant.

"EVERYTHING HAS A SHELF LIFE"

After Neil ignored me about the award nomination, I became convinced that leaving me off the program at La Costa was not just a forgivable mishap. The two incidents were too much alike. In baseball, it's three strikes and you're out. In my book, Neil now had two big strikes against him.

His third strike could have come straight from Yogi Berra's playbook. It was "*déjà vu* all over again." I had been busy working with my consultants and getting through the June 1974 BMOA convention—the one when Johnny Williams came up from Texas and unintentionally turned us into a national organization. Meanwhile, preliminary plans were being draw up for the next Chicago business retreat, set for February 1975. Nobody could complain about the choice of location—Acapulco, Mexico.

I can't remember when I first saw it, but the agenda for the meeting was circulated sometime in the late fall, and all the department heads, including the other field service manager, were on it—everybody except me. Unlike the previous year, I had the chance to correct the oversight, if it was an oversight, so I went to Neil. Again, he claimed it was an error and said it would be corrected. When the final agenda came out, shortly before the retreat, my name was there. The problem was that Neil had also assigned the topic for my presentation, and I wasn't going to do it. After La Costa, I had put the Chicago market mini-co-op concept on the back burner; I knew that Neil would block such a plan, so it seemed wiser to hold off for the time being and wait for a better opportunity. (Wrongly as it turned out, I thought Neil couldn't last as regional manager for too much longer.) But once again, I planned to talk about the future of our market and the role of field services. Neil, however, had me down for a presentation he had titled "BMOA and What It's All About." Usually, I couldn't talk enough about BMOA, but in the context of the retreat, where the audience was *all* Chicago-area owner-operators, a speech specifically about BMOA was too narrow and not that meaningful to most of the operators. Whatever I said, it would be difficult to get the white attendees to pay attention. It was plain that Neil wanted to sideline me by making my speech irrelevant.

I confronted Neil. It wasn't an angry meeting, but I was firm. I had no intention of letting Neil off the hook this time. I wasn't going to negotiate. I told him that unless I could speak on the subject I had prepared, I wouldn't go to Acapulco.

People unfamiliar with McDonald's may wonder why a speech at a regional retreat was worth such a fuss. There were several reasons. One was that addressing the operators was a traditional privilege of department heads, and as one of two field service managers in the region, I was a department head. To leave me off once might have been a mistake; twice was a deliberate act, and it displayed both professional jealousy and racism. It was disrespectful of me and also of my position in the company. But the more important reason was that the retreat was the one opportunity a field service manager had to communicate directly with all the operators at one time. I knew the McDonald's owners in my territory, and I knew most of the owners in the other half of the region. But the speech was my chance to introduce myself, in a leadership role, to everybody and to show them that a black field service manager was not limited to the issues of black operators. A field service manager had a great deal of influence on what happened at the customer level and at the cash register; he and his consultants were the key people linking the company and its resources to the store owners. If I had made the presentation that Neil wanted, sticking strictly to BMOA, I realized that I would come off as championing the black owners at the expense of the others. Such a speech, to that audience, was very likely to confirm misconceptions that blacks in the company were exclusive, sticking together for their own self-interest. I would have been undercutting the core goal of achieving real diversity and racial integration throughout McDonald's. It may even have been viewed as racism in reverse.

I could have tricked Neil by accepting his topic and then giving the speech I originally planned. But deception and equivocation were his methods, not mine. In addition, Neil could easily have made such an act seem like a rebellion against the company itself—a good example of what happens when a black man gets "out of place." I wasn't about to give him that opportunity. After La Costa and the Rigo Llamas incident, I was ready to make my stand and make it openly.

Neil didn't believe my promise not to attend the retreat. As the date approached, he made repeated comments about looking forward to my talk and the good times we would have in Acapulo. Every time he said something, I told him that I was not going if I couldn't make the speech I had prepared. It was as if we were doing some kind of weird dance; I was taking the lead, but he was doing his own steps. Right up to the day before the departure for Mexico, when Neil said, "I'll see you at the airport tomorrow morning," he maintained the fantasy.

I didn't go to Acapulco, and when Neil came back to Chicago, he found my resignation on his desk. It wasn't an empty threat; I was ready to leave. I felt that I had hit a stone wall, and there was nothing I could do to bring it down. I had tried everything to get along with Neil and establish a positive working relationship. I had used all the recommended human resources approaches. Nothing worked.

I didn't want to be his friend, but I had often worked successfully with people I didn't admire personally. That's commonplace in business. Sooner or later, nearly everybody has to deal with a difficult boss. I believe that the way to handle the situation is to find *a common goal* that is greater than the areas of dissension. It takes persistence and creative thinking. It begins with a question, "What does this manipulative (or bumbling or ignorant) so-and-so want that I also want?" In every other difficult-boss experience in my life, that question has been pivotal. The answer might be anything— getting the workplace better organized, improving customer relations, lowering the rate of employee turnover, increasing sales and profits. But once I had the common goal identified, I could adjust my own thinking and begin to work with the boss or manager or supervisor to make the goal happen. We would have something to talk about, and when the boss realized that I wanted to achieve a goal that would benefit him, we could communicate and interact—at least on that one subject. In the best of all worlds, finding a common purpose would lead to improvements in other areas of the working relationship. At minimum, having a common goal tended to reduce conflict, lower the stress level, and make it easier to show up for work every day.

The problem with Neil was that we had nothing in common. Not one thing. He didn't care about the company. He didn't care about his employees, beyond keeping them quiet and acquiescent. He didn't care about the owner-operators. He didn't get any pleasure or satisfaction from work itself. The only conceivable goal we might have shared was *his* advancement, but I didn't want to see him move up because it would mean inflicting his brand of mismanagement on even more people. I wasn't about to violate my basic principles or abandon my loyalty to the betterment of the company for the likes of a man like Neil.

I also knew that if I stayed, he would continue to play his games and undermine my effectiveness. After Acapulco, there would be more 'mistakes' and more deceptions. He wouldn't fire me, I was sure, but he could impede my work to the point where I would eventually have to quit. I had once attended a McDonald's-sponsored seminar titled "Adventure in Attitude." In a discussion of dealing with problematic people, we had been told that there are three basic options: 1) change yourself, 2) change the other person, or 3) change the situation. I couldn't change Neil; I'd made adjustments, but I wouldn't make the kind of moral and ethical changes that might make it easier to get along with him. So I had to change the situation. I had been thinking about becoming an owner-operator at some point, and it seemed to me that the time might be right.

Neil didn't question my resignation, although he started a rumor that I was leaving to go to Burger King, which was regarded as high treason in the McDonald's culture. He took my letter to Bernie

Hall, who had become zone manager in the restructuring. (When the original regions were broken into geographically smaller regions, under regional managers, the country was also divided into zones that each included five of the new regions. The position of zone manager was added—a level above the regional managers in each zone.) Bernie, good guy that he was, didn't want me to go, so he took the matter higher, to corporate. The first thing that happened was that Bernie met with Neil and me, and Bernie asked me to reconsider. Neil didn't say too much, most likely because he didn't know yet which way the wind was blowing in the Ivory Tower. After I refused to withdraw my letter, Neil may have figured it was all over. Then right after lunch that same day, I got a call from the Ivory Tower. It was John Cooke, senior vice president for people and organization, and he set up a meeting with me. We spent several hours discussing the reasons for my resignation, and John finally concluded that the situation was beyond repair. But he scheduled another meeting the next day, and he had another offer for me.

For several months before my resigning, I had been one of a three-man team assisting an owner who was taking over a number of McDonald's restaurants in Puerto Rico. The restaurants had been owned by John Gibson, who was Oscar Goldstein's partner in Gee Gee Distributing, my first employer in Washington. In fact, Gee Gee had been the very first McDonald's overseas franchisee, back in 1965, when the company licensed Gibson and Goldstein to develop the Caribbean market. That deal had not gone well, but John Gibson retained some of the stores and was now selling. The incoming owner still needed help—particularly with understanding the market, developing his business strategy, and training his director of operations. John Cooke told me that it would take about two months. Then he asked if I would go. I finally said "yes," on the condition that

I could return to Chicago whenever I needed to.

John Cooke is an incredibly perceptive and persuasive man, with all the virtues of a great diplomat. He had experience as a management negotiator with labor unions and had become a management consultant. Back in 1964, June Martino hired him as a consultant to organize McDonald's salary and compensation program, and, more important, to try to calm the contentious relationship between Ray Kroc and Harry Sonneborn. John was not successful at the latter task, but no one could have been. In 1967, when Mr. Kroc briefly took over as president, between Sonneborn's resignation and Fred Turner's appointment, Mr. Kroc brought John in full-time as his assistant and "go to" guy. John soon became a vice president, then senior vice president. His main area was labor relations, but he was also working with Ed Schmitt on problems with the franchisees, and in 1975, Ed appointed him as the company's first ombudsman. (They selected the Scandinavian term "ombudsman," which hadn't been used in American business before, because it was unknown and didn't have negative connotations.) Over the years, John's reputation for absolute fairness in settling disputes between franchisees or employees and the company was never questioned. People may have been disappointed by some of his decisions, but nobody doubted his integrity.

In my case, John had sound business reasons for making the Puerto Rico offer. I was already familiar with the multi-store franchise there and had a good relationship with the new owner. My experience in Chicago and knowledge of operations in poor, racially mixed locations would be valuable in gauging the Puerto Rican market. John also saw this assignment as a kind of cooling-off period, when I could think through my decision to leave the company and the company could find opportunities to re-position me in a more advantageous

245

regional or corporate job. (I learned later that there were several highly placed executives in the corporation who were keen to keep me in the corporate management structure.)

I wasn't thinking about what might be going on behind the scenes. I went to Puerto Rico convinced that this would be my last "inside" assignment for the company. It was a good experience, and before the two months were over, the franchisee made me a very generous offer to stay on and work for him. I didn't want to move permanently to the Caribbean, but his offer raised my confidence level; whatever came of my desire to become a McDonald's owner, I would have other good options after I left regional.

I had traveled back and forth between Puerto Rico and Chicago several times, and each time I was in Chi-town, I met with John Cooke and reported on the island stores. On my last trip home, John told me that Ed Schmitt wanted to see me. It had been some time since I'd been able to sit down with Ed and just talk, so I was eager for the meeting. We met in his office on the eighth floor of the Ivory Tower, and even though he had recently been elevated to executive vice president and chief operating officer of the corporation, our conversation began as easily and amiably as it always had. I briefly told him about the progress in Puerto Rico, and we discussed some general issues related to my resignation. Then Ed surprised me. He said, "I would like for you to stay," and he proceeded to lay out an amazing proposal. He wanted me to come into corporate for two years as director of Urban Operations, an entirely new corporate department. My primary responsibility would be to organize and lead an initiative to help others do what I had done in the Midwest. I would be accountable to him and only him. My first year would be devoted to setting up the department, establishing key regional relationships, and developing and implementing our plan. Ed went on to say that the

second year would be spent solidifying the program and also recruiting and training my replacement.

This last part of the assignment showed me once again how astute Ed was about people. He understood better than anyone that I was serious about leaving the corporate environment and didn't make any effort to change my mind. He was asking me to delay my departure, so the company could benefit broadly from the expertise in urban operations I had gained in Chicago. He thought two years was adequate to get the department up and running, and he wanted me to pick a successor who was highly qualified and fully prepared to take over when I left.

During the more than six years I had been in Chicago, the company had truly committed itself to urbanizing and diversifying. Cities were now essential to the company's continued growth, and winning over black and ethnic urban consumers was critical to the company's success in the cities. I had played my role in that shift, and I knew that I could turn down the job, walk out of Ed's office, and leave McDonald's with a genuine sense of satisfaction in what I'd accomplished.

Looking back, I have to say that I'm grateful, in a strange way, to my nemesis, Neil. He was the one person in my career from whom I thought I'd learned nothing positive. Yet because of our difficult working relationship, I did learn a valuable lesson in business and in life. Put simply, it's that *everything has a shelf life*. I'd never been a quitter, but through my experience working for Neil, I had become a wiser man. I realized that there's a big difference between quitting and knowing when to bring something to its logical conclusion. During my brief stay in Puerto Rico and through my talks with John and others, I came to understand that I had reached the point at which I was ready to move on. As that line in a popular Kenny Rogers song goes, "You've got to know when to hold 'em and know when to fold 'em."

When I wrote my letter of resignation and put it on Neil's desk, I knew that his behavior was really just the shove I needed to bring a chapter in my life to its end. My conflicts with Neil had made me realize that there is value in conflict, and I remembered an old saying, "You can't light a fire without a spark." The friction between Neil and me had sparked changes in my thinking, and I understood that those changes were good. I wasn't breaking up with McDonald's; I was making a breakthrough, and on the other side, there would be new opportunities.

And now Ed Schmitt, the man I most admired in all of McDonald's, was offering me the chance to complete the work I had begun on that cold, January day in 1969 when I'd started my job as a regional consultant. He was handing me the opportunity to take the Chicago model to every corner of the country, educating every regional and field service manager in the hard realities of minority ownership and the successful strategies of collaboration and cooperation that we had proven through BMOA. He was asking me to create a new model of diversity for McDonald's as a whole, and he was promising me his wholehearted support throughout the process. He wasn't offering me a rose garden—just two years of hard, focused work. In essence, he was challenging me to begin a new chapter for myself and the company. If I turned down his challenge, I knew that I would always have regrets. So I accepted.

Chapter 10

Taking It Nationwide

To perceive a path and to point it out is one thing, but to blaze the trail and labour to construct the path is a harder task.

WINSTON CHURCHILL, BRITISH PRIME MINISTER

The new Urban Operations department was located on the seventh floor of McDonald's Plaza in Oak Brook—one floor below the Ivory Tower offices of Ray Kroc, Fred Turner, Ed Schmitt, and other top management. The department was easy to set up, primarily because it consisted of me and a secretary whose time I shared with several other executives. Sharing secretarial services was a tradition at McDonald's corporate offices, dating back to the company's beginning, when June Martino was secretary to Mr. Kroc and the first men he hired. I want to note here that the secretaries at McDonald's were a skilled and talented group, who handled complex multi-tasking long before anyone thought of that term.

Ed sent out a company-wide memo that introduced the department and me. The memo set out the main objectives of Urban Operations and established my credentials with the people I would be working with: the African American and other minority owners and the executives and staff inside the corporation and in all the regional

249

offices. (Though most of the minority operators were black, McDonald's also had a small but growing number of Hispanic American operators and at least one Asian American operator in urban locations.) People paid attention to communications from the senior executive vice president, and Ed's memo was a vital first step in smoothing the way for our new venture. Once his memo was circulated, I immediately started contacting regional managers and arranging to meet with them to discuss issues in their regions. I also began organizing road trips for Ed and me. We were going into the field to talk with black and minority owners about their situations and their concerns and to *listen* to what they needed and expected from the company. My visiting with owners was not unusual; my personal standard operating procedure was always to communicate closely and frequently with my "customers," who now comprised all minority operators in the United States, as well as their regional managers, field service managers, and field consultants. But for the senior executive vice president (Ed was also vice chairman of the Board) to travel out into the field to hear what was on the owners' minds—that got everyone's attention.

There's a larger context to the startup of Urban Operations. At the time we opened the department in the early spring of 1975, McDonald's was becoming embroiled in its most difficult internal crisis to date. As a consequence of the rapid and massive growth of the company, serious problems had emerged at the operator level, leading to the formation of an aggressive protest movement, formally named the McDonald's Operators Association (MOA) in mid-1975. (Despite the similarity in name, MOA had no connection with BMOA, the Black McDonald's Operators Association.) The franchisees who started MOA were experienced multi-store owners, like Max Cooper, who owned twenty-two stores in Birmingham,

Alabama. Prior to becoming an owner, Max Cooper had been the partner of Al Golin—the crackerjack public relations man who had been instrumental in making McDonald's a household name in the 1960s. MOA's first president, Don Conley, had been the corporate vice president of franchising before he purchased several McDonald's stores in Chicago. Men like these had long association with the company, and most came into the system early, became wealthy, and continued to benefit from the McDonald's new growth.

Despite their success, however, they were very worried that the company's growth was adversely affecting their chances for further store expansion in their markets. A number of them had long enjoyed virtual monopolies until the corporation began licensing new owners in their local markets, but with McDonald's restaurants seeming to pop up on every other corner, the old-line owners feared that the competition would damage their sales and profitability. They believed that as established owners, they should have first dibs on expansion stores and also have input into decisions about where to locate new stores in their markets. MOA members were concerned as well about McDonald's re-licensing policy. The company licensed its franchises for twenty years, and while it was difficult to rescind a license except for gross and persistent violations of company standards or malfeasance, there was no guarantee that a license would be renewed at the end of the twenty-year period. Owners who'd come into the company in the 1950s and early 60s were now into their second decade, and uncertainty about renewal was very real to those who weren't ready for a comfortable retirement. Many of their stores were old, and some were substandard; a lot of them were the original red-and-white tiled, walk-up operations—not the modern structures with inside seating, drive-thru windows, and the latest innovation, Ronald McDonald playgrounds. McDonald's strict re-investment guidelines—that owners fund improvements from the cash generated by their stores—was another source of contention. MOA members resented that they had to foot the entire bill for all upgrades and replacements.

Underlying these specific concerns was a deeper issue—the distance between operators and the corporation that was a natural but unsettling consequence of rapid growth. The older owners, who were used to being able to pick up a phone and call Ray Kroc or Fred Turner when they had a problem, now had to deal with lower levels of management and regional decision making. To owners who considered themselves senior members of the McDonald's family, the family had become unwieldy and less personal. The company's immediate need for more regional managers and field consultants meant that the people closest to the owners were sometimes too inexperienced to be effective in making the multitude of decisions that affected a franchisee's business. Owners' complaints frequently involved poorly trained and unresponsive regional people who often enlarged problems, didn't understand the markets, and rarely consulted with the owners except when they conducted performance reviews. I had occasionally seen the problem for myself in areas outside my own territory. I understood that field service managers and consultants who were not prepared to do their jobs effectively could feel very insecure and doubtful of their competence. These feelings too easily came across to operators as arrogance and indifference.

Fred Turner wasn't inclined to take MOA's complaints seriously, and he derisively referred to the dissenting owners as the "*Millionaire* Owners Association." Fred and some other executives saw the group as rich troublemakers who were using protest to coerce the company into buying their stores at higher than market value. Although Fred okayed the formation of the National Operators

Advisory Board—initially Operators Advisory Panel—as a counter-measure to MOA, it was a weak effort on his part. The panel members were all owners appointed by the company, so they were perceived by other owners as powerless puppets.

However, Ray Kroc and Ed Schmitt both realized that, while a number of the MOA members had self-serving motives, there were some hard truths in their complaints. Although MOA had only about two dozen active members, mostly in the Southeast, the group had many sympathizers throughout the system. McDonald's had weathered other crises, but Ed knew that the MOA-led revolt had the potential to cause an irreparable split within the company. He understood that in order to avert a genuine catastrophe, it was not enough just to address specific complaints. The company had to revive its relationship with its owner-operators. Fairness dictated change. In his autobiography, *Grinding It Out*, Mr. Kroc wrote, "I've always dealt fairly in business, even when I believed someone was trying to take advantage of me." Some of the MOA members were clearly motivated by greed, but not all. The challenge was how to deal fairly with owners who believed that the company was betraying them.

The black and minority owned urban stores that were my chief concern did not play into the MOA dispute, but it was clear that in starting a department of Urban Operations, Ed was committed to forging stronger bonds between *all* owners and the corporation by returning to Mr. Kroc's fundamental principle that the owner-operators were the heart and soul of the company. When Ed visited with owners and real changes subsequently resulted, it was proof to the minority owners—and to other owners as well—that the company was not scamming them.

Ed wanted to meet with the minority owners in all the regions as quickly as possible. I scheduled the meetings to take place in neutral settings in the most central city in each region, which was sometimes the regional headquarters city but not always, depending on where the minority operators were located. We made two to three visits per month until Ed had met with every minority urban owner-operator in every region. I informed the regional managers fully of what we planned. Sometimes we'd get together for dinner with the regional manager prior to seeing the owners, but other than Ed and me, no other company representatives were included in the owner meetings. All of our visits were overnighters, and these helped me get a better feel for the regions I wasn't already familiar with. Whenever we had time, we tried to visit some stores in the different regions—the better to understand the owners' situations.

The majority of outlying owners paid their own travel and accommodations costs, if they had any, but there were some special cases when owners simply did not have the extra funds for the trip, so McDonald's paid their way. Since McDonald's had a long history of expecting operators to pay their own travel expenses to conventions, regional retreats, etc., this novel instance of corporate generosity was further proof to the owners that the meetings with Ed were in earnest.

Al Joyner was then struggling to keep his recently purchased store in Mobile, Alabama, afloat. The Mobile store was known as the second poorest performer in the McDonald's system and was in such bad condition under the previous white owner that no one wanted it. The restaurant had been taken over by the company before Al agreed to take it on. While trying to turn around a failing store, he was also coping with being newly divorced and the single, custodial parent of a toddler. Al let me know that he just couldn't afford a trip to Houston, where we were holding the meeting with the minority owners in the Dallas region. Al really wanted to be there, and Ed and I were anxious for him to attend, but in addition to the cost of airfare and hotel, he was hard pressed to find someone to care for his young son in his absence. Although I hadn't met Al in person yet, I knew that he was pretty much on his own—the first black owner in the Deep South—and getting little help from his regional management and field service staff. It was really important that he come to Houston and share his experiences with Ed, so I arranged for McDonald's to cover his travel costs. To this day, Al appreciates that the company made it possible for him *and* his little boy to make the trip.

In region after region, owners went out of their way to attend the meetings. Ed is a terrific listener, and he quickly put the owners at ease. They realized that we weren't there to criticize or tell them what to do, but to hear their issues and learn what they needed from the company. We were on a fact-finding mission, and Ed didn't hand down pat answers from on high or make empty promises. He might guide the conversation, but it was remarkable how he could draw people out just by listening and focusing on what was being said. He wasn't what you'd call a quiet man, but Ed Schmitt knew when to be quiet and pay attention.

The owners' problems varied from region to region and market to market. Al Joyner, for example, was dealing with old-style Southern racism in Mobile, but black owners in Los Angeles were coping with more recent hostilities between the races, resentments that had surfaced during a series of urban riots, beginning with the 1966 uprising in Watts. Hispanic owners in California markets faced different challenges from those in Harlem or Miami. However, there were also difficulties that many minority owners had in common—most notably, the financial burdens on owners of older stores in hardcore urban centers. As I already knew, a lot of these operators were working day and night to rehabilitate their stores and establish credibility in their communities while trying to make a living and eke out sufficient cash flow for re-investment. Just at the time when they most needed help from the company, the company seemed preoccupied with its program of growth. The question of market expansion, which triggered the MOA rebellion, was also becoming an issue for the veteran black owners, particularly those whose stores were doing well and who were looking to purchase more restaurants but felt locked out of suburban locations. Compounding such problems were those inexperienced regional consultants and managers I mentioned—company representatives who had little understanding of the unique difficulties minority owners were dealing with and, because of ignorance, seemed more of a hindrance than a help.

The meetings were invaluable. The information we got enabled me to develop plans and find solutions that would really work. I recognized that what we had done in Chicago—the owners' cooperative, the shared training and the training center, the store blitzes—couldn't be imposed wholesale in other cities. Individual situations varied too much for a one-size-fits-all approach. What good was a Chicago-style self-help group of minority owners or blitz visitations to Al Joyner, who was all by himself down in Alabama? How could owners in Brooklyn, New York, or Oakland, California, set up a comprehensive training center without easy access to the corporate department heads and Hamburger University professors who contributed so much to BMOA's training program in Chicago? It simply wasn't feasible to start a joint training program unless stores were clustered close together.

What I had to do was *concentrate on the fundamental principles* that were the foundation of the Chicago model: collaboration for mutual benefit, teamwork rather than competition, free flowing and open communication among owners and managers, improved communication with regional and corporate management. *The concept of collaborative self-help could be applied broadly*, even though the specifics would vary from place to place. I also knew we already had the mechanism to spread the concept to every minority owner in the McDonald's system—the Black McDonald's Operators Association. The regional meetings with Ed weren't intended to promote BMOA, and Ed himself didn't recommend BMOA membership to anyone. But this wasn't because he didn't support the organization. (I, of course, had it in the back of my mind to promote BMOA membership, and Ed was fine with my doing so, as long as it didn't compromise his purpose in meeting with owners.)

Ed was a long-range thinker, and many people who know what he achieved for the company regard him as McDonald's first genuine *strategic* thinker. Ray Kroc was a business visionary but not, as he himself understood, always adept at planning how to achieve the vision. Fred Turner was a brilliant organizer and aggressive about growing the company, but his genius was for process; his concept of operations was conservative, and he mistrusted innovation. For example, Fred fought for years against the inclusion of drive-thru windows in the restaurants. Even when it was demonstrated how dramatically drive-thru service increased sales, he balked, contending that drive-thru windows were for "crackerbox" operations, not McDonald's. As a consequence, when McDonald's at last adopted the drive-thru, everybody had to hustle to catch up with the competition.

It always seemed to me that Ed Schmitt combined the best of both men—Mr. Kroc's ability to visualize the future and Fred's attention to method. Ed possesses a powerful intellect, an open and curious mind, and an understanding of people that made him more skilled at delegating authority than either Mr. Kroc or Fred. He understood clearly where the company was in the present; he could envision where it needed to go in the future; and most important, he understood that getting from 'what is' to 'what can be' required strategy. He gathered information and studied the marketplace before he arrived at a long-range plan; then he left the specific tactics to the tacticians.

It was not his way to make recommendations about what people should do. He trusted people to handle their responsibilities within the strategic framework, though he always made himself available to guide when guidance was needed. I'm sure he also understood that 'recommendations' and 'suggestions' from someone in his senior position often came across as 'orders' to people on lower rungs of the corporate ladder. Ed wanted the people who worked for him to have plenty of room for creativity and innovation; in my experience, he was always ready to listen to new ideas, and his style brought out the unedited best in people.

During our regional tour, Ed never brought up BMOA—though when asked about the group, his brief answers clearly implied approval. Yet the visits had the effect of legitimizing the organization. With Fred at the helm (Mr. Kroc was very active as chairman and *numero uno*, but he was no longer much involved in day-to-day operational decision making) and making his feelings about the MOA revolt clear, some operators were still fearful of anything Fred might perceive as a disloyal "splinter group." Ed Schmitt, however, was just one step away from the top of the ladder. By leaving the Ivory Tower to meet with minority owners in their home regions, Ed was sending the message that minority concerns mattered to him and the company. As we went out into the field, word got around about the open nature of the meetings, Ed's sincere commitment to diversity, his concern about the minority owners' issues, and our commitment in Urban

Operations to support and facilitate self-help initiatives by the owners. Without promoting any one solution, Ed's visits were like a stamp of approval for BMOA. Black and other minority owners who may have been hesitant about joining BMOA for fear of offending the corporation now felt free to participate. It was a kind of *empowerment*—not a word I use lightly—for all the minority owners and for BMOA.

Many of the minority owners we met with already knew at least something about the Black McDonald's Operators Association. When they asked me about the organization—its goals, its structure, how they could take part—I made sure they were well informed. Pretty soon, operators were calling me and asking how they could start BMOA chapters or attend the next convention or do both. By the time of the 1975 convention, held in July in Kansas City, Ed and I had covered every region except those on the West Coast. BMOA chapters were being formed in a number of cities, and the list of convention attendees included owners from most of the regions.

Before I move on to the impact of all this on BMOA, I want to recall another corporate executive who deserves a tremendous amount of credit for the success of black and minority ownership— Gerry Newman, who was a senior executive vice president and the company's chief accountant. He was already involved in the MOA problem; he had studied the numbers and determined that the rebellious white owners in MOA had a legitimate, though exaggerated, issue in their concern about new McDonald's franchises putting competitive pressure on their older, established stores. Gerry was doing something very similar to Ed's and my field trips; he was traveling to all the regions and meeting privately with every owner, not just MOA members, who had problems. And he was coming up with answers.

Rents and service fees paid to the company, plus local and national advertising fees, came off the top of gross sales, not profits, but when a store was running on very narrow margins or losing money, the cost of leasing often eliminated cash flow that might be re-invested in upgrades and improvements. Many owners felt themselves trapped in a Catch-22; they didn't have adequate cash for re-investment in improvements that would increase sales, and they couldn't increase sales without cash to put into improvements. Gerry extended McDonald's rent relief program, used very cautiously since the 1960s to help seriously troubled stores, and in 1975, McDonald's gave more than $5 million in rent relief to around three hundred operators. He was also developing a generous loan plan for owners to finance capital improvements, such as the addition of drive-thru windows and playgrounds, to their stores.

I was already working with Gerry on the financial problems of the minority owners while Ed and I were still on our road trips. Sometimes, I would call him from a meeting site and inform him about an owner's difficulties, and he would get straight to work on the situation. During my time in Urban Operations, Gerry and I made a number of trips into the field to talk one-on-one with owners. Like Ed, Gerry understood that the financial troubles of urban stores required creative solutions. A few years earlier, Gerry and his department had worked with owners and their lenders on re-financing the "salt and pepper" stores, especially those in Los Angeles. So he was well aware that many of the African American owners were weighed down by debts inherited from previous owners; the minority owners needed McDonald's clout to get access to white lending institutions in order to re-finance poorly structured initial loan agreements. Gerry also understood that circumstances differed from store to store and owner to owner; he studied each case individually and based his decisions on actual needs.

260

Gerry Newman was nothing like the stereotypical number-crunching accountant. He was smart and inventive, he was outgoing and likeable, and he cared about people. If Gerry had a fault, it was his determination to find solutions for every owner, and he would sometimes labor too long over situations that were beyond help. He hated to write off anybody, though this could compound the financial problems facing the next owner after a failure. I think his optimism was also his gift because it made him flexible. The general corporate mindset failed to recognize the obvious fact that it cost more to operate in some areas than in others. The company didn't see the difference between purchasing a new store in a prime suburban location and purchasing a dilapidated, over-priced older store in a hardcore urban neighborhood where consumers, often with good reason, mistrusted McDonald's. Gerry understood these realities, and while he had to function within the company's parameters, he would always bend and flex those limits as far as he could to save an owner. Rent relief, re-financing, and capital improvement loans became important means of enabling black and other minority owners to rehabilitate older stores and push their profit-and-loss statements out of the red.

At this time, the company had a new reason to strengthen its urban markets. Gasoline prices had soared during the oil boycott in late 1973 and early 1974, when the Arab states banned the export of their oil to the United States. The ban was lifted after six stressful months of shortages, rationing, and rising costs, but the price of gas continued to go up at the pump, and the threat of more boycotts seemed imminent. Wall Street and other investors worried that another interruption in the oil flow would negatively affect Americans' driving habits and reduce the frequency of their visits to fast-food restaurants. Being the biggest franchiser in the industry,

McDonald's would suffer the most. To placate jittery stockholders, Fred Turner said publicly that the company was preparing for such a contingency by strengthening its presence in "walking" neighborhoods. That meant increasing and fortifying its city stores, a business imperative that probably gave Gerry Newman more room for his creative financing of minority-owned urban restaurants.

For a variety of reasons, not all the black urban operators succeeded. Some failed because of their regional management's tendency to blame the owners for problems the owners didn't create. Yet I think a lot more might have failed without the intervention of Ed Schmitt, Gerry Newman, and others in senior management who didn't just pay lip service to the goal of integrating the company and forging strong, beneficial links between minority owners and the Ivory Tower.

"Brothers Standing on the Shoulders of Brothers"

Just before the July 1975 BMOA convention, I got involved in a dispute about one of our guest speakers. We had invited Tom Burrell to make a presentation updating BMOA members on the progress of advertising to the black consumer market. Tom accepted gladly, but as the convention date approached, he got back to me and said that the corporate Marketing department had decided to do the presentation instead of him. I was shocked.

I talked to Paul Schrage, head of Marketing, and after some discussion, Paul decided that he and Tom would both make presentations. It was a reasonable compromise, but I was still upset that any corporate department would impose itself, uninvited and without consultation, on BMOA (or any independent association of owner-operators). It was later that I learned what Paul had been trying to achieve. He wanted to build a trusting relationship between the black owners and his department by letting them know what Marketing could do for them. He also wanted the owners to become comfortable dealing with Marketing and not feel it necessary to go directly to Tom. Like Needham Harper & Steers and other ad agencies that worked for McDonald's, Burrell Advertising was a contract supplier. Marketing was responsible for everything that Burrell and the other agencies produced. Paul wanted to make the case that the Marketing department should be the black owners' first resource, and he was disappointed that the department hadn't been included.

I understand now that our disagreement also traced to my sensitivities. The struggle to get marketing directed to black consumers was still a sore spot with me and many of the BMOA members. When John Perry, who was president of the Chicago BMOA that year, heard about the change in the convention agenda, he also thought the company was attempting to cut Tom Burrell out of the loop. Although I knew operations inside and out and was very familiar with the way most other departments worked, I didn't know that much about Marketing. I didn't realize that going straight to Tom without consulting Paul and his department might cause hurt feelings—especially after Paul had bucked his primary national ad agency, Needham, to establish a direct reporting relationship with Burrell Advertising. Paul hadn't intended to offend the black owners by substituting his department for an agency he hired. And I hadn't intended to offend Paul by asking Tom to speak. There were no negative reasons why I hadn't invited Marketing to participate in the convention; it was simply that the BMOA members felt that Tom was closest to the action and the most knowledgeable expert on the African American consumer market.

As it turned out, both Paul and Tom gave great presentations. Paul did a terrific job of educating us about the different responsibilities of corporate marketing—national advertising, local advertising, national and local public relations—and how Marketing coordinated each of these functions and worked with owners through their local ad co-ops and the Operators National Advertising Cooperative (OPNAD). Tom spoke the next day, updating us on his agency's latest efforts and future plans based on new research.

I see now that our problem arose from a lack of communication. Paul hadn't gotten in touch with me because he assumed I would understand his motives. He didn't think he was cutting Tom out, and I don't think he realized how invested the black owners were in their relationship with Tom and Burrell Advertising. I had jumped to the conclusion that corporate was trying to undermine Tom and maybe, by extension, BMOA. We were both wrong, but somehow our mistakes were translated into a win-win situation, which was the springboard for the mutually beneficial relationship of NBMOA, the corporation, and Burrell Advertising that has so far lasted for more than thirty years.

Aside from this misunderstanding, the Kansas City convention went like clockwork. In addition to black owners from around the country, we also welcomed the first Hispanic owners to BMOA. For the first time, the agenda included a presentation on affirmative action, a proactive policy intended to redress the past wrongs of discrimination and give blacks and other minorities equal access to the workplace. (Minority quotas, which have caused so much dissension in recent years, were not originally part of affirmative action. The standard then was fairness, not percentages.) We had sessions on cash control, bank services, and minority licensing, and workshops that included preparing single store owners for expansion. My fondest memory of that convention was presenting a special tribute to Carl Osborne—"The Man With Indispensable

Roots"—in recognition of his pioneering efforts in Washington, D.C., to open the way for blacks in McDonald's and his unwavering support of the men, and eventually women, who followed him in the company. When I handed the award to Carl, the room was filled with clapping, cheering people who had benefited from Carl's trailblazing. Over the convention weekend, however, the main buzz was about the attendance of owners from so many regions and the possibility of making BMOA officially a national organization.

The idea of taking BMOA nationwide was fleshed out in the business meetings of the BMOA leadership that followed the convention. It was decided that BMOA would officially become the *National* Black McDonald's Operators Association (NBMOA) at the 1976 convention, which was going to be hosted by the Philadelphia owners. When this news reached Detroit, the owners there—Don Forney, Ralph Kelly, Bill Pickard, Bernard ("B.J.") Price, Ray Snowden, Tommie Watkins, Clayton Norman, and Melvin Garrett— decided that a national group needed an efficient organizational structure, and they took the lead. I still wonder how they all managed to fit inside B.J.'s tiny apartment and get any work done.

A key strategist was Bill Pickard, who had been a professor at Wayne State University before becoming a McDonald's owner and was a charter member of the Detroit BMOA chapter. A few years earlier, Bill had been brought into Hamburger University to develop a program to improve the company's employee relations, a difficult area at that time, when the company's growth required more workers than the market could supply and turnover was very high—more than 100 percent a year in many stores. Respected for his skills in training and personnel management, Bill put together McDonald's People Action, a program focused on employee recruitment, selection, retention, motivation, and discipline. The program was adopted into the Hamburger U curriculum and became the basis for a company-wide focus on human resources—a critical aspect of management that had been largely ignored by corporate during McDonald's early years.

Bill was kind of an oddity among the black owners; he was a Republican with a Ph.D. and considered conservative, though by today's standards, he's a moderate. Yet he was also one of the guys because he was outcome-focused like everybody else. A strong believer in free enterprise, Bill used to say that no one "can be independent with dependent thinking." BMOA's commitment to self-help fit right into his philosophy, and he was the perfect man to strategically assemble the chapter members' input into an effective organizational structure.

The selection of the Philadelphia BMOA chapter to host the next convention had special significance in several senses. The whole country was celebrating our bicentennial year in 1976, and while black citizens were only beginning to taste the full freedoms guaranteed in the Constitution, it seemed appropriate to go to the nation's birthplace for the birth of our national organization. We also wanted to expand our regional outlook beyond the old Midwest boundaries. We had already held three conventions in Chicago and one in Kansas City; it was time to set a new precedent. (After Philadelphia, our next six national gatherings were convened in Detroit, Cleveland, Los Angeles, Chicago, Houston, and New York City.) Another reason for the choice was to show support for the Philly owners, who were dealing with some of the most serious urban problems in the system, including nearly insurmountable financing difficulties that contributed to a high rate of failures and turnover among black owners.

The convention was actually held in Cherry Hill, New Jersey, a bedroom suburb where the Philadelphia regional headquarters of

McDonald's was located. The Detroit delegation presented their organizational plan, and as I recall, it was accepted unanimously. Ralph Kelly of Detroit was elected as the first national chairman of the executive committee, and Matt Mitchell of Philadelphia as the vice chairman. The officers and at-large members were impressive, not just for their individual abilities but also for their geographical distribution. Ramon Hardy of Richmond, Virginia, was secretary; Paul Guttierrez, an Hispanic owner from Huntington Park, California, parliamentarian; Cirilio McSween of Chicago, treasurer; and at-large committee members were Caesar Burkes of Cleveland, Bradley Hubbert of Atlanta, Roosevelt Stroman of Valley Streams, Long Island, New York, John Williams of Houston, Ken Mayes of Dallas, and John Perry and Walter Pitchford from Chicago.

It was hard to believe that we had come so far, and how much further we were capable of going. In 1972, when BMOA's first convention was attended by thirteen owners from Chicago, St. Louis, Kansas City, and Milwaukee, the black operators were barely a blip on the corporate radar. Their combined sales amounted to just $9 million. By 1979, NBMOA members would come from twenty-eight states, plus the U.S. Virgin Islands, the Bahamas, and Canada. Their stores would be ringing up more than $204 million in combined sales.

NBMOA inspired the Hispanic operators who attended the 1976 convention to start their own organization the following year, to meet needs specific to their markets. Over the next few years, NBMOA's self-help model would be applied by Asian American owners and other minority groups and finally by women, who, as a group, were the last to gain entry to full ownership and corporate management. In BMOA, we had a kind of unofficial motto: "Brothers standing on the shoulders of brothers." It was an adaptation of a quote from the civil rights leader Benjamin Hooks, and to us, it expressed our commitment to lift each other up and never to forget the people who came before us. It was more than a decade after the first black man became a McDonald's operator that we were able to change the words of our saying from "brothers" to "brothers and sisters."

IN THE TOWER AND ON THE ROAD

I enjoyed working in the Ivory Tower, even though I was rarely in the office for more than one or two days a week. The building's interior space design was still something radical in American business when I moved in. There were no offices in the traditional sense. There were no floor-to-ceiling walls and no doors separating people. Traditional desks had been eliminated in favor of work units, familiar to office workers today but really 'out there' in the 70s. People were amazed that even the offices of the most senior execs, on the eighth floor, were door-less—a physical affirmation of the company's open-door policy. But the area that drew the most comment from visitors was the "think tank," added to the original design at Fred Turner's request. The think tank was an enclosed place roughly centered in the seventh-floor work area. It consisted of a glassed-in workroom and the actual tank, which had a waterbed as its floor. The lighting was low, and office noises were absent. Soft music was piped in. Anyone who needed a place to contemplate or just chill in private could go to the tank. Fred used the room, though it was too calm for Mr. Kroc. However, I do remember once seeing the chairman bouncing across the waterbed as he hurried to find someone on the opposite side of the enclosure. The workroom was a good place for brainstorming meetings, and I also went there sometimes to write and to practice speeches. One of the few rules governing use of the space was that men and women couldn't go into the tank together. There was no hanky-panky in the tank.

The open plan layout wouldn't surprise anyone today, and the think tank would probably strike most people as a quaint 70s fad, like love beads. But at the time, the office design was intended to promote productivity, creativity, and collegiality, and it worked. Everybody was on a first-name basis, though I and a few others could never bring ourselves to call Mr. Kroc "Ray." People were less conscious, as I recall, of titles and ranks, and nobody could get away with snubbing a fellow worker. Even when people were having heated disagreements, there was something about the atmosphere in that office that facilitated speaking and behaving respectfully.

What kept me away from the Ivory Tower was mainly the time I spent in the field, meeting with owners and regional people. A critical part of my job was to help regional managers and field service managers understand the realities of inner city operations, especially in the hardcore urban areas, and the special concerns of urban owners, whatever their color and ethnicity. The success stories of the company's first generation of suburban operators had been recounted so often that they had evolved into a corporate mythology. At the heart of the myth was the belief that a McDonald's franchise was a virtual license to print money. When a store was in trouble, it was often assumed to be the fault of a lazy and incompetent operator, and that was sometimes true. But a lot more operators, especially in the cities, were struggling with circumstances that would bring down the best CEO.

The success myth permeated the organization, but by the mid-70s, those of us who had seen the experiences of the black urban operators were painfully aware that the myth was full of holes. I had to educate quite a few regional and field service managers in the realities of urban ownership so that they could educate their field consultants. Because of the company's rapid growth and the increase of regions from the original five to twelve, a number of the consultants who had been hired in the early 70s lacked the kind of operational background and training in finances that had been the earlier standard. I often heard owners refer to their field consultants as "Joe College," and it wasn't a compliment. The last thing an owner needed was a fresh-out-of-college consultant who didn't know what time of day it was. If we were going to establish mutually beneficial relationships between the regional offices and the urban owners, the regional people had to recognize their own naiveté, learn what was really happening on the ground, and break through the corporate mythology.

Most of the regional managers and field service managers I saw were receptive to my message, but some were reluctant to take advice. Mistrust of me, as a black man, and of black owners came up on occasion, and in the South, I ran into the old prejudices. What surprised me there were managers who were not Southerners themselves but were so afraid of white consumer reactions—even in Deep South urban locations where the population was overwhelmingly African American—that instead of helping black operators, the managers and consultants actually created new obstacles. They couldn't blow me off, however; I was a corporate department head, and they all knew that my work had the blessing of Ed Schmitt. Even so, they could be very stubborn sometimes.

Urban Operations got a big boost when I was invited to speak to a Board of Directors meeting toward the end of 1975 and to report on the history, current status, and future outlook of minority ownership. I can't remember being nervous about addressing the Board, but I do recall how I excited I was to have the opportunity. I had a powerful story to tell, and I wanted to lay it all out—beginning with the situation in the cities in 1969 and the mistakes that were made at the outset. I wanted the Board members to know how some problems had been resolved and others, like the residual effects of the "salt and pepper" partnerships and the financing problems, were being dealt with.

I knew that numbers would be important to the Board, and I had good ones. We had started in 1969 with one minority operator, Herman Petty, about to take over one substandard Chicago restaurant. Now, with 1975 drawing to its close, we had eighty-nine minority owners and 116 urban stores. Based on the numbers of minority applicants registered to get franchises and the current minority owners who were ready to expand by acquiring additional stores, we had the potential to add as many as sixty more minority-owned stores during 1976. The average annual sales of minority-owned stores was now nearly that of all McDonald's stores, and the average rate of increase in sales in 1975 was running slightly higher for minority franchises.

I also presented census figures to demonstrate the value of black and other minority consumers to McDonald's future. Three-quarters of blacks now lived in major metropolitan areas, and the majority was concentrated in the city centers. The growth of city centers depended entirely on minorities. The black population was growing faster and tended to be younger than the white population. From the company's own research, we knew that the number of heavy users of McDonald's was higher among blacks than whites and that per person, blacks spent more than whites.

I then explained what Urban Operations was currently doing. On the corporate side, I was working with eighteen fast-track operations trainees, who would be in line to become regional consultants, to prepare them to serve minority operators in hardcore urban areas. Urban Operations was also cooperating with Human Resources in an aggressive recruitment campaign at black colleges

271

and universities, with the long-term objective of bringing more blacks into corporate middle management.

For new and prospective licensees, I had implemented a strategy that—in addition to the required in-store training, basic and advanced Hamburger U courses, and BMOA training—was designed to head off the kinds of problems we had experienced in the past. For prospective licensees, I set up a special training program that comprised seven video sessions followed by discussions focused on issues specific to minority franchisees and their operations. I also arranged for each in-coming or prospective minority operator to be placed in a store similar to the one he would be running. When the owner took over, I personally selected an experienced operator to work with him and continue his training, supplementing the assistance he received from regional field services.

The videotapes, by the way, featured a number of our pioneer owners—Herman Petty, Walter Pitchford, Carl Osborne, "Doc" Ben Davis, Ralph Kelly, and Chuck Johnson—who were now experts in the complexities of urban operations, from managing crowds of school kids during the hectic lunch hour to keeping on top of the routine paperwork. Lee Dunham, a former New York City police officer and the first McDonald's owner in the Big Apple, did an eye-opening video presentation about store security, which included the topic "How do you recognize a drug addict, and why is it important?" I had learned something about drug users back in D.C., when I used to find heroin needles dropped by our next-door neighbors in the trash cans at the Bladensburg Road store. Since that time, the drug epidemic had exploded across the country, and urban businesses like McDonald's were particularly vulnerable to the crime that always followed drugs. To people of my generation, including most McDonald's owners, drug addicts and their drug-inspired thefts and assaults were as alien as little green men from Mars. I'd never even caught a whiff of marijuana until I was in my thirties, and then somebody had to tell me what it was. Lee's presentation was a wake-up call alerting all of us to this new danger to urban operations.

Maybe the most important thing I told the Board about was the improvement in morale we were seeing among the minority owners. The pioneer owners had struggled against the worst kind of odds, and in the beginning, they often felt that the company didn't care about them or their communities. But things were changing; the company had owned up to its mistakes and was correcting them as rapidly as possible. Ed Schmitt's listening tour and Gerry Newman's work on re-financing and rent relief were inspiring a new and highly favorable attitude among the minority operators. As I told the Board, minority owners were no longer thinking, "McDonald's is a bad company with a few good guys." The new attitude was that "McDonald's is a good company with a few bad guys who are hiding themselves from top management."

I was about to bring two more "good guys" into the Ivory Tower. I began talking with Cosmo Williams about coming into Urban Operations. Cosmo and I went all the way back to D.C. In 1968, Cosmo was attending graduate school at Howard University and driving a taxi to support his family. Then the riots after Dr. King's murder drastically affected tourism and reduced foot traffic in the city, and Cosmo remembers that suddenly there were "more taxis than passengers" in the capital. One of the passengers he did get happened to recommend that Cosmo look into employment with McDonald's. When his cab business went bust, Cosmo talked to a friend who recommended that he contact Carl Osborne, who then referred him to Gee Gee Corporation's director of Personnel. Cosmo was hired as a manager trainee, and it wasn't long before he decided to give up his graduate studies and pursue a career in McDonald's. He had been one of the group of D.C. men who remained second assistants for more than a year; then he was put into the company's fast track management training program. By 1973, he was McOpCo's regional operations manager in Washington, but serious injuries suffered in an auto accident while he was visiting his native Trinidad sidelined him for seven months. Mike Quinlan, who was D.C. regional manager at the time, promoted Cosmo while he was still on his sickbed. Cosmo didn't get the chance to do the job, however. Before he had fully recuperated, he was sabotaged by office politics and demoted back to operations manager in Washington.

It didn't take too long for me to convince Cosmo to come to Chicago. My own future was up in the air—whether I would leave my position at the end of two years or stay on longer—but part of my agreement with Ed Schmitt had been for me to hire someone who could take over the department when I did leave. I knew Cosmo was the right man. He accepted and started in Urban Operations at the beginning of 1976.

Not long after Cosmo came on board, I recruited Art Smith, the talented young man who had replaced me as field consultant when I became field service manager in Chicago and who was doing such an outstanding job with the BMOA training program. With Art hired, Urban Operations became a three-man team. Our combined experience included store management, field work with urban franchisees, Art's and my work with BMOA, Cosmo's thorough knowledge of McOpCo and the operation of company-owned stores, plus my time inside corporate management. We had contacts in every department and every region in the country, and we were closely linked to every minority operator in the system. We had the backing of Ed Schmitt, the company's newly appointed president/chief administrative officer. In other words, we were positioned to nurture a nationwide network of minority franchisees, McOpCo personnel, and corporate executives.

The "old boys' network" is, I guess, as old as human history, though the term goes back to the English upper class and their elite boys' schools. In the United States, you didn't have to be born into the ruling class to be part of the old boys' network, but you did have to be male, white, and preferably Protestant. It was (and to a surprising degree, remains) one of the most effective tools white businessmen had for getting, holding, and perpetuating control. White American men have always been less rigid about who gets into their network than their British cousins. A person's family tree, for example, is not so important, nor is attending the top prep schools and colleges. Religious exclusion is less obvious than it once was. In the 1970s, however, the old boys' network still closed ranks against people of color and women. (We could work at their country clubs, but we couldn't join them.) If we wanted the kind of system that would elevate qualified minorities up the ladder of success in the company, we had to create it ourselves.

There were precedents for what we wanted to achieve. The Chicago BMOA was the obvious role model for networking. Cosmo also had experience with a group that had been formed in Washington just after I moved to Chicago in late 1968. It was after McDonald's had bought the forty-two D.C. area stores owned by Gee Gee Corporation. Called the United Black Managers' Committee, the group consisted of African American store managers, and Roscoe Coleman, who was then managing my old store on Bladensburg Road, was the leader. The managers had a number of concerns, but their immediate, specific objective was to get Carl Osborne, the first black area supervisor in McOpCo, promoted to director of operations. The committee had come together in secrecy, and Carl knew nothing about it initially because the group didn't want to jeopardize his position with the McOpCo executives.

By August 1969, the store managers had firmed up their goals, and they requested a meeting with the regional executives. Their issues centered on promotion opportunities for black store managers and clarification of the company's real commitment to blacks. On the morning of the meeting, the executives offered Carl the job as director of operations, and he took it. He realized then that the black managers must have been doing a lot of lobbying for him. In fact, the managers had made it clear that they were prepared to walk out if the company continued to drag its feet about Carl's promotion. After that, the United Black Managers' Committee continued for a short while, until most of its original members were brought into the regional offices, McOpCo management, or to Chicago. Cosmo had been part of the group, and he brought this different experience of networking into Urban Operations.

Cosmo's special 'baby' was the development of a Big Brother program to provide a network for nurturing black talent in the company. The idea was to match up minority employees at the assistant manager level and management trainees in McOpCo stores with experienced mid-management people of color (primarily McOpCo area supervisors and regional field consultants) in business mentoring relationships. Company-owned stores were the training ground for both regional and McOpCo middle management and ultimately for corporate positions. We had seen how black store managers employed and trained by Gee Gee in Washington became the management 'farm team' when corporate McDonald's first decided to integrate its urban store ownership. We also knew the toll that employee turnover took, constantly depleting the pool of young, black assistant store managers who had the potential to become store managers and then move up. Turnover of junior store managers in urban areas was ridiculously high; Cosmo has said that "they were hired in the front door and kicked out the back door." Bright black kids left the system because the system hadn't offered them much chance of advancement. But now that more and more positions in regional, McOpCo, and corporate management were opening up to minorities, black store managers were moving up. We knew that once a store employee became a store manager, he had a very real chance of promotion and was unlikely to leave. Our focus was on training and retention at the assistant manager level to the feed the pipeline to McOpCo store management and eventually into key regional and corporate positions.

As Cosmo organized the Big Brother program, the mentors would make themselves available to promising assistant managers and help them navigate the system. The responsibility of minority mentors would be to help the "little brothers and sisters" learn how the system worked, what obstacles to expect and how to overcome them, and how to achieve their career goals in McDonald's. The Big Brothers—one per region at that time—would keep track of what was happening at the assistant manager level and use their own networks, including store managers, to provide support, education, and encouragement.

I should make clear that this was a *business mentoring* program. Today, the name Big Brother might conjure up images of groups like Buddies and Boys' and Girls' Clubs, which foster helpful friendship relationships between children and caring adult volunteers. While friendships often evolved from Big Brother relationships, the primary purpose of the program was to identify assistant managers with potential and keep them in McDonald's by preparing them for leadership.

277

Cosmo, Art, and I worked together to develop a list of possible Big Brother mentors and invite them to a meeting in Atlanta. Almost everyone we talked to was interested, and to a person, the participants in the Atlanta meeting were ready to give their time to the creation of a minority mentoring network. Largely due to Cosmo's persistence and careful tending of the group, the Big Brother program thrived while I was in Urban Operations and continued to flourish when Cosmo took over as director of the department. Not only did it facilitate the promotion pipeline we hoped for, but the relationships formed carried over into a new informal network as mentors and "little brothers and sisters" eventually became colleagues and peers throughout virtually all levels of the company.

Unfortunately, when Cosmo left in September 1979 to become a franchisee in the U.S. Virgin Islands, the Big Brother program itself was allowed to die off. But that wasn't the end of the story. Mel Hopson, director of the Affirmative Action department from 1980-2000, was one of the company's most dedicated and effective advocates of diversity. He revived the Big Brother idea and in conjunction with Personnel created the Black Employee Network, which extended the mentoring concept from the store level into regional and corporate management.

Cosmo also was a friend and ally of women in the company. By the late 1970s, women were finally breaking into middle management. A lot of the credit goes to Ed Schmitt, whose unyielding commitment to diversity opened many doors during his tenure as president, and also to Fred Turner, who took a personal interest in the future of women in the company. Marge Cooke, who had been Fred's administrative assistant before being promoted to Personnel, and Kathy Spivey, also in Personnel, got together with Cosmo sometime in 1978 to discuss what was being accomplished in Urban Operations and NBMOA. The outcome was a meeting of women in management with the objective of forming a self-help network. Eleven women and one man—Cosmo Williams—attended that meeting. The background Cosmo provided about what blacks were doing, particularly the work of NBMOA and the Big Brother initiative, helped Marge and the others determine their initial objectives and approaches. Marge, who is regarded as the founding mother of the women's network in McDonald's, was a key mover and shaker until her retirement. She became an assistant vice president of McDonald's in 1976, later served as the company's liaison to the National Operators Advisory Board, and worked tirelessly for affirmative action in hiring and promotion. She is married to John Cooke, whom she met at McDonald's, and they remain two of the company's most vibrant and interesting alums.

I have to say that women in McDonald's had the toughest row to hoe. Blacks were brought into company management and store ownership during a serious crisis that white executives could not handle. We had some difficult battles, but the company learned quickly that black experience in and knowledge of minority markets was essential to preserve its urban operations and expand its growth in the cities. Even executives with personal reservations about racial and ethnic integration realized that minorities, as owners and in middle management, were good for business. However, there was no crisis comparable to the 1968 inner-city riots that would propel women into the company and up the corporate ladder. The new feminists of the 70s might be burning their bras, but they weren't burning restaurants or boycotting hamburgers. Suburban moms might be trading tea parties for consciousness-raising sessions, but they never stopped taking the kids to McDonald's.

Discrimination against women was by no means exclusive to

McDonald's. It was intrinsic to the national culture and psychology. My friend Lynn Crump started at McDonald's in 1972 as a sixteen-year-old crew person at a store in Portsmouth, Virginia. She went on to become an executive vice president, heading up Worldwide Restaurant Operations—the first black female to reach that level. When I talked with her as I began researching this book, Lynn told me about the kind of prejudice she encountered as she moved up the career ladder. I was surprised when she said that it was harder for her as a woman than as an African American. Men in general, she said, had difficulties working with women, especially women in authority positions. Another friend, Annis Alston, said much the same thing. Annis was employed by the FBI when, in 1974, she began helping her brother Ben, a McDonald's restaurant manager in the D.C. area, in his store. Two years later, she became the company's first female, multi-store supervisor. Annis continued to move up, becoming a vice president/regional manager in the late 1980s, and today, she is a multi-store owner. The more women, like Lynn and Annis, whom I've talked to, the more I have heard similar sentiments, regardless of their businesses and professions.

I was raised in a family of strong, determined women—my mother; my grandmothers, "Mama Totcy" Jones and "Gran-dear" Hattie Williamson; and my great-grandmother Henrietta Porter. The men in my family respected women as equals, and that became my ethic. My father, as a Baptist minister, was criticized for inviting women ministers to speak in his pulpit, but that didn't stop him. So I was well aware of the obstacles women faced in the 70s and 80s, but like a lot of my male peers, I didn't always see the worst of it.

Annis Alston recently said that blacks have a responsibility to educate whites, to open white eyes to the conscious and unconscious acts of discrimination committed against people of color every day.

The same is true for women, and thanks to a lot of smart, wise women, I had my own eyes opened. I hope that, someday soon, someone will tell the full story, warts and all, of the early history of women in McDonald's, the pioneers of female advancement, and the proactive role of the corporation. McDonald's can rightfully take pride in its leadership in promoting women, but there were many more bumps and twists in the road than are related in press releases.

Getting back to Urban Operations, our work wasn't all about program development and implementation. Quite often we were involved with situations in individual stores and locales. A good illustration of the kind of grassroots issues we dealt with happened in 1977. I had recently left corporate and Cosmo was the new director of Urban Operations, but he and I remained in close contact. He told me about going to Buffalo, New York, to handle a problem in the community there. A black owner with a grudge against McDonald's was stirring up local African American activists. There were rumors that the owner was trying to organize a protest against McDonald's on Wall Street. Nobody had forgotten the Cleveland boycott, so the purpose for Cosmo's trip was to talk with community leaders, evaluate the situation, and head off trouble before things got out of hand. The activists wanted to talk with someone higher than Cosmo, so it was immediately decided that Ed Schmitt would come to Buffalo and meet with them. Ed's involvement settled matters, and the activists realized that they were being manipulated by a disgruntled operator who was never a good fit for the system—not because of prejudice or discrimination.

I'm citing the Buffalo case, even though I didn't participate in it, because it exemplifies Ed Schmitt's willingness to get down in the trenches. He could have sent a dozen vice presidents to Buffalo to analyze and negotiate. But he trusted Cosmo's judgment. That wasn't the only time Ed used his people skills to help Urban Operations, and it didn't surprise me.

THE FORK IN THE ROAD

I had promised Ed two years to get Urban Operations going, and 1976 was my second year. I knew that Ed would have been happy for me to stay on longer. I also believed that I had other options if I wanted to stay inside corporate. We had accomplished more than I'd thought possible, and the temptation to carry on was strong. At the same time, my ambition to become an owner-operator was pulling at me, and I knew I was at a fork in the road. I had a big decision to make, and I needed advice.

One of my best friends then (and now) was Jim Schenk. A former University of Wisconsin football player, Jim was a McDonald's owner in Chicago, and he was a favorite "customer" of mine when I was in field services. Our friendship developed from the business association, and when we got together, we discovered that we had a lot more in common than McDonald's. Jim's a white Midwesterner who grew up in Ohio, and I'm a black Southerner. Somehow our different backgrounds and experiences have strengthened our friendship over the years. We used to have long talks about business and management, among other things, and Jim once brought up the topic of business life expectancy. His observations reminded me of my thinking that every job has a shelf life—an idea that had helped me when I resigned my regional position and put Neil behind me. I had to ask myself whether I was now approaching a similar end point in Urban Operations.

I was also talking with Ed about my future. I once told him that I would be willing to return to my old job as field service manager in the Chicago region, as long as Neil wasn't around, but Ed said it wouldn't be a wise choice. It would be perceived as a move backward. Did I have a chance at becoming a regional manager? Ed didn't rule it out, but he did what he had done for me eight years earlier—when I was still a store manager in D.C. and debating whether to accept his offer to be a field consultant and move to Chicago. Ed told me exactly what to expect. Company policies had changed a lot since 1968, but corporate culture was something else. He made me realize that the old boys' network was still very much in place and that promotion decisions were still made with almost as much attention to personal relationships as to abilities.

Ed gave me his full support, but I knew he wasn't the type of chief executive to use his authority to dictate promotion decisions to his key executives. We both understood that if Ed did force my promotion, it would stir up the worst kind of office politics and cause resentments that would make it nearly impossible for me to be effective. Basically, there were a few qualified white men ahead of me who had been mentored and groomed for leadership positions for many years. Blacks were playing a game of catch up that would continue for some time—until there were enough blacks, other minorities, and women placed high enough in the system to create our own networks. Minority networking was beginning to happen, through NBMOA and also the Big Brother program we had launched in Urban Operations. But what Ed helped me understand was that I was a leader in initiating minority networks but was unlikely to benefit personally from networking.

Jesse Jackson often said that "there are tree shakers and there are jelly makers." I realized that I was a tree shaker and that the fruits of my work would be gathered and turned into jelly by people who came after me. Women later coined the phrase "glass ceiling" for the invisible but very real point beyond which female businesspeople cannot advance. That's where I was. If I stayed in corporate, I had to accept that I'd reached the glass ceiling and that it might be years

283

before I could break through. But if I chose to enter the entrepreneurial world of McDonald's restaurant ownership, I would be able to set my own ceiling. (The first black man to shatter the corporate promotion barrier was Raymond Mines, when he became an executive vice president in 1998. Ray went on to mentor a young man named Don Thompson who was appointed President of McDonald's USA in August 2006, becoming the highest ranking African American in McDonald's history.)

Around the time Ed and I were having our discussions, I got a call from Roland Long, who had been my field service manager back in 1970 and was now the regional manager in Indianapolis. He asked me to visit a proposed store site in Tennessee, evaluate the site, and assist with matching a franchisee to the location. So I made my first visit back to Nashville in many, many years. The site was at 2805 Clarksville Highway—an area not too far from the city center and near my old stamping grounds when I was a greenhorn college student. Tennessee A&I had become Tennessee State University (TSU). The Nashville I remembered had changed; it was no longer the sleepy Southern river town of the 1950s, but a hustle-bustle New South commercial and financial capital. Still, many of my old landmarks were there too, and a lot of good memories came back to me. When I reported to Roland, I told him I might be interested in becoming the Clarksville Highway franchisee, but I thought there might be a conflict with my current job. Roland didn't think there was any problem and advised me to talk to Ed, who cleared the way if Nashville was what I really wanted.

WEIGHING THE OPTIONS

The last few chapters may have left the impression that I did nothing but work while I was in Chicago. My job was my preoccupation, but I had made time for other things. I socialized with Jim Schenk and other friends and their families. I played golf every chance I got. Nearly every month, I would fly home to Memphis to be with my family for a few days. I also saw my brother, Carl, who came into McDonald's in 1975 and lived in Chicago while he trained with Walter Pitchford at the Better Boys' store. When Walter opened his own franchise on the South Side, Carl continued training with him there. Carl then moved to Norfolk, Virginia, to become a franchisee, but the time we spent together while he was in Chicago was another touchstone. I had been away from the South for more than a decade, and being with Carl reminded me of the good things about home, family, and old friends.

On my personal and business trips to the South, I had seen the progress that was being made in racial integration. The Memphis schools where my mother taught were integrated. Here and there, black men and women were being voted into state and local governments. The citizens of Georgia had turned their backs on racist candidates and elected a soft-spoken, liberal peanut farmer named Jimmy Carter as their governor. Blacks could sit on juries. I also saw small changes that spoke even more eloquently to me than the political and legal changes. Black couples announced their engagements in the big daily newspapers, something that had been forbidden before, and young black men who died in Vietnam received the same tributes as their white comrades. I could sit anywhere I wanted in movie theaters and restaurants, and nobody questioned me when I checked into a hotel. I could watch black people report the news on local TV. The struggle was a long way from being over, and frankly, there were a lot of white folks who would never change their racist attitudes. But my years away from home had shown me that racism wasn't limited to the South. The focus for Southern blacks was shifting from securing legal equality to creating economic opportunity, and that was where I could make a positive impact.

I could stay in Chicago and continue to build Urban Operations, but if I left, I knew that the department would be in Cosmo's and Art's good hands. I would be leaving many good friends behind, but I was confident my friendships would survive the distance, and they have. In Tennessee, I would be closer to my parents, who were approaching retirement. My marriage was at its end, and I was more than ready to put it behind me. I spent many sleepless nights weighing my options and going over the pros and cons of staying or leaving. The outcome was that new challenges were stronger than familiar surroundings. All things considered, Nashville was the winner.

Chapter 11

Bringing the Lessons Home

You're only as good as the people you hire.

RAY KROC, FOUNDER OF MCDONALD'S

Returning to Nashville was for me a way to go home without literally going home. I had lived there for two years in my late teens, when I was a student at Tennessee A&I, and I still had friends in town. But my college experience was rather limited in scope, so Nashville was also new to me—familiar but unfamiliar—and I was looking forward to getting to know the city from the perspective of an adult and a businessperson.

I made my decision to leave Chicago in August 1976. However, I remained as full-time director of Urban Operations through October. During that time, I was also commuting to Nashville to work on getting the Clarksville Highway store, which was under construction, ready for opening. In November, I took some vacation time and made the move to the South. My resignation became official at the end of the vacation period, and I made one more, brief trip to Chicago to clean out my desk and wrap up a few final details with Cosmo Williams and Art Smith. By time, I had mentally as well

287

as physically relocated, so it was a real surprise when Fred Turner called me and asked if I would reconsider. Fred's call was in earnest; he wasn't just being kind when he told me that "it's not too late" to rescind my resignation. Looking back, I appreciate his call for two reasons: It affirmed for me that the job I had done in the corporation was effective and valued. It also affirmed my decision to leave, because even Fred—a man I didn't always agree with but greatly respected—couldn't shake my conviction. I had a new vision now. After eleven years of working my way up the ladder, from management trainee to corporate department head, I was eager to put all the lessons I'd learned into action. I had spent eight of those years in Chicago, helping other owners and hammering away at the fundamentals of quality, service, and cleanliness. I was ready to practice what I had been preaching.

I expected to get out of Chicago without a lot of fuss, but my co-workers in the Ivory Tower threw a surprise going-away party for me, and almost all of my colleagues from corporate and regional were there. To this day, I feel honored that Mr. Kroc attended. He didn't try to talk me into staying. More than anyone else in the company, he understood my desire to get back to the store level. He had grown a fledgling business into the largest food service company in the world on the principle that the most important people in the company were the restaurant owners. Owner-operators are the direct link between the company and its customers; they control the everyday quality of the product and service and, ultimately, the fate of the corporation. When Ray Kroc wished me well in my new venture, I knew he meant it.

The going-away party also made me realize what I was leaving behind—friends and colleagues such as Cosmo and Art and especially Ed Schmitt, work I loved doing, daily contacts with owner-operators whom I admired and did my best to assist, my role in nationalizing successful minority ownership and pipelining black men and women into regional and corporate management. I knew that I would miss much of what I was giving up, but missing wasn't the same as regretting. There was nothing bittersweet about the party and the goodbyes. I left the Ivory Tower that day knowing that I was doing the right thing.

THE SITUATION IN NASHVILLE

Inside the McDonald's system, restaurants are identified by site numbers indicating when they come on line. My new store was officially listed as #3941. It was located on the north side of Nashville at 2805 Clarksville Highway, near the Cumberland River. The restaurant was built on the site of an old car wash, and the immediate neighborhood was pretty rundown. There were a few businesses within a half mile's distance—service stations, mom-and-pop stores, small restaurants, and some light industry—but no fast-food outlets. Behind the store site were low-income apartments, and a few blocks away was the Cumberland View Public Housing Apartments, often referred to as "Dodge City" because of the frequent gunfire in the project. Otherwise, there was no real residential neighborhood. The store was, however, about two blocks from the Bordeaux (now Martin Luther King, Jr.) Bridge, and on the other side the bridge was the blue-collar and middle-class area of Bordeaux, whose population was more racially mixed, though transitioning to a black majority. To the east of the store site, a major business park, MetroCenter, was being developed, and this would eventually bring a large number of white-collar workers into the area. About a mile away were the campuses of Fisk University and Meharry Medical College, both private, historically black institutions. Tennessee State University (TSU)—

now integrated since my days there, when it was still A&I, but still predominately black—was about two miles away. I believed, rightly, that these schools would be a great resource for recruiting store employees.

At the time the restaurant site was selected, what sold me on the location was its position at the intersection of two major thoroughfares that carried a constant flow of traffic into and out of the city. The flow represented a highly diverse potential market—city workers, including thousands of state and metropolitan government employees who commuted from the suburbs; commercial drivers; shoppers, for whom downtown Nashville was still the major commercial center; students; and tourists. A substantial portion of people traveling to and from the northeastern direction would pass by the new McDonald's on Clarksville Highway. I knew that these commuters and travelers would be the store's main clientele, not the neighborhood.

It's important to understand that Nashville was unlike cities in the North and East primarily because the population wasn't so densely concentrated in the city center. White movement to the suburbs had been on the rise since the end of World War II. In 1962, the city and its surrounding county had consolidated—becoming one of the earliest unified metropolitan governmental entities in the nation. There had been calls for some kind of consolidation for decades, and certainly the restructuring promoted economic growth and expanded public services to county residents. But many people still believe that a primary motive for ratification of the new city-county charter (which had been rejected by popular vote just four years earlier) was to dilute the power of the black population who lived inside the old city limits; in the 1960 U.S. Census, blacks made up 43 percent of the city population but only 19 percent of the county. The fear was that, with sweeping changes in federal civil rights and voting laws, blacks would gain control of the old city government. Consolidating the near majority black city with the majority white county meant that blacks could be elected to the new Metropolitan Council, but they could never control it. If reducing black power really was an underlying motive for consolidation, it worked. Blacks were reduced to about 20 percent of the new Metropolitan Nashville-Davidson County—Metro Nashville—which is about where the number stands today. Although there have been many outstanding African American council members and local public officials, there has never been a serious black contender for mayor.

Nashville's story in the context of the civil rights movement is also relevant. The city, especially the black universities, was an important training center for civil rights activists in the 1950s and 60s, but it had not been a major battleground in the struggle. In 1960, students began to hold lunch counter sit-ins in city department stores (which welcomed their black customers' purchases but denied them access to in-store luncheonettes, restaurants, and dressing rooms) and to picket movie theaters and other segregated businesses. These protests and black consumer boycotts against central city businesses, combined with loss of white trade, quickly convinced white business owners that the city's African Americans had real economic power. Led by a group of department store owners, most businesses were soon integrated. A 1961 *Time* magazine article titled "The Nashville Lesson," commented on the business community's response to the civil rights protests: "If Nashville's white merchants remain segregationists at heart, they have at least learned to become pocketbook integrationists." There were some segregationist holdouts, so the civil rights demonstrations and boycotts continued for a number of years, but the city experienced little of the violence seen in Birmingham, Atlanta, and the Deep South states. Nashville's city fathers did not want a repeat of the first days of school integration back in 1957, which were accompanied by angry, rock-throwing white mobs and the bombing of an elementary school that had been integrated by one, small black child.

Nashville was unusual because its integration proceeded relatively quietly throughout the 1960s and 70s. Pragmatic leaders on both sides of the color divide took a kind of "win some, lose some" approach that facilitated compromise. By the time I returned to the city, integration was an everyday reality, though racism was hardly dead and black people in general remained at the bottom of the economic ladder.

During my years with McDonald's, I had become an expert in big city, urban operations. But Nashville was a different kind of environment, and I had to adjust my thinking. The city didn't have the kind of hardcore urban center that I was so familiar with in D.C., Chicago, Detroit, and other Northern and Midwestern cities. Nashville had no large ethnic or national communities comparable to the Polish in Chicago, the Puerto Ricans in New York, or the Cubans in Miami. Nashville didn't have youth gangs or, as yet, the drug-related crime rates of the North. It was residentially segregated, but blacks lived in clusters scattered in different areas of the city. In the South, people didn't use terms like "ghetto" and "hardcore urban." They would say "the black parts of town." Nashville had four large "black parts," and the area roughly bounded by the TSU campus to the south and Bordeaux to the north, where my restaurant was located, was the largest. Sometimes these clusters included public housing, and poverty was widespread, but there were also a few middle-class and upper middle-class black neighborhoods. Thanks to TSU, Fisk University, and Meharry Medical College, Nashville had a strong, black professional class—educators and administrators, physicians, dentists—and many of these 'elite' lived in Bordeaux and would drive by my store every day. Though my restaurant was located in an area that was traditionally considered 'black,' my aim was to attract customers who were racially mixed and represented the full spectrum of social, economic, and age demographics. About the only Nashvillians who were unlikely to come my way sooner or later were the wealthy inhabitants of the country-club suburbs in the south and southwest of the county.

McDonald's came late to Nashville, not focusing on market development there until the end of the 60s. The fast-food inroads had been made by other major players including Burger King, Kentucky Fried Chicken, Dairy Queen, and regional chains like The Krystal and Krispy Kreme. (Kripsy Kreme, out of North Carolina, sold only doughnuts, coffee, and cold drinks but was a breakfast competitor.) In 1976, I was about to become the first black owner-operator in the city; the first in the state, in fact. My goal was to make my restaurant a model operation that Ray Kroc himself would be proud of. To achieve my goal, the restaurant had to become the preferred destination for a diverse clientele. The facility itself was brand new, so it would be a physical standout in the area. My key strategy was to hire employees who would reflect the diversity of the anticipated customer base and to make outstanding service our hallmark.

The restaurant was scheduled to open the week before Thanksgiving, 1976, and I was determined to make the deadline. Hiring a full staff from scratch, in a short time, isn't easy, but I knew exactly the kind of employees I needed: mostly college and high school students, plus a few mature workers and a few young adults from the nearby housing projects. I wanted my employees to be racially diverse—black and white. In addition to reflecting the

293

makeup of our anticipated clientele, this mix would promote several of my prime objectives.

First, I wanted to encourage mentoring relationships between the college and high school students, which would bring benefits that extended beyond the business itself. Both age groups would have the chance to learn and, hopefully, master essential job skills and discipline that would improve their future employment prospects. I would also be looking for employees who had the potential for store management. Mentoring younger workers was a good way for college students to develop the leadership and people skills necessary for management of any kind. Being mentored by their slightly older peers was an effective means to encourage high school kids to continue their education, develop a positive work ethic, and believe in their ability to achieve their dreams. A more direct and immediate consequence of mentoring would be to transform a group of individuals, who for the most part didn't know one another, into a cohesive team with shared goals and standards. It would also encourage them to form the supportive and collaborative mindset that would get us all over the inevitable rough spots.

Second, providing jobs for young adults in the housing projects who were truly seeking opportunities would help me build ties within the community. By hiring crew members from the projects, I would be creating employment for young black people whose traditional options were limited to menial and domestic work. At that time, the country was in an economic recession, and even positions like the dishwashing job I had gotten at Baptist Hospital when I was a college student were few and far between. Whites were competing with blacks for unskilled, low-pay employment, and guess who usually got the job. Racial discrimination in hiring was a daily reality for black people, especially young black men. I could at least make a small dent in the wall of prejudice and help break down the psychological barriers.

Third, I knew that including mature adults is a stabilizing factor. Over and over, I had seen the positive impact that older workers have on a young work force. For all their energy and seeming self-assurance, young people want guidance and look to their elders for their models of appropriate behavior—a fact of life that employers today might be wise to remember. At thirty-seven, I was an elder to employees in their teens and early twenties, but I needed more adults than just myself.

Word got around that I was hiring—thanks in part to the help of an old friend of mine who worked for Nashville's leading black radio station and got some on-air time for announcements of our opening. I received a large number of applications and was able to assemble a superb crew to open the store. The students I hired were split at about two-thirds college and one-third high school. My first hire was Carol Duncan, a TSU sophomore, who literally jumped with joy when I told her the starting salary was $2.20 an hour. Carol stayed with us through the summer after her graduation, when she left to enter medical school, and today, she is a health-care provider in Nashville. I take a lot of pride in the fact that McDonald's jobs helped young people like Carol finance their education and go on to successful careers in service to the community.

I was very fortunate in the quality of the older people who applied. I hired two men and four women. Two of the women were bank employees working to supplement their incomes, and two were public school teachers. I also employed two young black men from the housing projects. The only difficulty was finding qualified white applicants. This didn't have much to do with racism, as far as I could determine. Rather, it was because the pool of whites in the surrounding area was very small. Despite Nashville's then good public bus service, it was difficult for young people outside the area to get to our location, and white kids usually sought jobs closer to their homes. I suppose that some white parents were also nervous about sending their kids into a black area, especially at night. Still, I was able to hire six young white people, one of them a TSU student.

I personally did the initial hiring and training. As we approached the store opening, however, I had a ton of details to attend to, and my NBMOA friends stepped in. Herman Petty sent Willie Wilson, the Chicago manager who would later get his own restaurant after he tracked down and impressed Ray Kroc, to help with the pre-opening training of my new team. My brother, Carl, sent one of his managers from Virginia to lend a hand, and this manager stayed on for several weeks after we opened. I was getting great cooperation from the McDonald's construction superintendent, equipment representatives, and field consultant. All this help left me some time to devote to another of my objectives: connecting the store to the community. I visited other business owners in the immediate area, introducing myself and telling them about the restaurant. I was warmly welcomed, and they invited me to join the Middle Tennessee Business Association, an organization of black business owners in the North Nashville area. I promptly signed up. I also made contacts with the police (I'll get to the significance of that).

We were on schedule and proceeding smoothly. There were no delays, and both I and my new employees were excited about opening our doors to customers. When I had first investigated the Clarksville Highway site for Roland Long, some of the local community leaders I spoke with told me the area was too rough and that a McDonald's couldn't succeed there. Yet when we had our pre-opening run-through, with the families of the employees as our guests, I was sure that I was about to prove the doubters wrong. I was ready to open for business and have some fun.

A GREAT OPENING AND A BIG ERROR

Because of the tight schedule and changeable weather, I decided to forgo a grand opening, which would have involved more planning, time, and money than I could invest on an unpredictable situation. But our first day of operations was a grand day anyhow, in part because of great advance publicity on three local radio stations. I didn't arrange a Ronald McDonald appearance until several months later, but still, there were some very special guests—real "stars" in my book—on hand. My brother came in from Norfolk, and Cosmo Williams flew down from Chicago. Several other Nashville operators and the account manager from our local advertising agency came too. Carl Osborne, my friend and mentor, was still en route down from Columbus, Ohio, when he called to say, "Don't open the store until I get there! I've got to see the first sale." He walked in just minutes before we officially opened for business at 11:00 a.m. When the first transaction was completed, Carl grabbed the first dollar bill and had my friends autograph it. He took a photo of us all together, and he later sent me that photo and the dollar bill, handsomely framed.

My special guests pitched in, training behind the counter and anywhere else they felt the need. They understood that an operator has to be in the front of the store during an opening, greeting guests and concentrating on customer service. It is a critical time for an operator to make personal contact with his or her clientele, observe their reactions, and look for any problems from the customer's point of view. My friends watched my back by keeping food preparation and delivery going smoothly. Working hand in hand with restaurant

297

owners from Ohio and Virginia as well as Nashville and with Cosmo, now head of the corporate Urban Operations department, also helped my crew feel the team spirit. It was their first real-life, real-time experience as *members of the McDonald's team.*

I spent sixteen hours in the store, and the adrenaline was still flowing when I finally left. My life as an owner was officially a go. I didn't feel at all tired, but I knew we'd be serving our first breakfast the next morning, and I needed rest. Back in my apartment, I took a long shower and went to bed. I had gotten to sleep when, at about 1:30 a.m., the telephone rang. It was the night manager. The store had been robbed. He had everything under control, so I went back to bed, but I didn't get much rest.

That was the first of a series of armed robberies at the store over the next weeks. Security had been very important in my planning, and I thought I had factored in every possibility and contingency. What had I missed? I knew from my Bladensburg Road store in D.C. that the danger of holdups can't be eliminated entirely, but the incidents can be rare if the operator can determine why they happen and take preventive measures. I studied everything we were doing, and I realized that what had most attracted me to the site—its location at the junction of two major roads—was also an area of vulnerability. With roads leading north, east, and south, a low-income apartment complex on our western boundary, and public housing nearby, the location provided escape routes in every direction and made safe getaways too easy.

I would drive around the neighborhood at five in the morning and study the area. Although I had a lot of experience with security in urban areas, this situation was different in ways I hadn't anticipated. When a restaurant is located in an established residential neighborhood, I had always found that making strong ties within the community tends to reduce incidents of both robbery and employee theft. In the Nashville location, however, our closest neighbors were more likely to be the source of problems than part of the solution. On my pre-dawn drives, I realized that I needed to change my own thinking and that my best resources were the people who worked for me. I had been in Nashville for only a few months, and they knew the territory a lot better than I did. So I got together with some employees from the area, and we brainstormed.

The outcome of our unedited rap sessions was a set of measures to reduce our vulnerability. Some steps could be implemented immediately: We placed a police radio monitor in a cabinet out of customers' view and set the volume low. Most people didn't notice the sound, but would-be robbers were very likely to hear the scanner and think there was a cop in the restaurant or on the lot— a little psychological warfare. I changed my hiring policy so that all new hires were either referred by or had connections to my current employees. I also got police clearance for new hires. These measures greatly reduced the possibility of an inside set-up for robbery, with the bonuses of giving current employees confidence in anyone who joined the team and virtually eliminating the possibility of employee pilferage.

I began to establish good relations with police officers on the street and at higher levels in the department, and I hired officers who had the respect of their peers to do store security in their off-hours. Though I didn't have the budget to employ off-duty officers round-the-clock, their presence at different times of day attracted other officers to the restaurant. Pretty soon, cops were stopping by regularly. I was often invited to accompany the police when they patrolled the neighborhood, and this created the impression locally that I and, by extension, the store had a special relationship with law enforcement. I invited officers to speak at team meetings in the store, and in return, I spoke at police meetings about the security concerns of small businesses. (Later, I got Dick DeSoda, McDonald's corporate national security manager, to conduct a crime prevention seminar for all the Nashville area McDonald's owner-operators and store managers.)

In the long run, my employees were probably the most effective crime deterrent. In our training sessions, I emphasized how important it was not to let customer service slide at any time. Robbers don't want to attract attention, so they tend to hold up stores in slow periods, when few people are around and staff is often preoccupied with other duties. Greeting a customer the instant he or she steps across the threshold; making and maintaining eye contact; smiling and observing the customer's reactions; watching the customer as he leaves and inviting him to come back soon—these are the fundamentals of excellent service. They also unnerve robbers and discourage them from whatever wrongdoing they had in mind when they entered the store.

There's no way to calculate crimes that *didn't* happen, but as we put preventive measures in place, the robberies decreased and then stopped. My team was a determined bunch, and they stuck with me throughout our 'crime wave.' In all the years I was an owner, I never had an employee quit because of a robbery, attempted robbery, or fear of being held up.

TRAINING FOR BAREFOOT SERVICE

I came up with the idea of barefoot service when I was managing restaurants in Washington. McDonald's set high standards for production and service, but I wanted to raise the bar even higher. A "satisfied customer" wasn't enough; I wanted standout service so fast and good that it knocked the customer's socks off! I also had very specific ideas about the best ways to motivate employees to give barefoot service.

Service business operators have different ways of training employees. One is the "sink or swim" method: Give a new employee the briefest of orientations, hand him some instructions to read, and put him straight to work. This kind of trial and error training, however, rarely fosters positive attitudes and often results in higher than average employee turnover. Another approach is to assign the new employee to an experienced worker. I'm a great advocate of on-the-job mentoring, but I think this kind of employee-to-employee training produces uneven results at best. Some employers take a formal classroom approach, with the trainer lecturing or showing a training tape. In my experience, this method works best when the information is technical, but if the trainer isn't an effective teacher or the material in a video is unclear, there's always the risk that trainees will simply tune out.

I had used some elements of these methods in training, and over the years, I had developed my own approaches. Finally, in Nashville, I was able to consolidate everything I'd done in the past with my own philosophy of training to create a cohesive and ongoing program. Getting the Clarksville Highway store open on such a short deadline put me under the gun, and I focused on training the crew in the technical aspects of production, but that experience gave me the organizational pattern for all future training.

The basis for technical training was the McDonald's operations manual, station training videos, and hands-on instruction at each station in the store: grill, fries, drive-thru, etc., leading to counter service and cash register operation. For the Clarksville Highway

301

opening, everybody was trained for one station only. After things settled down, I rotated employees through all stations, so everyone could handle any job efficiently. However, technical skills alone aren't enough for barefoot service. Though I can teach just about anyone how to do mechanical tasks and do them well, a team must also be inspired with the genuine desire to be of service to others, including their fellow employees. *Each person is a link in a chain of service, and if the chain is going to be strong, every team member— from the operator to the newest employee—has to feel that he or she is essential to everyone else.*

The process of integrating individuals into a team began when new hires were oriented. In addition to completing the usual paperwork and W-2 forms, new workers received their uniforms and were instructed in the store's policies and procedures. They would tour the store and meet the station specialists—employees who oversaw operations at each station and did a good deal of station training. (Station specialist was the first level of advancement from crew level, and the responsibility went to employees who had developed expertise in multiple areas and had mastered a particular area of production or customer service.) I would meet with new people and talk with them in a relaxed format that fostered dialogue. I started by asking, "Why do you think we hired you?" Some would have an answer like "previous experience" or "good references," but most would be stuck for a reply. So I said, "We hired you because you have *personal pride*," and I explained how they had displayed that pride—in dress, speech, attitude, attention to details on written applications, and behavior during interviews. I think most were surprised that getting the job involved so much more than filling out an application form.

Then I would move the conversation to the idea of extending

personal pride into teamwork and introduce our motto: "We, us, our." As a team, we had to eradicate "I, me, mine" from our vocabulary. Our success depended on our ability to think and work as a team. We would chant, "We, us, our! We, us, our!" The trainees would be as fired up as a football team in the pre-kick-off huddle before a championship game. My approach was to make the orientation fun, to involve everyone in the conversation, to generate a sense of unity, and to introduce core principles. The fundamentals were teamwork, not blaming others for problems but concentrating on solutions, and realizing that solutions begin with self. One of my mantras was, "It's not *who*'s right that matters, but *what*'s right."

These activities may sound basic, and they are. That was the intention. I wanted new employees revved up throughout their training. I also wanted current employees to welcome each new hire as a team member, to help him or her learn the ropes, and to be role models of excellence. To achieve barefoot service, everyone had to understand that our success depended on the team.

Training in my stores was an ongoing process. There were two interdependent threads—the technical training and the principles of service. Both were equally important and were woven together in our training sessions. Even when employees were being instructed about operating a piece of equipment or preparing a new product being introduced to the market, the skills they were learning were also related to the quality of our service and the impression we made on our customers.

I conducted training sessions until I had managers who could take over, and I continued the dialog approach and the emphasis on principles. My first sessions with trainee employees expanded on the ideas I had introduced in their orientation. I would start with another question, "What's our job?" and someone would usually say, "To satisfy the customer." So I asked what it means to be satisfied. I would have the employees draw on their personal experiences, like going to a movie. When the film is satisfying, it lives up to our basic expectations, but it doesn't necessarily leave us impressed enough to see it again or recommend it to our friends. I would introduce the concept that success depends on going beyond satisfactory to *impressive*. How could we make the kind of impression that would not only bring customers back again but also encourage them to recommend our restaurant to others? When employees thought about what impressed them, they understood. *The difference between good and great is the quality of service.* And how do we ensure consistently impressive service? Individually and as a team, we cultivate the habits of success.

We would also discuss the fundamentals of McDonald's QSC standards—quality, service, cleanliness—and ways we could make our standards even higher. We talked a lot about SOP, or standard operating procedure, and why it was important to hang mops and position buckets in a uniform way. There were two basic rules of SOP: First, there's one way and one way only to do things. Second, there's a place for everything and everything should be in its place. If someone had a new and better idea, the procedure was to share it for consideration by the manager, discuss it with the team, and then test it in practice. If we knew an idea had been tried before without success, we didn't just dismiss it. That's a sure way to squelch creative input from employees. Instead, we took the time to explain previous experiences with the same idea, and we made certain that the team member was appropriately recognized for the suggestion. In training, we talked a lot about why details mattered and how even the smallest change in routine had to be communicated to everyone. There was a large bulletin board in the break room, a place to post messages, congratulatory notes, press clippings, and all information that would affect the team. For example, if a drain got clogged on the breakfast shift, the morning manager was expected to inform the lunch crew by posting a message. Reading the bulletin board before clocking in for work was a requirement and soon became one of our habits of success.

I continued a practice from my D.C. days—mini-training sessions. Whenever a situation or a question arose that everyone could learn from, I or the manager on duty would gather the crew or station workers and spend a few minutes discussing it. In addition to scheduled sessions and spontaneous mini-sessions, we held mandatory store meetings three times a year. (Everybody was paid for required meetings.) The agenda normally included updates on our progress and information about upcoming activities, such as a new sales promotion. Problems and potential problems were brought up, usually at the initiative of the employees themselves, and we would discuss possible solutions. In a way, these mandatory meetings were like gatherings of shareholders; there was an agenda, but the floor was open to anyone who had something to contribute. There was no penalty for airing complaints, and there was always a good deal of give and take.

Meetings and training sessions weren't usually lengthy, but they were frequent. My goal was to cement relationships and nurture communication up and down the line. I had seen owners who rarely entered their own stores and managers who spent more time in the back office than on the restaurant floor. That wasn't what I wanted. We had clear levels of authority—station specialist to crew chief to assistant manager to store manager to me—which everyone understood. Yet in terms of getting the job done, asking questions, and getting help, it was not a rigid hierarchy. Everyone was free to go to whomever was closest for assistance, whether it was another crew member or a manager. I characterize the everyday flow of communication as organic rather than bureaucratic; I wanted all employees to feel as comfortable speaking to me as they did with one another. This is the best way I know to promote individual responsibility, personal integrity, and creative thinking at every level. Without a rigid hierarchy, good ideas bubble upward. To me, the restaurant business, or any retail business for that matter, is analogous to a sports team. I was the boss, but I functioned more as the coach and often head cheerleader. *Whether we win or lose, we do it together.* This was our creed, and I focused on it in every aspect of training and operations. As I had seen my Daddy do for his students when he was a school principal back in Mason, Tennessee, I did my best to create a work environment in which every employee was encouraged to do his or her best for the customer, the team, and most of all, for themselves.

I didn't, however, fail to exercise discipline when necessary. Over the years, I had learned that some behaviors have to be governed by absolute rules; otherwise, an employer must make subjective judgments in every case, and questions about fairness and favoritism inevitably arise. So I informed all workers at the start that pilferage and theft would not be tolerated—ever. Anyone caught stealing would be arrested. I laid down the law on tardiness; anyone who was late three times in a month would be suspended. Not coming to work without calling a minimum of four hours in advance meant automatic dismissal, except in a documented emergency. Rudeness to a customer or fellow team member brought automatic dismissal. Being late for mandatory meetings (the doors were locked at the scheduled meeting time), resulted in dismissal; if the worker wanted re-employment, he had to reapply. Everybody saw how serious I was when an employee was caught putting a box of hamburger patties outside the back of the store, where an accomplice drove by and picked it up. The employee was arrested, convicted, and served thirty days in jail. That story and a couple of similar incidents were communicated throughout the team and always included in orientation.

I wanted the team to understand why we had firm rules and penalties, so we spent a good deal of time talking about how a business makes money and the effects of theft, habitual tardiness, rudeness, and so on. Younger team members and some of the more mature ones without a background in retail don't automatically connect the acts of a few bad apples to their own self-interest. They know that stealing is wrong, but teens in particular often believe that tattling or snitching is also wrong; they don't want to rat on a co-worker who is lifting cash from the register or pretending to be sick in order to skip out of work. In our discussions, most of them came to see how, for instance, the chronically late employee makes more work for her diligent team members, slows the system, and ultimately has a negative impact on customer service and earnings, which can mean fewer and smaller financial rewards. I explained how pilferage and waste affected operating costs, including insurance, just as outside robberies did. We also talked about personal responsibility and taking responsibility for co-workers. These discussions usually started with me talking but soon became group conversations, which was my objective. Our people often took matters into their own hands. I remember how they formed their own "wake-up service"—calling one another on the mornings of mandatory meetings, which began at six o'clock, so no one would arrive after the doors were locked. One of my former employees recently reminded me how his closing crew, which usually finished their work at around 1:30 in the morning, would pull an all-nighter, getting together to socialize at someone's house and then calling co-workers to get everyone to a team meeting or monthly breakfast on time.

Building a team doesn't mean ignoring individuals. I have a strong belief in the motivating power of praise, so I instituted a number of recognition programs and activities. Some of these ideas I borrowed from other owners, but many programs, like our monthly breakfasts, were original. The breakfast, which was initially started to recognize the Outstanding Employee of the Month, was held on the fourth Sunday of each month, and all employees, their parents, and families were invited. Though we started at 6:00 a.m. and the event was not mandatory, hardly anyone missed a breakfast. We often had guest speakers—one of my police friends, a local minister, city council member, state representative, or one of the team members' parents. The mayor came one Sunday, and the crew really got a thrill when Big John Merritt, head coach of the nationally ranked, Division 1-AA Tennessee State football team, had breakfast with us. Sometimes, I would do a motivational presentation. One of my favorites was inspired by a saying of my father's: Let down your bucket where you are. The theme was to find the opportunities in every situation, and I made the presentation whenever a group of trainees graduated to full crew status. I would start my brief remarks by saying, "You're sitting on opportunity right now, so get off your rusty dusty and find it." The graduated trainees would hustle, and it wasn't long before they would locate the shiny silver dollars we had taped to their chair bottoms. Some got several dollars; some got none. Either way, everyone was inspired. Back then, a dollar meant a lot and reinforced my point. Every customer who entered our doors was an opportunity to do our best.

The breakfast was also a time to recognize achievement. I had a number of ways for employees to earn praise—and they had to earn it. One was being named an Even All-Star; this was for cashiers. We had adopted a saying from Dianna Earing (now Dianna Alexander), a Nashville owner who became one of my best business friends and allies. Dianna often said, "Every dollar is a hundred pennies" to emphasize the importance of cash control and financial management. We applied her message to the cash register. We were still using manual registers, and little, repeated mistakes could add up to significant losses. The Even All-Star designation rewarded cashiers who were consistently careful with money and whose counts came out even at the end of their shifts. This award was an incentive to all employees. We also recognized employees for their accomplishments outside the store—often academic and athletic successes and community service work—and paid tribute to parents and family members for their achievements, which were unrelated to McDonald's but mattered a great deal to our team. Like most McDonald's stores, we gave an Employee of the Month award in every store. Employee of the Year was presented at the Christmas breakfast. I initiated the Christmas breakfast at Clarksville Highway. When I acquired more stores, it became a joint event; the employees planned the entertainment and the decorations, and it was always a blast for everybody.

The primary purpose of the monthly team-recognition breakfasts, the ongoing training, and other crew-oriented initiatives was to maintain enthusiasm and group cohesion. I rarely had a high school or college student who didn't enjoy these activities, and older employees were very responsive. In fact, some of my mature workers, like Thelma Watson, took mentoring to another level. Thelma was a retired university professor; she spoke four languages fluently and was a great communicator. She worked for me part-time at Clarksville

Highway as a swing shift manager, and she often came to the store in her free time to help young students with their school work. She did this on her own, as a volunteer. When she decided to become a full-time manager, Thelma accepted responsibility for the training department and later managed training for all my stores.

I always preferred to promote assistant managers from inside because we hired very smart people and they knew the system. I also wanted to retain them, and the most effective way to retain and advance good people is to give them more responsibility, along with higher pay. So I devised a plan that would involve assistant and swing managers (part-time assistant managers who worked shifts whenever full-time managers were unavailable) in more direct management roles and also provide more intensive training in all areas of store operations. We divided operations into departments and appointed "department managers." The departments included administration, personnel, bookkeeping, customer service, advertising/public relations, and maintenance. Under my direction, assistant managers were rotated through the departments. As I and my store managers worked with them in each area, we could see who had the ability, the personal discipline, and the interest necessary for advancement. A number of former managers have since told me how much they learned during their departmental rotations. For many of them, it was their first direct, hands-on experience in the multifaceted complexities of business practice and gave them knowledge that was valuable in their later careers, regardless of the fields they eventually entered.

As we proceeded, what I hoped for happened. Leadership and business aptitudes emerged, and I was able to determine which department managers were likely to be retained in the McDonald's system. The first manager to come out of the departmental system was a young woman who had been working in the admissions office at

Tennessee State University. She joined us as a part-time crew member, but when offered the opportunity to move to full-time, she grabbed it. She went on to be an outstanding restaurant manager. The system definitely facilitated retention and extended the shelf live of many of our best team members. It also saved me and my managers a lot of time and energy. The better the assistant managers/department managers understood the overall business, the more competent and confident they became. Crew members quickly began taking issues and questions to specific department managers, giving the store managers and me more freedom to attend to our duties. It was time-consuming to get the departmental system going, but the result was worth the effort. The only real difficulty was that, over time, we trained more potential managers than we had management positions to fill.

I did, however, create a problem for myself not long after our Clarksville Highway opening. The crew was doing a good job, but the speed of service, one of McDonald's core standards, wasn't acceptable to me. I repeatedly reviewed everything we were doing, and I could not for the life of me identify the source of the slowdown. I called on my field consultant for help, but rather than consult, he gave the store a performance rating of F in service and told me I had a serious problem. That was when I understood, at gut level, the complaints that other operators, including the rebellious members of the McDonald's Operators Association, were making about the incompetence and arrogance of so many field service representatives at that time.

At a loss for an answer, I thought about my friend Jim Schenk and his wife, Mary Fran, who were commuting weekly from Chicago to Birmingham, where Jim was working with an owner-operator. Both Jim and Mary Fran were disciples of the management principles of

Peter Drucker, and Jim had introduced me to Drucker's management theories when I was still in Chicago. The Schenks were both skilled at identifying obstacles that affected customer service, and Mary Fran was particularly adept at developing and implementing practical strategies. So I got in touch with them and shared my concerns. They volunteered to help, arriving in Nashville two days after my call. They spent a morning observing the store and talking with employees. When I joined them in the dining room after lunch, I had my notepad with me, ready to take copious notes. But Mary Fran said, "You don't need that notebook. The solution is simple, and it's no more than forty-eight hours away."

She and Jim spoke highly of the quality and dedication of my team members and their superior knowledge of operations. "But they're taking pride in their technical ability to run the store," Mary Fran said in her soft-spoken way, "not in their ability to take care of the customer." Jim told me to forget about mechanics—the temperatures and calibrations, the stock rotation, cleaning, and maintenance—because the crew had it all down pat. "The processes and procedures are in place," he said. "You've got it right; now leave it alone. You've got a team who will make sure new people get it. Start focusing on customer service only. That's it, nothing else." Mary Fran added that concentrating on customer service would also raise technical skills because the team would see how technical excellence improved service.

I recalled Walter Pitchford once saying, "Everything's so simple until it gets complicated." The obstacle wasn't in production; it was in my over-emphasis on production. Basically, I had complicated things by training my people too well in the techniques, and they were so intent on perfect production that the whole process was slowed. I had been searching for the solution in the trees, and the

312

Schenks had opened my eyes to the forest. When Albert Einstein had said that no problem can be solved by the consciousness that created it, he could have been talking straight to me.

I immediately communicated the new focus on service to all the crew who were in the store that day and put a notice on the bulletin board. I was excited and so was the team. A few hours later, after I had taken the Schenks to the airport, I returned to the store and could already see positive effects. The dayside crew was no less efficient, but they were faster. And exactly as Jim and Mary Fran had predicted, the daysiders were also explaining the change to the nightside crew members who were arriving. Within twenty-four hours, the service quality and speed were more than adequate. Over the next week, we had numerous mini-sessions and creative rap sessions about our responsibilities to the customer. That's also when I began to emphasize the service discussions in new employee training. As we picked up speed, service in general continued to improve from acceptable to superior. It became fun to get a positive reaction from every customer, without exception. When our customers began to comment favorably on the change, I knew that we had gotten the right balance between mechanics and principles. We were really knocking their socks off!

A Different Kind of Leadership

On a Friday evening about a year after opening the Clarksville Highway Store, I was at home when I got a call from Roland Long, the regional manager of the Indianapolis region, which included Nashville. He told me that on the following Tuesday, the company would be taking over the existing McDonald's in downtown Nashville, the business center of the city. He wanted me to be there

313

for inventory on Tuesday night and to open the store on Wednesday—as its new owner. As the cliché goes, my jaw dropped. *Whoa!* I thought. *What are they trying to get me into?*

It wasn't the offer of the store that threw me; it was the turnaround time. I knew about the restaurant and the difficulties the current owner had been dealing with. Located at 237 Fifth Avenue North, the Downtown McDonald's was walk-in only. There was no parking or drive-thru. It operated weekdays from 7:00 a.m. to 6:00 p.m. and on Saturdays from 10:00 a.m. to 6:00 p.m. It served basically a lunchtime clientele of city workers. Virtually no one lived in the center of the city, and there was relatively little night life. So the chance of increasing the store's already low volume was slim, yet occupancy, operation, and overhead expenses were high. Inside McDonald's, it was the kind of store known to most of us as a "dog" because of its history of poor performance, both operationally and financially.

Gathering my wits, I told Roland that I needed a little more time and that the following Thursday might work. I wasn't concerned about operating the store; I had managers and crew at Clarksville Highway who were anticipating opportunities for advancement and were well prepared to step in, and we could quickly adjust work schedules. But I needed to find out more about the economics of the deal, so I got in touch with Gerry Newman, the financing dynamo who had done so much to pull other faltering stores out of the red through financial restructuring and creative loan programs. I knew Gerry wouldn't lead me wrong, and he came through with a very satisfactory financing arrangement. I also knew that I was being offered a "dog" that nobody else wanted, and I decided that I could handle the challenge. Most important to me, the store would provide much-needed opportunities to promote talented managers and crew from Clarksville Highway and give them a challenge worthy of their skills.

We took over and opened under new ownership exactly one week after I got the call from Roland Long. The change went smoothly, and we immediately began implementing all the principles and standards that were working so well at Clarksville Highway. Because of its location, the Downtown store store never broke any sales records, but we worked hard to increase lunchtime traffic and had a lot of fun transforming the restaurant from a loser into a consistently profitable operation.

Practically overnight, I became a multi-store owner—a situation that required altering my personal mindset. I recalled a comment that Ralph Kelly, the Detroit owner and first president of NBMOA (the nationalized Black McDonald's Operators Association) had made in one of the training videos we produced in Urban Operations. Ralph said that every new operator should spend four seasons in his first store. I had done that: winter, spring, summer, and fall, I'd worked in the Clarksville Highway store, not only training and implementing policies and procedures but also rolling up my sleeves and doing whatever chores needed doing. I took a little time away to attend the inaugural master's class at Hamburger University in the spring of 1977, but for the most part, I had spent every day in my first store or out in the community making local contacts that benefited the store.

I remember being in the store one day when a car pulled onto the lot and a familiar-looking man got out on the passenger side. I thought he looked a lot like Ed Schmitt. Then I realized it was Ed, and Mike Quinlan was with him. The last time I had visited with the two of them together was back in Chicago when I was a field consultant. Now Ed was president of the corporation, Mike was a senior vice president, and I was an owner. When I showed Ed and Mike the store and introduced them to the crew and a few of our regular customers, I felt incredibly proud of what we were achieving. After our reunion, as my two special guests were leaving, Mike called out to me, "You need more whites on your crew." He hadn't forgotten my frequent complaints that we needed more blacks in the regional office. It was a joke we shared, but it also got me wondering how I could bring more diversity to the store.

As a result of Mike's joke, I called Dianna Earing, who, with her then husband, owned and operated three Nashville city stores. She came to dinner at Clarksville Highway, and we discussed ways to get more racial diversity in our stores. We put together an employee exchange program, sending workers to each other's restaurants during high traffic times. The success of that program was indicative of future collaborations and the start of a long and productive business friendship. And none of it might have happened if I hadn't been in my store when Ed and Mike paid their surprise visit.

Now, however, as the owner of two franchises, I had to think beyond the store and re-envision my role. Owning a single store is highly entrepreneurial in nature, hands-on, and grounded entirely in that one operation. Operating more than one store necessitates a change in perspective, and it wasn't long after getting the Downtown store that I came to grips with my new responsibilities as a businessman.

During my first year, I hadn't been too concerned about my financing, although I did want to keep my store out of my divorce negotiations, which were underway when I arrived in Nashville. Gerry Newman and Don Horwitz, McDonald's General Counsel, had crafted an agreement, similar to a lease-purchase contract, with the company, and this would bridge the period between my acquisition of the Clarksville Highway store and arranging a business loan locally. No one expected that I would have any difficulties getting the loan, but I did, and I am still not certain why.

I didn't know anybody in the city's banks, so a multi-store McDonald's owner, Frank Chalfont, personally introduced me to officers at his two banks. The first bank turned me down flat. The second bank offered financing at the maximum interest rate allowable under Tennessee law—an offer that made no sense, given that I was already operating a profitable restaurant with large average bank balances, had come to them on the recommendation of one of their valued customers, and had the full support of America's leading food service corporation. I understood that the offer was the bank's way of telling me they didn't really want my business, and I walked away from it. I ran into similar responses at every other Nashville bank I approached. To be generous, it's possible that the bankers were shy about financing a new business in a black area near housing projects with a reputation for lawlessness. Fear of a business failure? Concern about securing the loan? I don't know, because I was never given a clear explanation. Or was it because I was a black man seeking funds from white loan committees in large but still provincial Southern institutions? I don't like to jump to conclusions that can't be verified, but I have to believe that racism may have played some part in some of the rejections I got. Nashville's black-owned bank was not sufficiently capitalized to meet my total financial needs for the business and position me to maintain adequate cash reserves. I could have taken a smaller loan with them, plus a loan with one of the high-interest-charging white-owned banks, but I preferred to have one bank for all my business dealings.

I wanted to get my financing settled, so I decided to forget the local banks and approached Hyde Park Bank in Chicago. I had

317

established a relationship with their Urban Development department a few years earlier, when Herman Petty was financing the buyout of his "salt and pepper" partners. I had also referred a number of new franchisees to the bank, and those arrangements had worked out very well. When I was in Chicago, I had regularly communicated with the bank's Urban Development people in relation to minority economic issues. So I had no difficulty getting the financing from Hyde Park Bank. Still, I continued to pursue financing in Nashville, without success. Then Dianna Earing took up the cause.

Originally from Detroit, Dianna and her husband had come to Nashville about the same time as I and purchased three existing franchisees. They had gotten their loan from the same bank that offered me the high-interest loan, although their interest rate was substantially lower. Dianna was the driving force of their business. There were only two real differences between Dianna and me as owners: She was white, and my franchises were more productive. In addition to the employee exchange program, we had combined forces in other areas—she assisted me with administrative matters, and I helped her with store operations, management, and training. When a different bank in town courted her for her business, she asked if I wanted to come into the deal. I was ready to give it a try. Dianna made it clear to the bank that she would close on her new loan only if it included re-financing my loan, which was currently at Hyde Park Bank. I figured it would be a slam dunk, in light of the strength of my financial position after nearly two years of successful operations with large, daily cash balances, plus a strong equity position. (I was borrowing only for the Clarksville Highway store, since the financing arrangement for the Downtown store was with McDonald's Corporation.) Dianna's bank agreed to her conditions, and it looked as if I would finally get my local loan. But the loan officer had one more hurdle for me to jump.

My parents had recently moved to Nashville, and I had arranged a Veterans Administration loan for the purchase of their new house. Their house was therefore listed as one of my assets. Dianna closed on her loan, and I went to the bank a couple of days later for my closing. Before I signed, however, the loan officer asked me to include my parents' home as security. I told him I would have to think it over; then I left the bank with the papers still unsigned and went straight to Dianna's office. When she heard what had happened, she called the banker and pitched a fit. He apologized, and the next day I got a call asking me to come in "at my earliest convenience" and complete the closing on the original terms. From that point forward, my parents' house was never mentioned again. I had become a valued customer, and despite the shaky start, all my future dealings with the bank went smoothly.

I tell this story to illustrate two points: the importance of persistence when confronted with seemingly insurmountable obstacles and the value of *sincere* friendships in business. Dianna didn't have to go out on a limb for me, but she didn't hesitate to help when she saw the situation I was in. I would do the same for her. It seems to me that sincerity is often lacking in business relationships today. Networking has become a tactic, and too many people have lost the concept of mutual benefit. When the objective of a business relationship is "What can I get *from* you?" rather than "What can I do *for* you?" nobody benefits.

The financing hassle is also an example of the kind of issues I was dealing with as an owner. When I was in the regional and corporate offices, I had helped plenty of franchisees with similar situations, but I had never before done it for myself. That's what I mean about changing my mindset; I had to think like an owner and consider what was best for *my* business. In the early days of getting

319

the Clarksville Highway store going, I was focused on immediate concerns—daily sales, cash reserve, and heavy expenses that wouldn't wait for me to develop an adequate cash flow. Not long after the store opened, we were hit by an energy crisis, and the Middle Tennessee McDonald's Co-op responded with a drastic, across-the-board reduction in store operating hours. Established owners had the cash reserves to cover the losses in revenue, but I was the new kid on the block, and I was concerned about survival if the crisis went on for weeks or months. It was during those sleepless nights that I began to shift my thinking from *what is* (in this instance, an event beyond my control) to *what can be* (the return to regular operating hours, followed by huge sales increases and a big bank balance). Yes, I had to keep one foot firmly in the present, but I also needed to step into the future. I had to have a clear image of the future that would guide me through the problems of the moment. Fortunately, the energy crisis passed, and we returned to our normal hours after a week. Sales increased beyond my expectations. I'd had a scare, but by altering my vision, I hadn't panicked. I learned a lesson in leadership. As a business owner, I was the keeper of the vision.

One consequence of this change in mindset was that I became a lot more cautious about spending money. McDonald's was always offering owners new and innovative programs, but I remembered Fred Turner once advising owners not to buy everything the company was selling. Now that the financial risk was all mine, I finally understood the logic of his remark. Every new idea from the company had the potential to be rewarding, but not for every owner in every market all the time. Acquiring the latest piece of high-tech equipment, for example, is a temptation (the kid-in-the-candy-store syndrome), but a businessperson has to do cost-benefit analysis. He or she needs to weigh the cost of the new equipment against its potential to increase sales, and project its compatibility with long-term objectives. I found myself increasingly focused on setting long-term priorities and gauging every expenditure against those goals. It became much easier for me to take a pass on a shiny new piece of equipment or a novel, local store marketing program when I viewed it in the context of the actual, long-range benefit to my stores, my customers, and my bottom line. The vision of the future of the business became the baseline for my decision making.

Not all of my priorities could be measured in dollars and cents. Peter Drucker said that a healthy business cannot exist in a sick society, and I believe that. Contributing to local projects that would improve the community as a whole rarely produce immediate and tangible benefits. But I see the donation of time, talent, and financial support as an investment in the health of the community. With that in mind, it wasn't difficult to forgo expenditures that would have only marginal, short-term returns for the store and, instead, to direct resources to community-based projects and programs with the potential to make life better for my neighbors, my employees, and our customers.

Ray Kroc always said that a good business gives back to its community, and when McDonald's became successful, he was incredibly generous, personally and through the corporation, to worthy causes. I remembered how Herman Petty and many other black owners I had worked with had insisted on involvement in their communities. I guess I combined Peter Drucker's wisdom with the models of Mr. Kroc and owners like Herman. Well before I was financially secure as an owner, I made the community a priority. Maybe it went back to my dad's emphasis on living the Golden Rule and to my roots in a small, country town where people didn't have a lot but were always willing to share with a neighbor. I just didn't see how I could succeed if the people around me were failing. I had long preached that a standout business elevates its neighborhood. Becoming an owner and learning to think into the future, I enlarged my definition of "standing out" to include standing up for the betterment of the community. What was good for everybody was good for business.

As time went on, I felt confident that my priorities were right on track. I wasn't as active in day-to-day operations, which was my first love. But with smart, well-trained, and super-dedicated managers, I knew that both my stores were in good hands. To avoid isolating myself, I continued to be active in orientations and some aspects of training. My focus, however, was more and more on growing the business. For every franchisee, growth meant acquiring additional stores. For black and minority owners in urban centers— where populations in those days were either static or declining— growth also meant having the opportunity to expand into suburban markets. *Expansion was the key*, but as we entered the 1980s, that key was being dangled just beyond the reach of our black hands. Across the country, black and minority owners were trying to cross the old urban-suburban boundary line, yet the company was holding us back. Individually, we were stuck in place. Collectively? Well, we already had the organization.

Back to NBMOA

I had been a part of the Black McDonald's Operators Association since its beginning. Some people credit me with founding the organization, but it was a group effort, so I think of myself as one of the founding fathers, entrusted with a key leadership role. Until I came to Nashville, however, I had never been a member. The summer before I left Chicago, the association had gone national, and among the first things I did as a new McDonald's owner was pay my dues and sign on with NBMOA, and my fellow members were there to help and support me when I got my Clarksville Highway store going. That first year, I wasn't able to participate as much as I had when I was in Chicago, but I stayed involved in an advisory capacity. It was around the time of my one-year anniversary in Nashville that Ralph Kelly selected me to serve as NBMOA's first member of the McDonald's National Operators Advisory Board (NOAB); in that position, I represented all minority owner-operators. The next year, Carl Osborne succeeded Ralph as NBMOA president, and Carl soon had me hopping. Over the two years of his presidency, I advised other members much as I'd done as a field consultant, attended meetings with corporate management, traveled to help out members as they had helped me, and made a number of speeches for the organization. I also evaluated and trained a substantial number of potential minority franchisees for McDonald's Corporation in my Nashville stores. I didn't have an elected position, but I just couldn't say "no" to Carl, and besides, I really had fun getting back in the swing.

At the 1980 NBMOA convention, held in Chicago, I was elected president, and I almost immediately got into some hot water. Mike Quinlan, who had been elevated to president of McDonald's USA that year, came to accept an award for Ray Kroc, and I was on the stage when Mike made a few comments that I took issue with. He seemed to be saying, as a veteran owner later put it, that the corporation was doing us a big favor. Corporate people often projected the attitude that the company is the more important partner in the relationship with franchisees. I had thought that way myself before we got BMOA operating in the Midwest and Mideast regions. Working collaboratively with the BMOA members, however, I saw that the company and the owners are equally important to the success of McDonald's—just as Mr. Kroc said again and again. Without intending to, Mike seemed to me to be affirming the myth that owners were obligated to the corporation without acknowledging that the company owed an equal responsibility to the owners. There was no racism in Mike's comments, but I knew that for black and minority owners, the sense of being beholdin' to the head guys in Chicago can be demeaning, dispiriting, and, worse, disabling.

Since I was right there, next on the agenda to speak, I expressed my point of view. Later, I realized that my tone sounded more aggressive than necessary, but I was just talking to Mike in the way we had often debated similar issues in private. Mike didn't take offense, but some NBMOA members, especially new members who didn't know that Mike and I were old friends, perceived our exchange as a fight between the new president of the company and the new president-elect of NBMOA. They worried that my response might damage the relationship between the company and the organization and even affect the members directly. Nobody approached me, but there was a lot of behind-the-scenes conversation about "the fight." Somebody even theorized that Mike and I had been drunk, showing how little they knew about us. Older members did their best to explain Mike's and my friendship and put my comments in the context of the history of BMOA and NBMOA. But it was Ken Allison, a recent franchisee in Southern California and a new member of NBMOA, who really laid the controversy to rest. As it was reported to me, Ken told a group that "it's not wise to elect a president with knowledge and experience and expect him to keep his mouth closed." After that, common sense won out, and when Mike again addressed the convention in 1982, I introduced him by giving the members some background. I told them how Mike had participated in the first BMOA

324

convention in 1972 as a "lightweight field service manager" and that he was still with us as the "heavyweight president." In his remarks, Mike told the audience how I had trained him to be a field consultant. To this day, I remember the good feeling I got when my old friend said, "Without Roland Jones, you [NBMOA members] would be five, maybe even ten years behind where you are today. We all owe him a lot."

Something else unexpected happened at the 1980 convention that helped to set the tone for NBMOA in the new decade. Walter Williams, an African American economist, had been invited to be keynote speaker at the main banquet. Tom Burrell attended, as always, and he brought a guest to the pre-banquet reception. It was Benjamin Hooks—a Memphis native, a lawyer and former judge, an ordained minister, a former FCC commissioner, and the current executive director of the NAACP—whom we all knew for his leadership in the civil rights movement. I had first met Ben when I was a boy and he, then a young lawyer, came to speak in my dad's suburban Memphis church. I had heard him speak a number of times since, so Carl Osborne and I convinced him to stay for dinner and make a few comments to the group. Walter Williams gave his speech, which was as dull as a spreadsheet and full of conservative politics that didn't go down very well. It was Ben Hooks, talking off the cuff, who brought the members to their feet and left us with a message that stimulated me and others to think in a new direction. He told us to keep our focus on self-help and group solidarity, and he also challenged us to look beyond the group and use our growing strength as a black business organization to benefit the wider community. Before he left that night, I made sure to get Ben's commitment to speak at our next convention.

I had been thinking a good deal about what Ben said when I started my two-year presidency at the beginning of 1981. He'd made

325

me realize that NBMOA was growing and that the time had come to direct our attention outward. His remarks had reminded me of Peter Drucker's observations about healthy businesses and healthy communities. I had preached Drucker's wisdom to every franchisee I'd worked with and brought it to my own stores in Nashville—and I knew it was true. But how would it work for NBMOA? How could we look out our front door and see not only our individual neighborhoods but also our nation as our community?

My more immediate concern, however, was to carry forward the work of my immediate predecessors: Ralph Kelly, who had done such a superb job of implementing the organizational structure adopted when the group went national in 1976, and Carl Osborne, who had brought even more focus to the issue of black consumer marketing and forged closer ties between NBMOA and the McDonald's corporate structure. The organizational structure—officers and board, duties, and so on—was proving excellent, largely because the Detroit members had devised the overall structure to conform to the organization of McDonald's and, in particular, the National Operators Advisory Board. However, I had become aware of the need for improvements in the group's functional structure.

I was concerned that within the organizational structure, we now needed to function more professionally, firm up the membership, and put NBMOA on a solid financial footing. When I was so busy helping Carl during the previous two years, I had realized how much time and out-of pocket money the group's officers and the most active members were spending to make NBMOA an effective national organization. Membership dues were $200 a year, and even if everyone had been paid up, those dues were not enough to fund a travel and expenses budget. So anyone who traveled for NBMOA did so on his own dime. My own travel expenses prior to and during my presidency amounted to more than $20,000, on top of my out-out-pocket costs for other expenditures related to running the organization. And I can't begin to estimate how many thousands of dollars we all spent on long-distance phone bills. I didn't expect or want reimbursement, though several members graciously made the offer, because I didn't begrudge spending the money myself. But reimbursements wouldn't solve anything; we needed innovative ideas to arrive at a permanent solution. Without long-term changes, each president and every officer and board member who succeeded me would face greater personal obligations—time and money—as NBMOA grew, and there was a real danger that the organization would suffer when capable members were no longer able or willing to shoulder the personal and financial burdens on a voluntary basis.

It seemed to me that part of the solution lay in spreading responsibilities more evenly throughout the organization and making better use of the talents of our members. Because I wanted as many good minds as possible working on these and other key issues, I worked with the board to establish committees and task forces, each chaired by a board member and each focused on achieving goals set by the board. Committee and task force members were drawn from the general membership. We appointed standing committees for insurance and financial planning, government relations and public affairs, operations and training, communications, hospitality, and NOAB (this last committee charged with providing input on black owners' issues to McDonald's national owners board). There were also three task forces: corporate relations, employee relations, and purchasing. I won't go into the specific responsibilities, but in general, the assignments were designed to build and improve functional ties with the corporation and among NBMOA members, to increase awareness of and response to minority needs and concerns, and to enhance the flow of information to and from all NBMOA members.

One of the first achievements of this committee structure was the newsletter, which was developed by Osborne Payne, a multi-store owner in Baltimore who was secretary of NBMOA and chaired the communications committee. Osborne and his committee created a quarterly publication that functioned as an information clearinghouse. The emphasis was on articles that conveyed important information to owners and stories of owners who were making innovative improvements in the field. It was a means of introducing members to the organization leadership and to each other and informing members about whom to contact when they needed help. For example, if Mack Wilbourn, an owner in Atlanta, needed help with an operations problem, he could pick up the phone and consult with Ed Benson, co-chairman of the operations and training committee, in DeSoto, Texas. In the January 1, 1981, newsletter, put out when I took over as president, the officers and board members were profiled, and their addresses and phone numbers were listed. Looking over that issue of the newsletter, I remembered that we all included our home as well as our business numbers. That was before answering machines and caller ID, so no matter what time of day or night we got a call, we answered it. I don't think it occurred to any of us that we were ever off-duty when it came to responding to our fellow members.

The committee/task force structure enabled us to implement self-help among more members with wider geographical distribution. As the number of members increased, we also encouraged frequent contacts among owners in each zone—the management structure instituted by Ed Schmitt for the corporation and mirrored in the NBMOA structure. Open communication was the key to self-help, and we wanted it to flow in all directions.

Adequately funding the organization, however, continued to be problematic. At an October 1981 membership business meeting, our treasurer, John Perry, gave a stark accounting of our finances. He informed the members of the amounts of uncompensated expenses incurred by the officers and board members in the previous year—averaging above $4,000 per person, with my costs running three times that amount. John also explained how, for the previous five years, a few members had been subsidizing the group in the early part of each year, before dues came in, and how reimbursements of these expenses were often delayed for months. John emphasized the difficulty of continuing to run NBMOA for the amount of money paid in dues. Much of what John said that day was new to most members, and his pull-no-punches assessment helped set the stage for a major restructuring of dues. The board worked on the solution for several months, and we presented our proposal at a specially called meeting of NBMOA members held during the McDonald's operators convention in San Francisco in April 1982. (The NBMOA meeting was not part of the McDonald's convention; we simply scheduled our activities to coincide with the larger gathering.) The increase in dues was steep—from $200 a year per owner to $500 for single store owners, $700 for owners with two stores, and $900 for owners with three or more stores. It was a real tribute to the importance of the organization that the members agreed to the change unanimously. Not just that; they all paid the new dues in record time. By the end of my presidency, we had 100 percent member participation.

With our revised functional structure, improved communications network, and sound financial position, I felt that NBMOA was now ready for the challenges of the new decade. I had not forgotten Ben Hooks's impromptu remarks at the 1980 convention. The time was ripe for NBMOA to begin looking outward

329

as well as inward. We needed stronger links with organizations and individuals who were serving blacks and other minorities in the business, political, and social arenas beyond McDonald's.

My first convention as president was held in October 1981 in Houston, Texas, and our theme was "Building Profits and Progressing Together." Ben Hooks came, as he'd promised to a year earlier. Other special guests included U.S. Congressman Mickey Leland of Texas, Dr. Ben Wright, the associate director of the federal Small Business Administration, and NBMOA's own Bill Pickard of Detroit, who had been elected vice chair of the Michigan Republican Party. Bill was part of a very interesting panel on the relationship between the federal government and black-owned businesses. That panel also included Cliff Raeber, vice president of Government Relations for McDonald's, and Bill Armstrong of Fort Lauderdale, who was vice president of NBMOA and chaired the government relations committee.

We also marked a kind of milestone—a somber one—at the 1981 convention. Dr. Ben Davis of St. Louis had died, the first NBMOA member to pass away, and we were all shocked and grieved. "Doc" Davis had been one of the first BMOA members outside of Chicago, and no one had given more unselfishly of himself to assist other black owners as they learned the realities of business. He had been a friend and a mentor at every turn. Losing him went so much deeper than his contributions to the organization. It touched our hearts, as "Doc" had touched our lives.

In 1982, we convened in New York City, and again our list of guest speakers included influential business and government leaders. Walter Fauntroy, a Baptist minister and civil rights activist who had represented Washington, D.C., in the House of Representatives for more than a decade and was chairman of the Congressional Black

Caucus, was the keynote speaker at our banquet. Clarence Mitchell III, a Maryland state senator and chairman of the National Black Caucus of State Legislators, addressed a luncheon session. So did Edward Frantel, president of the Seven-Up Company and a vice president of Philip Morris. Speakers of this caliber helped us improve our understanding of the interrelatedness of business, government, and social policy. Just as important, I think, was the impact that learning from and sharing with national leaders had on us, as a group. Though most of our activities focused on helping one another succeed as McDonald's operators, it became clear that NBMOA was gaining national stature. Almost without our realizing it, we had created one of the country's first, unified, national networks of black businesspeople, and movers and shakers outside McDonald's were paying attention. As a group, we were rubbing shoulders with the traditional "old boy" business organizations and acquiring the kind of clout that would benefit us and create opportunities for others.

We also continued to strengthen our ties with the corporation. Our new committee structure, which mirrored the departmental divisions in McDonald's, made communication much easier. NBMOA committee members consulted directly with the corresponding department executives in the company, peer to peer. NBMOA now had a permanent seat on the McDonald's National Operators Advisory Board, and we began looking forward to the day when a black person would be appointed to the corporate Board of Directors. Another key link was forged during my days as director of Urban Operators. I had very close ties with senior management, and those working relationships continued during my NBMOA presidency. Recognizing the importance of such ongoing communication with NBMOA's leadership, McDonald's soon instituted a policy of designating a senior executive to serve as liaison

331

with future NBMOA presidents. This made collaboration between the company and NBMOA official. Our corporate partner stayed in close contact and channeled information about the organization's needs and concerns to other senior managers in the company. Don Horwitz was the first corporate liaison, followed by Pat Flynn. I still consider these guys and Mel Hopson, the corporate Affirmative Action director, to be as much a part of the NBMOA team as our members.

People who do the hard work deserve recognition, and we had honored our own over the years with various awards. By 1982, however, we realized that we needed to consolidate. As Osborne Payne, the board secretary, said, NBMOA awards should be few in number, hard to earn, and precious to recipients and the membership. So the board instituted three annual awards: the Outstanding Store Award and the Special Achievement Award, both given to members, and the Corporate Award to honor an individual in the McDonald's Corporation who had demonstrated superior understanding of and commitment to NBMOA and all black owners. There was no question who should receive our first Corporate Award—Ed Schmitt. The next year's recipient was Gerry Newman. Although both men held lofty positions in the company (Ed was president and Gerry was executive vice president and chief accounting officer), there was nothing political about their selection; no one in NBMOA was trying to curry favor. We wanted to express our gratitude publicly to the two men who had championed black and minority ownership at every step on the road to integration and who continued to be our strongest corporate allies. Those of us who had been around for a while knew in our hearts that without Ed's unwavering support, NBMOA might never have come into being. Without Gerry, the business survival of our members would have been a lot more difficult.

When I handed over the presidency to Lee Dunham at the end

of 1982, I was confident that NBMOA was in very good shape in terms of structural organization and our relations with the corporation. Far from being the splinter group that Fred Turner and a few others in the company had once feared, NBMOA had established a collaborative relationship with the company and maintained clear, open lines of communication with most regional and corporate management. We were well prepared to tackle the challenges ahead, and we already had a good idea about what those challenges would be.

Chapter 12

Expansion on the Front Burner

To succeed, one must be creative and persistent.
JOHN H. JOHNSON, COMMUNICATIONS ENTREPRENEUR

During my term as president of NBMOA, an issue that had been simmering for years began to come to the boil—expansion. The ability to expand by acquiring more stores in one's market was the carrot that always dangled at the end of the corporation's stick. Every owner in the system, regardless of his or her color, knew that expansion spelled the difference between SUCCESS and **SUCCESS!** McDonald's owners who reaped the largest financial rewards were multi-store operators, so whenever a store became available, the competition to get it could be fierce. For us black owners, expansion was also the key to developing a strong pool of trained and skilled black managers at the store level and maybe even feeding the pipeline into McDonald's regional and corporate management, which was now a major concern for NBMOA.

Expansion had been one of the issues that sparked rebellion by a number of white owners—the MOA revolt—in the late 70s. My first experience of the power of expansion came in 1972, when the veiled

334

threat of denying expansion was used to prevent black owners in the Mideast region from participating in that year's Chicago BMOA convention. Expansion really became a serious concern for the early wave of black owners, however, after they had stabilized their urban restaurants and were financially and operationally prepared to take on additional stores. With the increasing number of black owners and the company's overall growth throughout the 70s, inner-city black ownership was approaching a saturation point, at which the number of viable locations for hardcore urban stores would plateau. To expand, black owners needed access to city business districts, the urban fringes, and the suburbs. The hitch was that McDonald's showed little inclination to give experienced black owners the opportunity to purchase stores outside the hardcore urban areas. Understandably, a lot of NBMOA members viewed this unwritten policy as blatant racism. But after I became an owner, I began to understand that expansion was a much more complicated problem.

Based on what I saw and what I experienced, I have to say that *politics* played a greater role in expansion than racism. I don't mean governmental politics. I'm talking about the kind of political maneuvering, manipulation, and plain old brown-nosing that goes on in most large businesses. "Neil," the Chicago regional manager who nearly ended my career in McDonald's before Ed Schmitt stepped in, was a classic corporate politician, though to the degree that he relied on politics instead of actual performance, he was not typical of McDonald's corporate management. As head of Urban Operations, I had heard a lot about owners' difficulties with regional management. The lesson really came home to me when, as an owner in Nashville, I started seeing the game playing first-hand and then became embroiled in it myself.

Basically, the problems were at the regional level, where the regional managers had total autonomy in decisions about site location and franchisee selection. The corporation set the general criteria for determining whether an existing franchisee could acquire additional restaurants. These criteria included an owner's financial capability; a positive track record of operating his or her existing store, or stores, at an average grade level of B; and management depth and training adequate to handle expansion. I always knew that the goal of McDonald's senior management was to protect and maintain the integrity of the system, the brand name, and customer loyalty. The general guidelines came from the top, and they made good sense to me. But the guidelines were enacted lower down the chain of command, and a great deal of control rested with field service managers and field consultants. Regional managers made the final decision about store locations and franchising, but they relied on information provided by field service managers and field consultants.

The consultants controlled the grading of the stores, which opened the process to political games. Most field consultants didn't play politics and did their job well. But a few used their inspection and grading power to reward or punish franchisees. More often, however, some field consultants would use their power to push their personal agendas for advancement or what they perceived as the agendas of the higher-ups or to gain favor with white owners, who made up the majority of owners in most territories.

I really think that the old unwritten policy of keeping black owners in the urban centers and the white owners in the suburbs was fading away at the senior corporate level and among most regional managers. Despite McDonald's open door communication, however, the executives in the Ivory Tower didn't always know the details of what was happening in the field, where most of the game playing went on. But it also seemed to me and other black owners that management at all levels did want to keep black ownership confined to the cities, especially the hardcore urban areas. It was difficult to place white owners in most urban stores—in part because white owners were still reluctant to go into predominately minority communities and in part because minority owners were generally much better at establishing strong ties with minority consumers and avoiding the kind of protests that had flared up in Cleveland in 1969. Memories of the 1968 riots after the assassination of Dr. Martin Luther King and the violence in Cleveland were still vivid for many of McDonald's senior managers.

From the mid-70s into the early 80s, corporate management was also dealing with the rebellious, white MOA owners, and in the aftermath of that threat, no one wanted to ruffle the feathers of any white owners who were trying to expand. To give a new or existing store to a black owner in a market where everyone wanted to expand ran the risk of alienating white owners. The upshot was that black owners were essentially *ghetto-ized*—held back from acquiring profitable or potentially profitable locations in middle-class and upper-class neighborhoods, even when those areas were inside the cities. About the only time a black owner was allowed to expand to a location beyond a hardcore urban area was when white owners expressed little or no interest in the site. I think this was part of the reason I was handed my second restaurant, in Nashville's downtown business district, in 1977. None of the other Nashville area owners showed any desire to take on such a troubled store. It's possible, too, that at the regional level and in some corners of the Ivory Tower, an old stereotype was still kicking around—that putting black owners, managers, and employees into certain white communities would offend white customers. Whether it was racism or just an outworn business mentality, McDonald's did what they thought was best to protect brand loyalty.

There was also an attitude problem among owners: Regardless of their color, too many felt that the company was doing them a favor when they were awarded additional franchises. Black and other minority owners were especially vulnerable to this kind of thinking and frankly too fearful of biting the hand that fed them. Out of the fear of losing future expansion opportunities, some owners took over poor performing stores, and this actually hurt their chances for further expansion. In the 1970s, few black owners raised a ruckus when they were denied expansion or given "dog" stores. But in the 80s, that attitude began to change, as more black owners starting standing up and demanding fair treatment.

Lee Dunham, who succeeded me as president of NBMOA, had been the first black owner in New York City, opening a store on 125th Street in Harlem in 1972. Lee was born in North Carolina and moved with his family to the Bedford Stuyvesant section of Brooklyn when he was a young teen. After a stint in the Air Force, he joined the New York City Police Department, and during his years with the NYPD, he also studied business and management. By the time he took early retirement from the police force, due to a back injury, Lee knew the city like the back of his hand. His McDonald's ownership, which had grown to six hardcore urban restaurants by the early 80s, and his generosity to the community demonstrated his commitment to what were then the most impoverished parts of the city. Lee, however, wanted to expand into Midtown and/or Lower Manhattan, which were the demographic equivalent of white suburbia in other cities.

There was probably nobody in the whole McDonald's system more qualified for expansion. By 1980, Lee's stores had received more of McDonald's coveted Outstanding Store Awards than any of the three hundred McDonald's in the tri-state area of New York, New Jersey, and Connecticut. During the time he was struggling to expand

338

and hitting brick walls, Lee was receiving the corporation's highest accolades including the Ronald McDonald Award for outstanding community service and the most prized honor an owner-operator could get, the Golden Arches Award for overall excellence in all categories. Lee exceeded every standard in the corporation's criteria for expansion. He was an influential leader in political and business circles in New York and eventually at the national level. When McDonald's needed help with some pending federal legislation, Lee would get a call from the corporation because he had the direct contacts with the Washington power brokers. Yet he was not granted a franchise in Midtown Manhattan until 1988—fifteen years after he first asked to expand his ownership into more desirable markets.

Osborne Payne ran into similar obstacles in Baltimore, where he owned four inner city stores. Osborne was the first black owner to receive the Golden Arches Award. He also received the Ronald McDonald Award, and his stores consistently got Triple A awards for operational excellence in QSC (quality, service, cleanliness—the McDonald's trinity). Osborne repeatedly requested expansion opportunities and at one point filed suit against the company, yet it never happened. When he sold his four stores and retired in the 1990s, it was out of frustration.

It's impossible to pinpoint a single reason for situations like Lee's and Osborne's and the many other black owners who had similar experiences. Some or all of the factors I have noted played into each case, especially the effects of regional-level politics and the company's reluctance to cause friction with the white owners. The variables in each case differed, and on occasion, the rationale became personal. That's what happened to Al Joyner, the Mobile, Alabama, owner who had brought his little boy to his first meeting with Ed Schmitt and me back in 1975. Al had saved two low-volume

McDonald's restaurants in Mobile, but primarily because of their locations, the stores were never going to be great performers, and Al needed to expand or relocate. Sometime in 1985, he had heard about the possibility of some stores becoming available in Jackson, Mississippi, so he wrote to Ed Rensi, the president of McDonald's USA. (Ed succeeded Mike Quinlan, who had moved up to president of the corporation.) Al didn't expect a phone call from Ed, but that's what he received. Ed didn't know Al personally; he was basing his judgment on reports from field people in the New Orleans region, which included Mobile. Al remembers exactly what Ed said to him: "Hell no, you will never expand. You've got to run AAA stores to prove that you're worthy."

Al had never gotten an F on a field report, and he knew his stores were operating well. He figured, correctly, that somebody in the region wanted him out of the system and was feeding bad information up the line. Al wasn't going to leave McDonald's, and he worked on relocating to California. When that didn't pan out, he set his sights on Birmingham, where one white owner had all the stores in the market. The Atlanta regional manager, who had charge of Birmingham, let Al know that he had enough black owners in his region and the best Al could hope for was one store. That's when Lee Dunham and I got involved. We went down to Mobile to see Al's stores and found out they were in fine shape. Then we went on to New Orleans and reported to the regional manager there, recommending that Al be allowed to expand or relocate. Al's problems also got attention from NBMOA, and Pat Flynn, our corporate liaison, stepped up to the plate, throwing his support behind Al. When Pat overrode the Atlanta regional manager's "one store only" dictate, Al sold his Mobile stores and got his first new store in a small rural town outside Birmingham. In the early 1990s, he began adding stores, assembling a chain of ten successful restaurants in the Birmingham area. In late 2004, he sold those stores and purchased twenty-two McDonald's restaurants in Jackson, where he had wanted to go in the first place. The story has a happy ending, but Al's struggle to expand stretched out for over a decade, and a less determined (or less loyal) owner might not have made it. It took a lot of character for Al to stick it out with McDonald's.

Ed Rensi recently confirmed his role in Al's story. Ed is one of the straightest shooters I know, and when he told Al to forget about expanding, he was not playing games. Unfortunately, he was trusting false or at least misleading reports from his regional field people. Ed must have come to have doubts about those reports, because sometime after he had basically written Al off, Ed sent Gordon Thornton, the director of Urban Operations, to investigate the situation in Mobile. Gordon returned with a very good assessment of Al personally and his operations, and Ed changed his mind. Not long ago, Ed told me that he had been completely wrong about Al, and he asked me to put that statement in my book.

What Al Joyner went through involved just about every problem black owners faced when they tried to expand: political intrigues at the regional level, regional concerns about offending white owners (in this case a long-time owner in Birmingham), and misperceptions about the objectives of senior executives that led to serious troubles for a black owner. The racism appeared to be real on the part of several regional managers. But in this instance, a persistent black owner, backed by his brothers and sisters in NBMOA, overcame. It didn't always work out that way.

Bill Armstrong, a former Bell Telephone Company employee in Detroit, opened his first McDonald's franchise in Ft. Lauderdale, Florida, in 1975. By 1978, he had been ready to expand for more than a year. A store just a few miles from his restaurant was available, but it was in a predominately white area. Instead of that nearby store, Bill was offered a franchise in a mostly black community in Miami. Bill was prepared to protest, but his regional consultant, Clint Gulley, advised him to take the offer in order to protect his future expansion opportunities.

Clint, who is African American, had moved into regional management from a supervisor's position over several company-owned stores in the St. Petersburg area. Well educated, with a master's degree in sociology—which gave him a good understanding of group dynamics—Clint came to McDonald's from Eastern Airlines. He had experienced a good deal of overt racism in his early days with McDonald's in Florida. He was very familiar with the regional political games and determined to buck the system when he could open more opportunities for black owners in Florida. His advice to Bill Armstrong was smart, in the context of what was going on in Florida in 1978. Clint knew that if Bill turned down the Miami expansion offer or made a fuss, he would be categorized as a troublemaker and possibly sacrifice any chance for future expansion. At that time, it was a matter of picking the right battles, and fighting against the Miami offer was a lost cause.

By 1985, however, Bill Armstrong was ready to stand up and fight when a new McDonald's, located four miles from his original Ft. Lauderdale store in an area that was approximately 70 percent African American and 30 percent Hispanic, was up for grabs. Bill wanted that store, but it went to another black man. The reason was pretty clear: The regional decision makers wanted more black owners but didn't want black owners in white areas. Bill's loyalty to the company and his track record as an owner didn't matter. If management gave the new Ft. Lauderdale store to him, they would have to find another store for the other black franchisee, and that would require them to put the franchisee in a white neighborhood. But if they awarded the new store to the other man, they would have two black owners in Ft. Lauderdale, both in minority locations. Presumably to appease Bill, they offered him another store in Miami—in one of the city's most notorious high-crime, hardcore areas. Bill wasn't about to let it go this time. He rejected this Miami offer and took his case to the corporate ombudsman, John Cooke. After reviewing the situation, John reversed the regional office's decision, and Bill Armstrong got the new store in Ft. Lauderdale.

At first glance, Bill's story also seems to have a happy ending. Not so. After the ombudsman's ruling, Bill wrote to his regional manager, recapping his expansion experiences. (Clint Gulley wasn't around at this time; he had gone to Chicago as a field service manager in 1982. For family reasons, Clint resigned from McDonald's in 1983, although he later came back as a McOpCo senior supervisor.) Bill's letter got a response that was laughable; the regional manager claimed that he had no idea that Bill wanted stores in white areas and that he thought Bill could do a better job in black areas. Later, Bill was told that although regional management was confident that he could run multiple businesses—Bill had acquired an Oldsmobile dealership in 1985—other black owners couldn't, and they didn't want to set a precedent. So they offered to buy out his three stores. In 1987, Bill sold to the company, for a price that was more than double the stores' actual value—showing just how far a few people at the regional level were willing to go to get him out.

Bill, who was my vice president when I headed up NBMOA, says that the problems and biases he encountered in McDonald's are very similar to those still plaguing minority franchisees in the auto industry, especially in the awarding of inferior and failing dealerships to blacks. Drawing on his experiences in NBMOA, he joined the Ford Minority Dealers Association and was almost immediately named to its executive board. He also serves on the executive board of the National Association of Minority Auto Dealers and has testified before Congress on the exclusion of minority owners by foreign-owned auto companies.

These stories could be multiplied many times over. The better we black owners did, the more obstacles were thrown in our way. I saw it happen again and again to black and minority owners, and I did everything I could, personally and through NBMOA, to help my friends and colleagues. Then it happened to me.

My Expansion Story

My expansion problems began after I opened a third store in Nashville early in 1980. Located in a predominately white but mixed, blue-collar neighborhood, the restaurant was referred to as the Richland Park store, because of its proximity to a popular public park. Parts of the neighborhood were regarded as pretty rough, and none of the white owners in Nashville was interested in the location, so it was offered to me by default. Being an optimist, I saw Richland Park as an opportunity for me, my managers, and our team. I was sure we could make it a standout store.

My third McDonald's restaurant, as it turned out, was my last. Throughout the 1980s, I did everything I could to expand my ownership, and by all of McDonald's traditional standards, I was an excellent candidate for expansion. My stores consistently performed at a high level in all categories and were truly representative of a model Ray Kroc operation. We had reclaimed the Downtown store from the operational failure of the previous ownership, maximized

344

sales and profits in all three stores, and maintained more than adequate cash reserves for expansion, as well as excellent banking relationships. Except for an occasional and brief operational valley, we were always at our best and among the best—at least, that's what our customers were saying.

Moreover, with our ongoing training program and opportunities created for employees to take on additional responsibilities and enter management, my stores had an unusually stable workforce in an industry characterized by high employee turnover. This meant that we were always prepared for expansion, with skilled managers and crews ready to go at virtually a moment's notice, as we had done with the Downtown store. A huge part of my desire to expand was to create new opportunities for my people and to retain those with potential for advancement *inside the McDonald's system*. I believed that, given the quality of the people we hired and promoted, we could be a significant source of minority and female candidates into the company's regional management pipeline.

So why was I stuck at three stores in the growing Nashville market? My own experiences and those of fellow NBMOA members, as we struggled to expand, were a daily reminder that the weak link in the corporate management structure was at the regional level, where expansion decisions were rife with politics. When I had been a regional consultant and then a field service manager, I had not participated in the kind of political jockeying I have described. Regional politics were part of the "old boy" mindset, and since black regional consultants and managers weren't "old boys," we were, for the most part, excluded from the power games, though they could affect our progress. (I didn't confront a serious game player until my encounter with "Neil" in the Chicago regional office.) In the early days, I think that being left out of the day-to-day petty politics was an

345

advantage. We could focus our energies on helping African American and other minority McDonald's owners succeed. We knew that every individual success opened the door wider to everyone else, and this understanding created extremely tight bonds between black owners and black regional consultants. As we began to move higher in the company, the bonds of loyalty strengthened—loyalty to each other and to McDonald's.

I've said before that I don't think the white corporate leadership ever fully comprehended the cultural differences between whites and minorities (or between men and women, for that matter), although NBMOA played a major role in identifying and creating awareness of the importance of diversity and encouraging the corporation to respond to our wishes and recommendations. When we had a convention or meeting with corporate, someone often got promoted, as in 1984 when Bob Beavers, a senior vice president by then, was named the first African American corporate board member from inside the company.

In the same vein, I don't believe the corporate leaders truly understood or appreciated the degree of loyalty that black owners, managers, and consumers felt for McDonald's. For most black owners, however, not being able to expand their ownership beyond hardcore urban areas tested that loyalty.

NBMOA became deeply involved in the expansion issue and the companion issue of parity as the 80s progressed. Parity for blacks and other minorities had actually been a concern even before the company had black owners, when blacks first achieved store management and then supervisory positions in McDonald's in D.C. I define parity as a level playing field, within McDonald's or any other organization. Parity is about *fairness*. The concept is a system driven solely by performance, with equal access to the system and equal opportunities within the system. Parity does *not* mean equal outcomes. It means that everyone starts on an equal footing, and what individuals achieve from that point forward is their own responsibility.

Ed Schmitt was a superb example of an executive who promoted and practiced unconditional people parity at every level. As long as I worked with him, I never knew Ed to get hung up on racial, ethnic, or cultural differences, much less petty politics. He hired the best people he could find, gave them the resources and support they needed, and let them do their jobs. When Cosmo Williams and I got the Big Brother program started in Urban Operations—with Ed's blessing—the plan was to mentor black assistant managers to prepare them for entry into regional and eventually corporate management. In other words, we were creating a network to get talented, young black people onto the playing field. We couldn't guarantee that each person would succeed; our goal was to give them the opportunity, on a par with white people, to try.

For owners, parity revolved around a number of issues: sales volume, cash flow, profits, number of stores, the consumer marketplace, and marketing. Beginning in 1969, when black owners were first brought into troubled hardcore urban areas, they had been at a disadvantage in all these areas. It was a lot harder to succeed in old and frequently rundown stores, which had often been purchased at prices higher than actual value, in low-income areas, where consumers didn't have much disposable income. Most senior executives in the corporation failed to comprehend that the financial and operational obstacles facing black and other minority owners in hardcore locations were very different from the situations of owners in the predominately white, middle-class suburbs. If ownership were a football game, minority owners were in the position of a team starting the game without helmets and padding. Lacking the essential assets, too many minority owners were being tackled even before the ball was put in play.

Over the years, various fixes had been applied to specific problems, such as Gerry Newman's innovative program of financial restructurings and rent adjustments for struggling minority owner-operators. But there had never been a broad consensus in corporate that the playing field was not level for minority owners in general. The demand for advertising that appealed to black consumers was the first instance of black owners actively seeking parity. Carl Osborne introduced us to the word then, and he continued to emphasize parity in consumer marketing during his NBMOA presidency and his entire career with McDonald's. Yet as the number of black and other minority owners increased and we went into more markets (often into the most difficult locations in a market), the disparities became more obvious and more galling. Although parity concerns varied from place to place, there was a general lack of access to the assets, resources, and opportunities—including expansion—that were routinely available to white owners.

Because I stayed very active in NBMOA, I saw how the lack of expansion affected individual owners, like myself. It wasn't an isolated problem; it impacted owners throughout the country—men and women who had struggled for years, against the odds, to save McDonald's position in the cities and who had earned their shot at the financial rewards that expansion offered. There were a few exceptions here and there, but why were most of us black owners held back? I don't believe there was a single motive, and I know there was not any kind of official corporate policy against black expansion. McDonald's corporate leadership had committed to diversity in the 1970s and had taken risks that other major national businesses were afraid of.

348

McDonald's black consumer marketing is a good example of corporate risk taking. I was recently reminded that McDonald's was also the first to feature disabled people in its national advertising, which was another risky move back then. Perhaps, if expansion decisions had been made at the highest level of the company, the situation might have been different for minority owners.

There's no question in my mind that racism did play a role in a number of decisions at the regional level. However, it was a different, more subtle kind of racism than I had run into back in the 60s. I believe that many regional consultants and managers were still afraid of angering white owners, who were also seeking to expand, by allowing black owners to have stores in urban fringe and suburban areas. At the same time, white owners had not shown themselves willing to take on stores in hardcore urban locations, and some regional managers feared the consequences of letting minority owners have access to traditionally white areas: If we left the city centers, who would fill the void? There was also a more paternalistic attitude that we black owners should be content to continue serving the urban poor and not dilute our resources by running suburban stores. There were, as well, implications that we couldn't compete successfully in white areas because white customers would not patronize our stores.

But the country was changing, and average Americans of all colors were moving beyond racial and ethnic discrimination. A generation of young people had grown up in an integrated environment, and they were now raising their own children to get along in a multi-hued society. Admittedly, we were a long way from fully achieving Dr. King's dream of a nation where all people are judged not by the color of their skin but by the content of their character, yet real progress was being made at the grassroots level, where folks interact day to day.

I saw the change in my stores, all of which had integrated staffs. One incident stands out. We had hired mostly young white people (high school students and recent high school graduates) for the new Richland Park store, but I also employed several black college students and transferred an experienced black assistant manager— Donnie Cox, a Tennessee State University graduate who had worked his way from crew level to management while in college—from Clarksville Highway to Richland Park. This mixed crew functioned beautifully as we prepared the store for opening. There were no indications of problems until the day someone left this note on the bulletin board: "Let's buy Mr. Cox a one-way ticket back to Africa." Some employees found the note and removed it. I wasn't told about the note at first; later I learned that the employees didn't want to upset me but had talked it over among themselves. Then a similar message appeared on the morning of our first Sunday team breakfast, and again the employees removed it. We had just completed a great motivational session, and everyone at the breakfast, including the family and friends who were our special guests, was in high spirits. When a young lady stood and asked to make an announcement, I figured she was going to say something about operations or maybe a group activity. Instead, she said that she was speaking for the whole team, and she held up the offensive note. She directed her announcement "to the person who wrote this," and she said, "We don't want you on our team, and we wish you'd resign now." Her words got a standing ovation. That night, two male workers—white and in their early twenties—didn't show up for their shift. They never showed up again.

I was so proud of the team. They had taken the lead and handled what could have become an explosive situation with cool efficiency. They had driven the racists out, and their action had made their bond even stronger. Word soon got around the community, and

350

our customers expressed the same pride I had in these young people, most of whom were local kids, the children of white, working-class parents. That pride extended to the restaurant, and we never felt anything but welcomed by our neighbors in Richland Park. This, I thought, was real change. This was the New South, where good people were standing up against the old prejudices.

Still, old stereotypes persisted, and there seemed to be an entrenched feeling among regional personnel that white McDonald's consumers would react negatively to black ownership in their neighborhoods. Black owners knew this wasn't true. We all served mixed clientele; as long as the food and service consistently met their expectations and the pricing was reasonable, few customers probably cared who prepared their meals or owed the business. We also saw again and again how Tom Burrell's black consumer advertising campaigns appealed broadly to the general consumer market and increased everybody's sales. Even in the South, there was little evidence that the vast majority of whites had problems dealing with black-owned businesses. These were the everyday realities that we experienced in our stores.

The problem was that from the consultant level upward, too many regional people had become detached from the grassroots. Except for an occasional and perfunctory drop-in or drive-through inspection, most field consultants came into a store only a couple of times a year to grade performance. That was about it. They no longer observed the actual dynamics of a restaurant at work or took the time to talk with customers. There were plenty of exceptions, but as a general rule, consultants had ceased to be innovative thinkers and hands-on problem solvers; they were mostly preoccupied with new-store openings and fault-finding. In the process, they had lost touch with the heart and soul of McDonald's success—the people who bought the burgers and fries. This detachment flowed upward, from consultant to field service manager to regional manager to zone manager.

McDonald's was by no means the only corporation drifting away from its customer base in the 1980s. That decade saw the rise of the "bean-counter"—the accountants and the merger and acquisition specialists—as the emphasis in American big business shifted from customer to shareholder. Increasingly, more attention was paid to the performance of a company's stock than the performance of the business. The needs of customers, the traditional backbone of any corporation's success, began to take second place to the interests of stockholders. McDonald's wasn't immune to the Wall Street versus Main Street conflict (although the company didn't make the mistake of abandoning its core business). McDonald's Old Guard leadership was handing over the reins. Ed Schmitt retired as president in 1982. After suffering two strokes, Ray Kroc died in January 1984. Fred Turner remained involved as board chairman and then chairman emeritus into the 1990s, but his influence was waning. These three men—each in his own way—exemplified the "customer first" philosophy that had guided the company from its founding. Many of the men who replaced them were consumed with growth and drawn to the Wall Street side of the equation, and Mr. Kroc's entrepreneurial spirit and customer focus began to fade. The company's priorities were on the *macro* level, focused principally on expanding by opening new international markets. At the *micro* level, at home in the United States, the expansion problems of individual store owners were too often left to inexperienced, uninterested, or self-serving regional people.

NBMOA did everything it could to support members in getting equal access to franchise expansion opportunities. I still have a file full of letters sent back and forth between black owners and regional managers. An owner would make his or her case, in hard numbers, for expansion. Fellow NBMOA members would add corroborating testimony. The company would respond vaguely, and little or nothing would happen. For instance, Lee Dunham, one of the most productive owners in the system, never got the ten stores that were his goal. He continuously communicated his wish to expand to his regional consultants, managers, and senior corporate decision makers, all the while watching as white counterparts with less experience and fewer qualifications expanded into areas that Lee repeatedly expressed interest in. Worn out by the difficulties of operating hardcore restaurants and determined to upgrade the quality of his assets, he finally sold his stores in Harlem and other hardcore areas of the city and began operating fewer stores in New Jersey, where he continued his outstanding performance record. It was only after he had moved his interests to New Jersey that Lee was finally offered a store in Midtown Manhattan.

In a few cases, the lack of expansion opportunities literally forced some highly effective black owners to give up on McDonald's. Mack Wilbourn was a sharp businessman who acquired his first McDonald's franchise in Atlanta's inner city in 1971. He got three more urban stores, all in difficult locations and all but one with low volume. Mack built up his restaurants and made them productive. It was a tough climb, and he knew that three of his stores would never be more than marginally profitable. To secure himself and his existing stores financially, he needed more stores in higher volume areas—the predominately white city fringes or suburbs. Mack was a driving force in the Atlanta owners' co-op, and despite having only four stores, he became the face of McDonald's in the city. He was Atlanta's go-to guy, whom marketing people, suppliers, and even the media usually called first when they needed information or wanted to pitch their wares and services to the co-op. In other words, Mack was an outstanding McDonald's owner, and there was no good business reason to justify denying him expansion. But it didn't happen, so after more than two decades with the company, Mack made the difficult decision to sell his stores and leave McDonald's. Today, he operates the number one and number two Popeye's Chicken franchises in the country, along with several other high-performing outlets for other national franchise and licensing companies. Mack gave up on McDonald's reluctantly, and the company lost a good businessman through its own narrow thinking and intransigence.

Mack's story, like that of Bill Armstrong in Florida, was exceptional in that they left the Golden Arches behind; most of the black owners who sought expansion stayed in the company in the hope that their efforts would pay off. Some, like Lee Dunham, did get more stores, but rarely in the prime locations that would have been the logical reward for years of hard work, productivity, and dedication. As a group, it seemed that we had been confined to a box. Unlike the late 1960s and early 1970s, when the predominately black, urban markets presented McDonald's with a serious challenge that demanded creative, even visionary, solutions, it seemed that the company now regarded the old "urban problem" as settled. Instead of visualizing the future and thinking ahead, as Ed Schmitt had done in 1968, regional managers weren't thinking much at all about the specific needs of black and other minority owners. It was a mistake, and I would be gone before it was corrected.

Chapter 13

Still Making Waves

Winners must learn to relish change with the same enthusiasm
and energy that they have resisted it in the past.

TOM PETERS, MANAGEMENT THEORIST

The first time I lived in Nashville, back in the mid-1950s, I was a
sixteen-year-old college freshman, full of energy and idealism and
with only the vaguest concept of my future direction. More than two
decades later, I returned with much of my energy and idealism intact.
Now, however, I brought with me a clear sense of purpose and more
than two decades of experiences to guide my next steps. I had made a
series of life-altering decisions—leaving my corporate position with
McDonald's, ending my marriage, giving up my comfortable life in
Chicago, and putting literal distance between myself and most of my
friends and colleagues—in order to create new opportunities and face
new challenges. I was a couple of months shy of my thirty-eighth
birthday, which is a pretty good time of life to deal with major
changes.

I arrived in Nashville in the fall of 1976 with one goal: to
become a successful McDonald's owner by making my new store the

best run and most productive store it could be, operating with integrity, and having a positive impact on the people who worked for me and the people we served. When I acquired a second restaurant and then a third, I brought the same goal to each of them, and thanks to the hundreds of people who worked with me and helped me along the way, I met my goal as an owner. In the process of building a single store into a successful business, however, my life changed in ways I hadn't anticipated. At first, just about everything I was doing was directly related to my stores, my people, and McDonald's. Without my realizing it, however, my vision was enlarging as I set down roots in my new community. For the first time since I left my parents' home—after my stint in the Army and a year of teaching in Memphis—I was settling into something beyond a job and a career.

About a month before I actually made the move to Nashville, I drove down from Chicago on a business trip. First on my agenda was attending a meeting of the Middle Tennessee McDonald's owners' co-op at the Roadway Inn near the city airport. I had some other business matters to attend to during my visit; I also wanted to see the Tennessee State University neighborhood where I had lived when I was in school. But Nashville had changed so much that I needed directions to the campus. At the co-op meeting, I asked several of the members how to get from the meeting site to the TSU-Fisk University-Meharry Medical College area. They weren't very helpful because they hadn't heard of any of these institutions. Finally, somebody remembered seeing an interstate exit for Jefferson Street (the main east-to-west thoroughfare through the "black part" of the city where my Clarksville Highway store was being constructed), and with that clue, I made my way to my old stamping ground. I saw there were clear directional signs to TSU, Fisk, and Meharry on the expressway and wondered why these names had never registered with the Nashville co-op members.

The TSU campus, though expanded, was also familiar and welcoming; many of the buildings that had been part of my daily life when I was a student were much as I remembered. But when I searched for several of my favorite off-campus hangouts—the Hayes Rendevous Lounge, Driver's Diner, and the dry cleaning store where I had learned my first lessons in business ethics from Gene Story, the owner—they were gone. I saw, too, how drab and decayed much of the neighborhood around the three schools, especially Fisk and Meharry, had become. Although Meharry now had a modern, high-rise hospital, the construction of I-40, the interstate linking Nashville and Memphis, had sliced through the heart of the area, and streets that I remembered as busy throughways had become dreary dead ends. Once well-maintained residential sections were shabby and deteriorated. If I hadn't spent so much time in the hardcore areas of Chicago and D.C., what I saw in this part of Nashville would have been intimidating. Far from the safe and vibrant area I had loved so much in the 50s, this part of Nashville was in decline, largely as the result of being left out of the progress taking place elsewhere in the city. The area around the universities had been transformed into the kind of place that most people didn't visit without a good reason, and I understood why the co-op owners didn't know how to get there.

After I moved to Nashville, I renewed my friendships with people like Gene Story and John Driver, whose diner had been one of my favorite eating places when I could afford it. Some years later, I also caught up with Luster "Brute" Hayes, who had owned the Rendevous Lounge, where he had sold nothing stronger than beer to patrons of legal age and colas to us minors. These old friends had been early influences on my understanding of the importance of service. But during that October business trip, I made my first new friend in town.

Ralph White, an executive at Meharry Medical College and TSU alum, was applying for a McDonald's franchise. We were scheduled to discuss his application, which, as it turned out, was the last application I approved before I left Urban Operations. (Ralph later became a multi-store owner in Atlanta and president of the NBMOA chapter there.) During our meeting, I mentioned my upcoming move to Nashville. I must have told Ralph that I didn't yet have a place to live because he called me the next day and offered to help me find an apartment. It was a Saturday, and I had wrapped up my business, so we had plenty of time to look. One of the complexes we visited was Creekwood Apartments, located on Highway 70, about twelve miles southwest of the city in a suburb called Bellevue. In the days when my dad drove me over from Memphis to school, Highway 70 was the main route, and I remembered the Bellevue countryside as farmland and cow pastures. Now it was growing with the rest of Nashville, and many of the old farms were being sold and broken up into housing developments. There were fewer cows, but even with the changes, the landscape was still natural—open fields, rolling hills, and more trees than I had seen in a long time. For a guy who had spent so many years in urban centers, it was enchanting.

At the Creekwood complex, I was shown a very nice two-bedroom, two-bath apartment that overlooked a green, park-like space. Within an hour, I had signed a lease and paid my deposit. When I moved in a few weeks later, I knew I had made the right choice. I could have gotten a place closer to my new store, but I very quickly came to value the drive between Bellevue and the city. The scenery, beautifully restful in every season and at every time of day, was like a decompression chamber where I could slow down and leave work behind me. Whatever had happened during the day, I felt good returning home to my apartment in Bellevue. I guess you could say that the boy had come back to the country. Five years later, I bought my first house in a forested area just a couple of miles away from Creekwood.

I have said that I had very clear objectives, but life has a habit of throwing us unexpected curve balls, knocking us off-stride, and teaching us a thing or two about our limitations. There's no predicting when life (or fate or God or whatever you want to call that power beyond our control) will step in. I had been in Nashville for about six months, and things were going pretty well. There were difficulties, which I've already described, but for the most part, I felt I was on track to achieving my goal for the store. I was working long hours, getting the Clarksville Highway restaurant to the level of consistency I wanted, and I was probably pushing myself a little harder than was good for me. I tried to set a reasonable work schedule for myself, but there were many days when sixteen or eighteen hours on the job seemed reasonable and necessary to get everything done. Although it wasn't usual, I didn't mind occasionally closing the store at 1:00 a.m. and then opening four hours later, with just enough time in-between to go home, shower, and grab a catnap. I had done it before. But one early summer morning in 1977, I overslept and had to hustle. The man who focused so much attention on the importance of punctuality with his employees had to be on time himself. It was still dark when I left my apartment and tore out of the parking lot in my Oldsmobile Tornado. I was doing sixty miles an hour on the two-lane road that would take me to the expressway. There weren't many people out yet, and I was so intent on making up lost time that I didn't think about how fast I was going. The on-ramp to the expressway came up before I expected, and I jammed hard on the brakes to make the turn. I lost control, and the car went into a full spin. After what seemed like an age was really just seconds, the car came to a stop across both lanes of the road. I managed to steer the car to the side of the road, and I just sat there for fifteen minutes, shaking and struggling to regain my composure.

I had been incredibly fortunate. I was okay, no one else was hurt, and the car seemed in good shape. It was dumb luck that had prevented me from causing a terrible accident. After my grandfather Yerger Williamson had nearly died because he ran back into a burning house to get something, he used to warn me again and again: "Haste makes waste. Haste makes waste." As I sat in the car, I could hear him saying it, and I thought about how I had nearly wasted my life—and jeopardized others—just because I didn't want to be late to the store. I knew what my dad would say: "Never bite off more than you can chew." I'd tried to do more than I could manage, depriving myself of sleep in order to open the store four hours after I had closed it. It was a foolish and unnecessary choice and could have had horrible consequences. I could have died just to make a point about being punctual.

When I finally got back on the road, I headed for the restaurant, driving ten miles an hour below the speed limit the whole way. The members of the breakfast shift were waiting for me to unlock the store, and after some good-humored ribbing, they accepted my apology, and we got to work. Yet I didn't forget what had almost happened, and I never have. We can't always control what life throws at us, but I had been reminded that I can control how I respond to the unexpected and learn from it, as long as I'm open to change and to new ways of thinking. One of the first, tangible outcomes of my near-accident was that I developed a new series of employee seminars on the themes "Haste makes waste" and "Never bite off more than you can chew." The discussions that emerged in these sessions were enlightening, especially for younger workers, who don't tend to give much thought to their vulnerabilities.

Personally, I began to re-examine my own thinking about what it means to be a leader. And I re-evaluated my ideas about teaching by example. On the morning of my spin-out, I was rushing to work in order to get there before anyone else and exemplify my lessons on punctuality. But it would have been more effective—and a lot less risky—to call the assistant manager who was on schedule and lived nearby, tell him I was running late, and ask him to get to the store a few minutes early and open it for me. That's what I expected my employees to do in similar circumstances. I didn't want any employee to ever risk life and limb for the job, but I had done just that. What happened that morning had dramatically reinforced the lesson I learned from Jim and Mary Fran Schenk, when they told me how to speed up restaurant operations by changing my emphasis from perfect production to customer service. The Schenks had taught me to stop looking at every tree and see the forest.

I didn't dwell on the incident in the car, but it did impel me to expand my perspective and to be more aware of my options. For instance, six months later, when McDonald's offered me the Downtown restaurant, I took time to consider all the implications; I delayed accepting until I had explored the pros and cons and assessed the long-range benefits to me and my people. I think that my experience that morning in the car also helped me make the mental transition from store manager to store owner and soon to business owner, which involved letting go of my intense hands-on involvement in store operations. In a strange way, I became a better team leader and role model by becoming less concerned about day-to-day details and more inclusively focused on the big picture. I became more adept at pushing the details down to responsible people at the store operational level. Although I had always emphasized delegation in the workplace, it was now easier for me to identify team members prepared to assume leadership roles, with new levels of responsibility and authority.

The Grassroots Connection

In truth, I didn't have much of a personal life those first few years in Nashville. During my time in D.C. and Chicago, I had been so focused on McDonald's and my work with BMOA/NBMOA that I probably qualified as a workaholic, and that didn't change overnight when I became an owner in Nashville. But through my initial contacts with people in the community, I started to see that interesting things were going on all around me.

Nashville was in the initial stages of a period of rapid growth and economic development that was affecting all the major Sun Belt cities of the South and Southwest. For a number of reasons— including the milder climate, lower energy and living costs, an educated skilled workforce, and a general free enterprise work ethic— our part of the country was beginning to boom, attracting industry away from the North and Midwest. It had started in the 70s, when the steep rise in oil prices drove manufacturing businesses to look for cheaper energy sources and a less expensive labor market. The once sluggish economy of the region was looking up, and it seemed that new opportunities were emerging everywhere. In 1980, Nissan, one of Japan's auto giants, chose the sleepy Nashville suburb of Smyrna (previously best known as a costly speed trap for unwary drivers) as the location of its huge North American plant. A few years later, General Motors selected a small country town to the south of Nashville as the site of its new Saturn manufacturing operation.

Hospital Corporation of America (HCA)—a home-grown enterprise started by Jack Massey, the entrepreneurial genius behind the national expansion of Kentucky Fried Chicken, who teamed with a local physician, Dr. Thomas Frist, Sr.—had become the world's largest for-profit hospital company and was transforming Nashville into a magnet for health-care-related business. Major corporations like Nissan, GM, and HCA brought more business—suppliers, support services, real estate developers—into the area, creating a range of job opportunities and new business growth that, frankly, the South had never seen before.

Within this context, average Southern folks were getting chances to improve their lives in ways that were really extraordinary. It was harder for poor and poorly educated blacks to get a foot in the door than for their white counterparts, but as President John F. Kennedy had said, "A rising tide raises all the boats." A new generation of employers, many from outside the region, were helping to change attitudes about employment, looking past race and ethnicity, and making performance the standard. As the 80s progressed, many of the old walls of institutional discrimination began to crumble.

In the early 80s, my attention was concentrated on growing my own business. After the acquisition of my third store and the completion of my two years as president of NBMOA, I could focus more on the strategies of success. I had two key objectives: First, I wanted to maximize the benefits from our daily cash bank balances by getting the most return from high interest rates and the proliferation of cutting-edge banking opportunities, like the new money market accounts. In those days, money management wasn't a high priority with most owner-operators, but I thought about something Dianna Earing often said: "A dollar isn't a dollar; it's a hundred pennies." That piece of wisdom reminded me of the time, when I was a little boy back in Mason, that my Grandpa Jimmy Jones raked through the ashes on the hearth to retrieve a lost penny. Dianna's words and the memory of my grandfather's object lesson inspired me to take more innovative approaches to my cash flow. Interest rates were soaring, and it no longer made sense to simply park cash in low-interest savings or no-interest checking accounts. I studied the financial markets and searched for the best opportunities to earn interest while keeping my funds liquid. I also emphasized cost control even more in the training of employees and managers and encouraged them to find ways we could reduce waste and improve efficiency. We weren't pinching pennies, but we were paying much closer attention to how they were spent.

My other, equally important strategy was to strengthen the relationships among my employees, our customers, other McDonald's owners throughout Middle Tennessee, and in our market. I wanted the McDonald's brand to stand out not only for quality, service, cleanliness, and value but also for good citizenship. For personal and professional reasons, I was determined to follow Ray Kroc's dictate and give back to the community. Ironically, my involvement got its first big boost from a conflict in the community.

Not long after we opened the Richland Park store in 1980, I got into a dispute with Nashville's zoning authorities about erecting a high-rise road sign at the nearby expressway, I-40. Past requests for a sign, made by McDonald's regional real estate and construction departments, had been denied because of strong neighborhood opposition, and my first application was also rejected. People in the area weren't comfortable with the idea of outside traffic and worried that attracting strangers from the interstate would have negative consequences, including an increase in crime. But as we established good relations in the Richland Park area, the opposition to my request for a sign melted away. Our Metro council member, Ralph Cohen, was our champion. He convinced the residents and business owners of Richland Park that everyone would benefit from business generated by having McDonald's in the area, with expressway visibility, and that my store was a great addition to the shopping district. With community support, I appeared before the Board of Zoning Appeals, and they reversed their earlier decision. We got the sign, which did increase business, and we always went out of our way to repay Ralph and our neighbors by being the best, most conscientious business citizens possible.

Shortly after the sign incident, I was appointed as a commissioner of the Metropolitan Board of Zoning Appeals by Mayor Richard Fulton; I held that post for six years and served as vice-chair. I also chaired the next mayor's Nashville Amateur Sports Committee, and I was appointed to the governor's Appellate Court Nominating Commission. These experiences brought me into the worlds of politics and public service and taught me a lot about the impact, for good and for ill, that political decisions have on the daily lives of average folks. When, at one point, I was approached about entering the local political arena and running for office, I was a little surprised to find myself interested in the possibility. I considered it seriously. The prospect of applying my knowledge and experience to the difficult problems of managing growth in the state and the city was very tempting. Yet I knew how time-consuming political office is, when the politician wants to be effective and responsive to his constituents. I also asked myself if I had the temperament to make the compromises that are the essence of politics. I respect the good people who hold office, but politics isn't a particularly conducive environment for innovation, vision, and entrepreneurial spirit. So after a great deal of consideration, I finally decided that elected office wasn't my thing. What really interested me was helping people maximize their abilities and to take full advantage of the opportunities offered by Nashville's new economic development. I figured I could do more by concentrating my energies on areas that provided opportunities for creative innovation and by working at the grassroots, through groups that dealt directly with issues and problems at the individual and community level.

Instead of seeking office, I got involved in a number of business and charitable organizations, particularly those focused on community and youth services, and I was soon doing a lot of motivational speaking to high school and college audiences and numerous business and civic groups. I was invited onto the board of a local financial institution—the first of three bank boards I've served on over the years. I was already a member of the Nashville Area Chamber of Commerce, and I became more involved, chairing a couple of key committees and then serving as vice-chair. I joined the Downtown Partnership, a group promoting the revitalization of the old city center; the Business Incubation Center, which consulted with and assisted small businesses to get off the ground; and other civic organizations that put me on the inside track regarding developments and trends that could directly affect my stores, my employees, our customers, and our neighbors. I became very active in the local McDonald's advertising/purchasing co-op, serving as treasurer at a time when we began making cash management a major priority, which benefited all the owners, and also on the advertising committee.

Through my work with the co-op, my community involvement, and my frequent speaking engagements, I became so closely identified with McDonald's that I was often called "Mr. McDonald's." Many people thought I actually owned all the McDonald's in town—a slightly bitter irony given my failed efforts to expand. Not too long ago, I learned that a number of Nashville advertising agencies, all of which were at one time or another interested in getting the co-op's lucrative media account, thought that I was the guy who made the decisions, a false but flattering perception. I guess I could have used my local 'celebrity' to vent my frustrations about expansion, but I didn't. No matter how upset I was about some of the company's current decisions and representatives, I always felt intensely loyal to McDonald's, to Ray Kroc's vision, and to the corporation's capacity to correct its errors and change its ways. In fact, I don't think I would be writing this book if the company had not changed. It would seem too much like telling secrets out of school. But McDonald's did change after the 1980s, and many of the mistakes in judgment were and are being set right.

All these activities conformed to my business strategy of establishing strong ties between the community, my business, and McDonald's. They also had an effect on me personally, although I wasn't conscious of what was happening at first. My perspective was enlarging; my field of vision was widening. The shallow roots I had planted in Nashville in 1976 were growing stronger and deeper. My community involvement was changing me from a McDonald's owner located in Nashville to a Nashvillian who was a McDonald's owner. For the first time in many, many years, I was becoming a man with a home.

EXTENDING THE FAMILY

My parents had moved to Nashville in 1978, though for several years, my dad continued to commute to Memphis every weekend to serve his church there. It was good to have my folks close by, where I could see to their needs as they had done for me. But I should have known that my parents weren't about to settle into the typical, peaceful retirement. Pretty soon, they insisted on working for me! They both worked part-time in the stores—Daddy on the breakfast shift and Mother during lunch—and they were great models for our young employees. My immediate family was fully reassembled when my brother, Carl, moved to Nashville from Virginia. He had left McDonald's by then and gone in a different business direction.

After several years, however, I still didn't take a lot of time to socialize outside of work. But everything I was doing brought me together with a lot of good people and led to many new friendships. When people talk about the South, the phrase "Southern hospitality" generally crops up sooner or later, but a person has to experience it to know what it really means. Real Southern hospitality isn't the kind of superficial, back-slapping, big-grinning heartiness so often portrayed in the movies and on television. I would say it's a welcoming attitude and a willingness to reach out to a stranger and give him the benefit of the doubt.

I remember a day not long after we opened the Clarksville Highway restaurant. A man came into the store and introduced himself as a city councilman. He wanted to welcome me and McDonald's to Nashville and offered to buy me a cup of coffee. We were in my restaurant; I owned the coffee. His offer, however, was genuine—the kind of friendly courtesy a Southerner shows to a newcomer. I got the coffee and had the first of many enjoyable and informative conversations with Vernon Winfrey. As I recall, he told me about his daughter, Oprah, who had graduated from TSU and become the first black female reporter and news anchor on Nashville television. She had recently moved to Baltimore to host her own TV show, *People Are Talking*. I was impressed, but not nearly as impressed as I was by the fact that Vernon Winfrey—a very well-known community leader, a highly respected businessman, and a role model for youth and young adults in the community—had come by to see me. I don't have to tell anybody about Oprah's subsequent career and about how proud Nashville is of her. But the first star in the Winfrey family was her father. Knowing Vernon and benefiting from his wisdom and encouragement over the course of our friendship remains a blessing to me. I've had many similar experiences, and I wish I had enough pages to name all the people who have reached out to me the way Vernon did.

Although I didn't have much interest in getting into a serious relationship—the kind that leads to marriage—I guess the power that was watching out for me when I spun out in my Olds Tornado was still on duty. I attended a political conference in West Tennessee in 1984, where I first met a lawyer named Susan Short. A native Texan, she had been an attorney with Legal Services and then an assistant attorney general after graduating from Vanderbilt University Law School. In fact, she had come to Nashville to enter Vanderbilt at about the same time I arrived in town to open my first store. When we met, she was serving as general council to the state Board of Regents, the body that oversees all state colleges and universities outside the University of Tennessee system. Susan was *very* smart and *very* attractive, and I was intrigued, but I didn't think of her as a potential social partner. Then in early 1985, I accepted an invitation to join the next class in Leadership Nashville, a nine-month-long educational program that prepares a select group for leadership roles in city government, business, education, non-profit institutions, and so forth. It is an honor to be tapped by Leadership Nashville because each class is made up of people who are already considered leaders in their various career fields. It's not an honorary program however the work was intense, requiring a substantial commitment of time and study, with the inner workings of the city as our curriculum. When I got the list of my classmates, there were many names I already knew, including Susan Short. At our first brief meeting at that political conference in Jackson, Tennessee, I had sensed that Susan was a remarkable person, and I found myself looking forward to seeing her again. The next nine months, I thought, could be even more interesting than I had anticipated.

Our first working session was part of an overnight retreat held at a mountain lodge about an hour-and-a-half bus ride southeast of Nashville, and Susan and I had a chance to get better acquainted. The activities included a picnic with a country music band, and when the band announced a square dance, Susan asked me to be her partner. I hadn't square danced in more than twenty years, so I hesitated. Susan was not about to take "no" for an answer, and she dragged me onto the dance floor. I guess square dancing is like riding a bike; once you know how, you don't forget. After a few missteps on my part, Susan and I were dancing with the best of them. In Memphis in the early 1960s, square dancing had been a required element in the physical education classes when I taught middle school, and back then I had wondered why. Now, as the movements came back to me, I was very glad of that requirement.

Susan and I started seeing each other often, but we didn't tell our Leadership Nashville friends. We didn't think it was appropriate, given the serious nature of the program. Our individual commitments to serve our community were an immediate bond, and over the next nine months, we discovered a great deal more that we had in common. By the time the Leadership Nashville course concluded, we were a couple, and at the final gathering of the class, we were ready to tell our friends. Only a few people knew, but at the closing retreat, Nelson Andrews, who founded Leadership Nashville, let the cat out of the bag, and all our friends were extremely happy for us.

Susan and I were married on June 6, 1987—exactly one year after the Leadership Nashville closing retreat. Benjamin Hooks, a longtime friend of my family, performed the service. There were more than four hundred guests at our reception in the grand ballroom of one of Nashville's most elegant new hotels. Instead of gifts, we asked our friends to contribute to the NAACP, and through their generosity, the organization received more than $20,000. Our wedding was widely reported in the local and state press, and to our surprise, was also covered by *USA Today* and several national magazines. I believe we symbolized something new in America: an African American couple, each of whom had achieved prominence and leadership positions and both determined to make their communities better for everyone. We probably represented what many good people hoped was a new direction in the South and the whole country. The attention was flattering, but what mattered to Susan and me was that we had found each other—and we both knew that it was a lifelong partnership. (After we got married, Susan told me how, following our first meeting at the political caucus in 1984, she had a dream that we were married and that she always just believed it would happen.)

We took our honeymoon trip to Europe and then settled into my house in Bellevue. Not long after, Susan started a new job. She became the first woman to serve as director of the Metropolitan Nashville Department of Law—a very high-profile position as the chief legal counsel for the city. She held this position for four years and then left to start her own law firm in 1991. She later scaled back her private practice and eventually became senior corporate counsel for a major international health care company. Susan has always managed to balance career and her public service activities, which have included organizing the Middle Tennessee chapter of the

Coalition of 100 Black Women of America. I was a charter member and organizer of the 100 Black Men of Middle Tennessee, an affiliate of 100 Black Men of America. There was one very hectic year when we both were serving as president of our respective organizations. There has never been a top dog in our household. We're both forceful people, and we've worked at balancing our interests and finding our happy medium. After almost twenty years together, we're still dancing to the same music, and whenever I miss a step, Susan takes the lead and gets me back on course.

MAKING CHANGES FOR THE BEST

When Susan and I were dating, I still had some expectation of expanding my McDonald's franchise ownership. There were occasional rays of hope, but they dimmed out quickly. Regardless of my efforts and those of other black owners and NBMOA, McDonald's regional management wasn't shifting our way. I was becoming increasingly frustrated with McDonald's foot-dragging about expansion, and I was also feeling the need for new challenges. I loved McDonald's and never wanted to consider leaving, so it was very hard for me to accept that my opportunities within the company were limited to three stores. The company had erected a wall in my path, and trying to climb over the wall or break it down was draining my enthusiasm. My feelings were in turn affecting my employees, and I could see the impact that frustration was having on our performance. I didn't complain openly, though I did explain the situation to my managers, whose chances of further advancement depended on expansion, and I'm sure our employees began to pick up the vibes.

We did not become less efficient or less attentive to service and our customers, but the spark was fading. I remember when a couple of my college student workers went home for their summer vacation, and over the break, they worked for their hometown McDonald's restaurants. They saw how other stores were expanding and how we, in comparison, were standing still. When they told me what they had learned, they expressed their dissatisfaction with our regional consultants and lack of growth. Among my managers, I was also noticing a new level of dissatisfaction with the general level of competence and the political game playing in regional. We had some good regional consultants, but because of frequent turnover, we also had more than our share of inexperienced, poorly trained, and incompetent ones. Through their interactions with this latter group, my managers' confidence was being shaken, and their resentment of regional began to include McDonald's Corporation as a whole.

I finally discussed the situation with my father, and he saw what was happening with his usual clarity. He didn't tell me what to do; that wasn't his way. He said, "If you can't always do your best doing what you love best, it's time to move on, because God has something better in store for you." With the one exception of my experience with "Neil" in Chicago, I had always succeeded by making my best better and setting a positive example for the people who worked for and with me. What my dad said helped me face reality; I could no longer do my personal best because I couldn't break through the wall. The best I could do was to continue running in place. Unless or until regional management changed its mindset, I was going nowhere. And how could I continue to set high expectations and standards for the people who worked for me when I was stalemated? How could I continue to inspire my team to improve and advance when my opportunities to advance them were so limited?

My friend Jim Schenk, back when he was an owner-operator in Chicago and I was his field service manager, kept a sign in his office that read: "Don't compromise yourself. You're all that you've got." After talking with my dad and with Susan, I knew that to continue as I was going would compromise my commitment to excellence. Sooner or later, I would no longer be able to run in place, and there was a chance I would start to slip backwards—settling for what was acceptable rather than striving to be superior. I thought about what the Green Bay Packers' famed coach Vince Lombardi once said: "When you're less than your best, you cheat yourself." I had seen what happens when a person settles for the status quo. Ray Kroc had a saying: "When you're green, you're growing; when you're ripe, you rot." People who cease looking for new opportunities and who stop making waves are telling the world that they've stopped growing. In business, it's pretty easy to recognize someone who is ripe. When they speak, no one pays much attention. They get a polite brush off and no greater recognition than what I call "a pat on the back and a peppermint stick." I wasn't going to let that happen to me and my business. I wasn't ready to stop growing. I had to envision success in a new way and make major changes.

McDonald's had set up a regional office in Nashville but had no local McOpCo, or company-owned, restaurants. Normal practice was to have a mix of franchisees and McOpCo stores in cities where regional offices were located, so I knew that the company would be looking to acquire existing franchised stores in Nashville, if possible. I decided to sell my Clarksville Highway and Richland Park stores to the company. I could profit very well from the sale (though in order to give the company a presence in Nashville, I sold for less than I had been offered by another owner in the market). More important, I would end my stalemate with McDonald's regional office. I also thought that my people would have better opportunities to move up in the McDonald's system via employment in McOpCo operations. I didn't see selling as severing my relationship with the corporation; in fact, it was possible that someday I might be offered opportunities to expand if I wanted to.

So in 1987, I sold my most productive stores, but I didn't burn bridges. I held onto the Downtown restaurant. Deep down, I was still sure that the expansion problem would be resolved and suburban ownership would be opened to blacks in the near future. When that happened, the Downtown store would give me a base for rapid expansion in the Nashville market. Meanwhile, I would focus on making the store a standout performer—which seemed possible to me, given new developments in the city. The dormant center of Nashville was waking up again. An area around the riverfront, where the Ryman Auditorium had been the home of the Grand Ole Opry until the 1970s, was being rejuvenated, attracting more tourists and suburbanites. A large convention and entertainment center and a new indoor arena were being built. Other new hotels were going up in and around the city, and one of Nashville's architectural treasures, the Hermitage Hotel, was getting a handsome makeover. The state capitol building and its surrounding area were being spruced up in anticipation of the state's bicentennial in 1996. Serious efforts to attract major league sports to the city were beginning. (It took a while, but in a cloud of controversy, the Houston Oilers relocated to Nashville in 1999 and re-named themselves the Tennessee Titans.) Rundown and abandoned buildings and warehouses were being renovated and converted into office, shopping, restaurant, entertainment, and residential spaces. With more people coming to the city center and a revival of nightlife, I was confident we could extend our operating hours and transform the store's sales from marginal to exceptional. Then we would be well positioned for future growth.

Those were my key business considerations, but there was

another, more personal reason for me to retain the Downtown store. I just didn't want to cut myself loose from McDonald's. I loved the company; it had been my life since 1965. In spite of everything happening to me and other black owners, I remained completely loyal to Ray Kroc's vision and the corporation's capacity to mend its ways and set things right. I had an emotional attachment to McDonald's that was now concentrated on my Downtown store on Fifth Avenue.

After the sale of the other two stores, I got lucky. Lynn Crump (now Lynn Crump-Caine) was made regional field service manager, and she was in Nashville for the next two years. For the first time since I had become an owner, I felt freed from having to deal with the politics of regional. I'd known Lynn since she was an assistant restaurant manager in Norfolk, Viginia, and was delighted to have her in Nashville, especially when she and Susan became friends. Soon after her arrival, Lynn asked me to do her a favor. She needed a Nashville store that exemplified the Ray Kroc standards of service and operations, and she wanted my Downtown store to be that model restaurant. I told her that we were on the same page. McDonald's was aware of the changes in the city and believed, as I did, that the city center had excellent growth potential. I was already working with Gerry Newman on financing a $250,000 renovation of the Downtown store, and we agreed on a joint project—I would finance half of the cost and McDonald's would fund half. The renovation re-energized me and my team. We were all working hard and having fun, and the expansion bug bit me again. When Gerry came to Nashville and visited the store, he was blown away. He strongly encouraged me to stay in the system, telling me that he was sure that I would have five stores within two years.

It might have happened, if Lynn had stayed in her position a little longer. But she was promoted, and we got a new field service manager, who, like Lynn, was African American. Our field consultant at the time was a little green and naïve, yet he was doing a good job, and I was very pleased with him. I assumed that the new field service manager would also be an asset, that he would know the history of black owners' attempts to expand and would be supportive of my ambition to grow. I'll never forget his first visit to the store. He came with the field consultant, who was there to complete his annual consultation report, grading the store. I didn't anticipate any problems, but when the three of us sat down together, the field service manager dropped a bomb.

He told me that as a single-store owner, I was now expected to work as full-time manager. According to him, I had to take the store back from my management team—in effect to go back to square one, where I had been when I opened the Clarksville Highway store a dozen years earlier. He said this was what I must do if I wanted to expand. I told him that my taking over as manager would destroy employee morale, deprive my best people of advancement, and drive them away. Besides, it didn't make financial sense for me to take an income out of the store. He told me to take the manager's salary. We continued to argue the points until he said, "I bet you don't even know the temperature of apple pies."

Maybe his remark was meant to be funny, but he was speaking to me as if I knew nothing about operating a store. I hit the roof. I remember yelling at him: "I've been fighting for twenty years to get blacks like you in management positions so you could help black owners. And here you are, standing in the way!" Then I shouted at him to "get the hell out of my store! Get out now!" He did.

The field service manager made a return visit to apologize. He admitted that he hadn't taken the time to review my history with McDonald's or my record as an owner in Nashville. I could see that his regret was sincere, and I accepted his apology. He turned out to be a likeable guy, and I didn't hold a grudge against him. But his superior attitude on his first visit to the store, his failure to inform himself about my situation before meeting me, his limited management vision, and his use of expansion to goad me into what I knew would hurt my people—it was the kind of condescending behavior that characterized all that was wrong about the regional approach to black owners. And it was the last straw. I'd had enough.

After talking everything over with Susan and also with Dianna Earing and some other close business friends, I made arrangements to fly to Chicago and meet with Gerry Newman and Pat Flynn. Pat, who had always been a staunch ally of NBMOA and the minority owners, was now an executive vice president. I told them what had occurred and that I was ready to go. I know how angry I appeared, but my feelings went much deeper than anger. I was terribly disappointed and hurt. This was one of the few times in my life that I felt victimized, and to make matters worse, the person who had done it was a black man. I wanted to know why a black field service manager knew nothing about the struggles and achievements of African Americans in the company. Why had he been insensitive to the issue of expansion? Why had he been so ignorant of *my personal history* inside the company and as an owner? Why wasn't he prepared to do his job? And how many times was I expected to go through this?

Nobody had to answer that last question. It was over. I wanted out. Gerry and Pat were good friends to me, and they didn't try to minimize my situation or make promises that couldn't be kept. Talking with them, I felt somewhat better about the company but no less certain of my decision to depart. I knew, and Susan knew, that my shelf life at McDonald's had reached its expiration date.

I sold the Downtown store to the company in 1990. There

were no negotiations over the price. I told them what I thought was right and fair, and the company agreed. The money wasn't a big issue to me. I wanted to leave with goodwill—in other words, to get out before more frustrations and disappointments destroyed my basic respect for and loyalty to McDonald's Corporation. I knew that I had done my absolute best, and I left with my sense of personal accomplishment intact.

My years with McDonald's remain the most important of my adult life, and I will always credit what I learned through my experiences in the company for making me a better businessperson, a better employer, and a better member of my community. Being a McDonald's man, steeped in the principles of service to others, taught me a lot about being a better man. Yet I wasn't sorry to leave because in my heart, I knew the time had come to move on. The story of *my* life in McDonald's was over, but the story itself hadn't ended. There were new chapters to be written for me and for McDonald's.

Epilogue

Live not to be known, but to be worthy of being known.

LEWIS CHARLTON JONES, TEACHER, PASTOR AND MY FATHER

The last thing I wanted to do when I left McDonald's was settle into an easy retirement. I couldn't imagine myself waking up every morning without a job to go to, and I still had goals to achieve. My brother, Carl, loved construction, so in the 80s, I had worked and invested with him in starting a construction company, which was expanded to include asphalt plants, building materials distribution, and real estate. These enterprises thrived for years, and even though my involvement was limited to marketing, consulting, and overseeing our wholesale printing operation, they introduced me to the realities of operating in areas outside food franchising. Not too long after I sold my Downtown McDonald's restaurant, however, the old itch for a customer-level service soon came back, so I started looking at what was new in franchising. I found an interesting possibility in a startup Florida company that had recently launched a burger-and-fries chain that was similar to Ray Kroc's original McDonald's, down to the ceramic tiles. The franchised stores would be built and equipped using the latest technology and cater to walk-up and drive-thru traffic only, offering a limited, standardized menu of high quality food and beverage products. I got in touch with the company and initially considered making a major investment in the corporation. But my objective was to get back to the customer, so I became a franchisee again.

What really attracted me, in addition to the company's sound business plan, was the chance to get in on the ground floor. I had missed the start of McDonald's by a decade, and I wanted to experience the challenges and exhilaration that drove Mr. Kroc, Fred Turner, Harry Sonneborn, and the few other entrepreneurs who had launched McDonald's in the mid-1950s. I opened two stores in the Nashville area, with the objective of future expansion throughout the state, and I helped several other franchisees in the region get going. I had a great time, but in my third year of operations, the parent company began to move away from its original concept. I had to decide if I wanted to go in the new direction. It was a pretty easy choice for me, and I sold my stores.

I had plenty to do. I was still involved with the construction business and was also doing some consulting for various clients. My community activities took on even greater significance, especially my work with 100 Black Men and a fun endeavor I had started back in 1981. Actually it began years earlier in Chicago when my dentist, Clarence Towns, inspired me to take up running. Although he was in his sixties, Clarence looked twenty years younger; he ran a minimum of eight miles each day. I'd always been athletic, but running for physical fitness was something new to me, so I set myself the goal of running two miles every day. I continued at that distance after I got to Nashville, and then on my thirty-ninth birthday, in 1978, I decided to run five miles. On my fortieth birthday, I upped it to ten miles, and the next year, I celebrated my birthday by running fifteen miles. By that time, I had joined the Nashville YMCA and was in a running group that ran nine miles a day. Several months before my birthday rolled around again, I asked the group to join me for a 20-mile run when I turned forty-two. That was the first Jones-A-Thon, an annual fun run that is now Nashville's oldest running event and the most prestigious among YMCA members and much of the Nashville running community. There's no entry fee, but we welcome voluntary donations, and all the funds go directly to the YMCA Youth Development Program. After several years, the day of the run was changed from my birthday, January 26, to the fourth Sunday in January, which has from that point forward been designated Jones-A-Thon Sunday—by proclamation of the mayor.

What appeals to me about long-distance running, in addition to health benefits, is that it mirrors in physical activity many of the principles that guide me in business. I've always had a strong competitive spirit, which I have learned to turn inward. Though other people set goals for me, such as McDonald's sales goals when I was a restaurant manager, I generally set higher goals for myself. When I compete, my objective isn't to beat someone else but to better my own personal best. Each goal achieved becomes the base line for a new and higher goal. When I run, I win not necessarily by being the first over the finish line but by doing my best meeting and exceeding my own performance expectations. I always tried to instill that attitude in the people who worked for me. I wanted my teams to "make our best better," to improve continuously within the context of strong personal and group ethics, and to support one another in our efforts to reach higher goals. After a quarter of a century, the Jones-a-thon still reflects this thinking: Everyone starts on an equal footing; going the distance is more important than coming in first; doing one's best is valued above finishing; concerns about age, color, gender, creed, and economic status don't come into play; and our participation and spirit reflect our love and respect for each other and our community.

After leaving McDonald's, I stayed in close touch with friends in NBMOA. I was especially interested to see if and how the conflict between the company and the African American franchisees over parity and expansion would be resolved. Throughout the 1980s, McDonald's had promised changes, but as my own situation demonstrated, little had been accomplished. Then under the presidency of Fran Jones, the first woman to head up NBMOA, a serious research study of parity was completed—detailing in hard numbers the inequities that black owners were struggling with, market by market. The statistics were even more lopsided than anyone expected: In all but one of McDonald's thirty-eight regions, black owners had fewer stores than the average for all owner-operators (attributable largely to lack of expansion), the lowest volumes, lowest cash flow, and lowest profits, yet they carried the highest debt and paid the highest percentage of gross sales in rent. The study also showed that in most markets with large black populations, black owners were seriously under-represented, as was the case in Nashville, which had no other black owners until several years after my departure.

When my old friend Reggie Webb took over from Fran, the membership of NBMOA had declined and was dispirited. Reggie himself had dropped out for a while, but when the board asked him to come back and take the presidency, he agreed. One of the first moves Reggie made was to set up a committee to negotiate with the corporation on parity. The eighteen committee members were among McDonald's strongest performers and had the most clout with the company.

There was a lot of back and forth between the committee and

McDonald's. The committee eventually approved a letter requesting the company's immediate attention to parity and included a list of specific results to be achieved within three years. A meeting was set up with McDonald's president, Ed Rensi, now McDonald's president, Tom Dentice, and other senior executives. Tom was executive vice president responsible for Franchising, Ombudsman, and Personnel. I had first heard about Tom when he was a field consultant in Ohio and helped carry out McDonald's agreement with the black community to increase black ownership after the Cleveland uproar in 1969. We had become friends, and when I was promoted to regional field service manager, Tom (by then the national field service manager) was the first to call and congratulate me. He was one of a small number of corporate 'cheerleaders' who welcomed and promoted diversity in the company, and I knew that Tom did not accept race or ethnicity as relevant issues in business.

Ralph King, a member of the parity committee, remembers almost every detail of the meeting in the corporate headquarters in Oak Brook. The corporate executives subjected the NBMOA members to four hours of tedious information, but there was no response to the parity request. Finally, Ralph interrupted Ed Rensi and said, "I'm tired of seeing graphs and charts. I'm ready for some action." Ed, who had always been known for his short fuse, appeared angry and asked what the owners wanted. In response, another committee member, Leroy Walker, stood up and told the execs in the room to take a blank sheet of paper and write down all the things they wanted for their company, themselves and their families, their children and grandchildren, and their communities. "When you finish your lists," Leroy said, "sign *our* names at the bottom." Leroy's words seemed to bring the message home: Black owner/operators wanted no less and no more than anyone else in the system. They didn't expect special treatment; they wanted McDonald's to level the playing field.

The NBMOA committee members left the meeting believing that nothing had been gained and that maybe they had put their own ownerships in jeopardy by challenging the executives. The general feeling was that Ed Rensi sincerely wanted to make changes but was hamstrung by the lack of support from his own people. As Ralph told me not long ago, "Ed's heart was in the right place, but his team wasn't with him."

What happened next was a total shock. Tom Dentice sent a letter to Reggie Webb, following up on the meeting. In his letter, Tom offered his personal apology and stated that it was time to do something. He promised that *he* would honor NBMOA's parity request. This personal pledge, which Tom had not cleared with Ed Rensi until after the letter was mailed, had been copied to the relevant corporate managers and licensing people. Tom was heavily criticized inside the corporation, especially by the licensing managers, for his unilateral move, and many people still believe that his letter played a role in his leaving McDonald's a couple of years later. But by taking a stand and keeping his promise, Tom had forced the issue, and his action broke the back of corporate resistance to parity for black and other minority owners. What Tom started, Ed Rensi pushed forward, and to its credit, the corporation honored Tom's commitment.

Over the next five years, the company implemented NBMOA's goals, and by the end of 2001, parity was achieved. Finally, minority owners had the same opportunities to expand as every other McDonald's owner. There was a concerted effort for every owner to be evaluated by the same criteria and given the same considerations. Total fairness became the goal. During the process of implementing parity, some black owners, whose stores consistently performed poorly, were weeded out. However, owners with good track records were given the opportunity to grow their businesses and expand beyond the traditional urban boundaries, leading to an overall increase in the number and the productivity of black-owned stores.

NBMOA also grew. Today, NBMOA represents more than 320 black franchisees and franchise groups that own more than 1200 stores with annual sales approaching $4 billion. There are now thirty NBMOA chapters, including one in South Africa. Black owners remain the largest minority group in McDonald's, with Hispanic owners a very close second.

McDonald's is a better system as a result of accepting the equality of all owners and expanding its commitment to diversity. Jim Skinner, the current CEO of McDonald's Corporation—and a friend of mine since we were golfing buddies in the early 1970s—filled me in on some impressive statistics: Almost 40 percent of the company's officers and nearly 30 percent of the Board of Directors are now minorities and women. McDonald's still leads the fast-food industry in the number of minority and women franchisees, and the company now spends 60 percent of its goods and services dollars with minority and women suppliers. Noting that "diversity is a vital part of our global business strategy," Jim says that McDonald's isn't resting on its laurels and is intent on continuing improvement. Talent development is one of his major priorities, including "identifying and developing diversity of thought as well as diversity of the population we serve."

I have included these positive numbers not as a happy ending—the story of McDonald's and diversity is not over—but as evidence of what can be accomplished when principled people persist in doing what they know is right, despite the personal consequences. Reggie Webb and the NBMOA parity committee stood up and took on a seemingly impossible task at a time when black owners in general were most discouraged. Tom Dentice put his career on the line when he followed his conscience and did what no one else in corporate could or would do. I wasn't there as a witness to their separate acts of courage, but I felt the pride of their victory.

MY PRINCIPLES OF STANDING UP AND STANDING OUT

When I was a kid, my grandmother Mama-Totcy Jones taught me and her other grandchildren to "stand out and don't blend in." The older I got and the more of life I experienced, the better I understood Mama-Totcy. By telling us to "stand out," she was encouraging us to become the kind of people who do the right thing, even when it's not popular, and to set the standard for others. She wanted us to know that doing right takes courage because it often involves going against the crowd and bucking conventional thinking. She was also giving us her support and letting us know that we wouldn't be alone when we stood up for what we knew to be right.

As I was choosing the title for this book, several people suggested I use the word "leadership" in the title. "Everybody wants to be a leader," I was told, "and that will sell your book." But I found myself thinking about Mama-Totcy's teaching and her influence on me and my career. I've been fortunate to work with outstanding leaders, like Ray Kroc, who created massive changes in business and in society. Yet many of the best and most successful leaders I've known are people who are great but not famous because they weren't recognized for wealth or celebrity. Only a relatively few people can be captains of industry or heads of state, but in our daily lives and careers, the opportunities for leadership are limitless. What makes real leaders is their willingness to stand up and do the right thing in any situation. Most of my own role models, particularly in business, were, on the surface, average men and women, but each of them drew strength from a deep core of principles that shaped their actions and inspired others to follow their lead. Somewhere in their lives, they had learned what Mama-Totcy taught me.

Though I believe we all have the potential for leadership, I can't tell anyone exactly how to be a leader. I can't give anyone a set of one-size-fits-all steps that guarantee success because I refuse to define success for others. In fact, my principles of standing up and standing out probably won't be of much use to anyone whose idea of success is merely the accumulation of money and fame.

What I have to offer are principles that continue to reward me with a fulfilling and enjoyable life that's filled with prosperity. These principles evolved from lessons I learned as a boy, expanded and refined by my own experiences. They are the yardsticks by which I measure every aspect of life. I have found them especially important and useful in business, where the pressures to get off course are frequent and often very seductive. Whenever I was tempted to stray and take the easy path by doing what was expedient, I could almost hear my parents and grandparents telling to me to stand up for what was right and stand out from the crowd. My family knew, and I learned, that high principles aren't worth a hill of beans unless they guide our actions and underlie our relationships. By passing these principles on, with some of my observations, I hope they will encourage and support others, in business and in every part of life.

"Do to others what you would have them do to you." The familiar words of the Golden Rule come from the Bible–the book of Matthew– but the message is universal. The Golden Rule has been my moral and ethical foundation since I was a boy. A lot of people today seem to believe that business, professional, and political ethics are somehow different from personal ethics—that business and politics are dog-eat-dog worlds in which the ends justify the means and almost any tactic is acceptable to achieve strategic goals. I don't buy into that thinking, and I have never known a truly successful leader who does. Treating others as I wanted to be treated has always produced desirable results and, in most instances, led to long-term gains that often exceeded my expectations.

Being governed by the Golden Rule produces rewards that can't be calculated on a profit and loss statement. My long friendship with Mike Quinlan, for example, began because he reached out and made me feel welcome when I first went to Chicago in 1969. Many of my co-workers couldn't get past my skin color, but Mike just saw *me*—the new guy who could use a friend on his first day inside Chicago's regional headquarters. His sincerity won my immediate gratitude and trust, and as we got to know each other, Mike and I both gave as much as we got from our friendship. We had plenty of disagreements during our years in McDonald's, but even when I thought he was wrong, I never doubted his word or his genuine desire to do the right thing.

I don't want to be treated differently, for better or for worse, just because I'm a man or because I'm black or for any other generic reason. I can't expect to be accepted or evaluated as an individual unless I respect the individuality of others. Growing up in a racially segregated society, I was labeled, and it made me angry. But it felt wrong to respond to anger with anger, even righteous anger. My father, who lived the Golden Rule, taught me to ignore stereotypes and avoid forming judgments until I made a serious effort to know another person's circumstances.

Secure, healthy, whole people honor and respect differences and regard them as assets that enhance our intangible net worth. I value differences in ethnicity, culture, intellect, physical abilities, age, and experience because I know the benefits that come from various perspectives. Diversity enhances and protects the whole. Effective leaders stand out by following the Golden Rule and by listening to, learning from, and showing respect for all individuals. They naturally build consensus, maximize mutual goal setting, and motivate diverse groups to work toward positive outcomes for everyone.

Strive for "barefoot service." Through his consideration for and his actions on behalf of everyone he encountered, my father showed me that willing service is the blueprint for a rewarding life. My dad faced serious obstacles, including discrimination; he never had a lot of money; he didn't gain the full recognition that I thought he was worthy of. Yet he often said, "A man can't miss what he never had." His happiness came from making others happy. He gave me the model and taught me that service is not just a career choice; it's a life choice.

It was Gandhi, the great pacifist and liberator of India, who said, "The best way to find yourself is to lose yourself in service to others." His words inspired Dr. Martin Luther King, Jr., and the heroes of the civil rights movement in this country. In turn, they helped change the meaning of service for countless more African Americans by demonstrating that service is not servitude. Serving others is a choice open to everyone no matter what path we follow.

I had seen the value of going the extra mile in business when my brother and I sold "the coldest beer in town" at our grocery store in Greenville, Mississippi. In McDonald's, that lesson was reinforced: Giving service means more than doing the bare minimum required to satisfy customers. As a management trainee, I watched Clarence Hoop, a high school kid at least ten years younger than me, delight customers with his efficiency, speed, and the genuine enthusiasm he brought to each sale. Clarence never failed to serve customers with respect, courtesy, and cheerfulness. Behind the counter of a McDonald's restaurant in Alexandria, Virginia, this young man lived Gandhi's words. He gave service that would impress his customers and "knock their socks off"—what I later called "barefoot service." It was clear to me that by giving more service than his customers expected, Clarence was making them and himself feel good. Through service, he created his own rewards.

That's the thing about service. The opportunities are everywhere in every person and every situation. If I hold a door open for a stranger or give my seat to someone on a crowded train, that person might not return the service directly to me, but there's a very good chance he or she will do the same for someone else. Being of service has ripple effects. Clarence Hoop served me by showing me the value of enthusiasm in customer service, and I took that value into my own work and brought it into every training session I ever led. I also taught my trainees that we don't just serve our customers. Life is an exchange of services, and we are all each other's customers. We serve one another by helping each other do our jobs to the best of our abilities, and that translates into barefoot service for the customer at the counter or the drive-thru window. When the customer is impressed and tells his friends about us, he's doing us a service, and the ripples spread.

In business, the rewards for excellent service, whether we're bagging an order of burgers and fries or directing a Fortune 500 company, are often measured in dollars and cents—a pay raise or a boost in share prices. The greater rewards, however, are not so easy to quantify. When I think about the rewards for service, I think first about my dad. And I remind myself of something George Washington Carver, who began life as a slave, said after he had achieved

391

worldwide acclaim for his accomplishments in science and education: "It is not the style of clothes one wears, neither the kind of automobile one drives, nor the amount of money one has in the bank, that counts. These mean nothing. It is simply service that measures success."

Never compromise personal integrity. My most rewarding compliment comes from people who say I am a person of integrity. To me, integrity means being an honest person with high quality intentions that are reflected in every decision and being impeccable with my word. I like the way Oprah Winfrey puts it: "Real integrity is doing the right thing, knowing that nobody's going to know whether you did it or not."

Integrity also means accepting responsibility for my actions. I have had outstanding role models of business integrity throughout my life; many of their names and stories are included in this book. What they have in common is a firm belief in themselves and their goals. People of integrity can make mistakes, and occasionally their mistakes are devastating. Integrity requires admitting mistakes, taking responsibility, making an honest effort to correct errors, and making amends in the event of harm. In the last few years, we have seen many businesspeople and politicians claim to be leaders, but their main talent seems to be blaming others. President Harry Truman probably put it best: "The buck stops here." Leaders with integrity take responsibility for the consequences of their leadership. When Ed Rensi apologized to Al Joyner for denying Al's request to expand his McDonald's ownership, Ed didn't pass the buck down to his regional management, who actually caused the misunderstanding. Ed acted with integrity and gave meaning to his apology by supporting Al's future expansion.

I have observed, in business and elsewhere, that really

392

outstanding leaders come equipped with some humility. They recognize that they don't know everything and that it's smart to seek help. Leaders have the ability to make decisions, but *good leaders know the difference between making a decision and arriving at a decision* through deliberation and consultation. Leaders who believe in themselves and their goals view seeking input from others as productive.

The most effective leaders I've known are also willing to defer to the judgment of others. I think about Ray Kroc, who would leave the room whenever his senior managers discussed Ronald McDonald. He knew that he didn't really understand how to market the popular character correctly, so he got out of the way and left the decisions closer to the knowledge. To me, that's an example of wise decision-making: Mr. Kroc *decided* to empower people he had hired to do what they did better than he. Then he got out of the way, let them work, and supported their decisions.

Unlike Harry Truman and Mr. Kroc, some 'lead' by passing the buck—a failure of integrity that creates confusion, undermines employee confidence, and ultimately damages product, service, and relationships.

Act, don't react. I believe in following my instincts, but only when my gut reactions are based on knowledge. This goes back to another of the principles I was taught in my youth: "Look before you leap." Back in D.C. in 1968, when I was managing the Bladensburg Road store and struggling to make it a superior McDonald's restaurant, I didn't hire a well qualified young man because of his hair style. Instinct told me that his Afro would offend some customers, but I hadn't yet studied my market thoroughly or familiarized myself with the changes in popular taste and style that were taking place in the

African American community. If I had been better educated, my instinct would have been different. That mistake, which I have regretted ever since, taught me an important lesson—instinct must be trained in order to be trustworthy. As a friend of mine often says, "An uneducated opinion is a dangerous one, especially if it's your own."

Good leaders learn by viewing the world as a classroom, keeping their eyes and ears open at all times in all situations. A student of the world is well equipped to recognize opportunities that others often miss and to prevent difficulties. Instinct is sharpened by awareness, and observation is the basis of awareness. We tend to focus our attention on a limited range of personal concerns, like walking over a crack in the sidewalk without being conscious of it, until we trip over it. That's a pretty basic example of the "box" that everybody is trying to "think outside of" these days. We tend to box ourselves into comfortable habits of thought, routines of action, and patterns of interacting with other people—limiting our knowledge and dulling our instincts. I did that in my first Nashville restaurant when I could not solve the problem of slow service. I had boxed myself tightly into a set of expectations, and my instinct told me that the difficulty was in the details of our food production. Yet my friends Jim and Mary Fran Schenk had the answer in a matter of minutes. Until I looked through their eyes and found a fresh point of view, it never occurred to me that my expectations were the source of the problem. I was narrowly focused on the details of production and failed to see how well my crew had mastered their jobs; I needed to back off and let them work. That was a forceful reminder that in order to improve a situation, I must *first seek the solution to all problems within myself.*

It's a truism in business that no one can manage what he or she does not understand. My own fundamental principle of good management can be summed up in three words—Think, Plan, Act—

in that order. Thinking involves adequately educating myself about a situation. Planning means viewing the situation from every angle and then determining the best course of action. Once I have a plan that I believe in, I can act, implementing the plan with energy and enthusiasm. Adequate education makes this process instinctive and tends to prevent and resolve problems permanently, thus making decisions more effective. When you get down to the basics, parents who think, plan, and then act in order to motivate their child to study harder are following exactly the same process as a company president determining the best way to motivate her employees to be more productive. The right *combination* of instinct and knowledge often starts the process and frequently warns us when our planning is insufficiently focused.

When Ronald Reagan was President and dealing with other world leaders, he was fond of saying: "Trust, but verify." Malcolm Gladwell, the author of *The Tipping Point* and *Blink,* made the same point when he wrote, "Truly successful decision making relies on a balance between deliberate and instinctive thinking." I generally trust my instinct because it's a road sign that points me in the right direction. However, a gut reaction can be wrong when it is based on ignorance and guesswork. Experience has taught me to strive for the balance by thinking and planning before acting on my instincts.

Respond to every obstacle as an opportunity. Whenever we encounter an obstacle in our path, we have options—turn back, stand in place, or go forward. My principle is to look at the obstacle, view it as an opportunity for creative problem solving, and seek ways to transform it into a greater opportunity. Usually, I find that the greater the obstacle, the greater the opportunity.

The one option I refuse to consider is giving up and going

back to where I started. That road leads to victimhood. I want to be clear. There are real victims—innocent people and groups of people who suffer real damage and loss as a result of crime, wars, and the cruelty and carelessness of others. Many years ago, the African American citizens of this country were victims of a legal system that deliberately excluded us from the full rights and guarantees of citizenship. I describe victimhood, however, as a state of mind in which people assume the status of victim in order to avoid responsibility for their personal faults and failures. This negates our inherent power to control our actions and reactions. Instead of seeking liberating opportunities, people who get into this mindset see obstacles as excuses to shift blame, seek attention, and gain sympathy. I don't have any sympathy for these false victims primarily because they demean real victims and trivialize real victimization.

The most successful technique that helps me deal with obstacles is to visualize the positive outcomes I want to achieve. I remember my early days as a regional consultant and my first visit with Herman Petty in his Chicago McDonald's. Everywhere I looked, I saw obstacles—the restaurant's disastrous physical condition, the poorly trained and larcenous staff Herman inherited, his own lack of business and food service experience, the absence of his franchise partners and adequate financing, and so on. But as Herman and I worked together, I realized that he had a clear mental picture of a standout operation that would be a source of pride to him and his community. That vision guided him as he confronted and overcame every obstacle. His vision soon became my vision, and knowing where we wanted to go made it easier to figure out the best ways to get there. It encouraged us to be creative and "think outside the box." With Herman's vision before us, we were able to set priorities and stick with each problem until it was resolved. Despite many frustrations, we made better decisions because Herman's ultimate goal was standing in front of us, beckoning us to move forward.

My experience with Herman and the other pioneer black McDonald's owners reinforced for me the value and power of vision—what most leaders mean by "big picture thinking." An obstacle doesn't seem so overwhelming when seen in the context of a larger goal.

After Ray Kroc got McDonald's off the ground in the mid-1950s, he visualized a great company dedicated to the highest quality of customer service. Herman Petty started by visualizing a single standout store, operated with the same commitment to quality and service. I believe what allowed both men, and most truly successful people I've known, to achieve their goals was *the magnitude and quality of their visions.* Neither Mr. Kroc nor Herman began with the objective of making themselves rich or famous. Mr. Kroc certainly enjoyed the perks of his phenomenal success, but I never saw any evidence that money or power motivated him; he cared about his company, and his customers were the key players in his vision, not him. I recently ran across a quote of Theodore Hesburgh, the much respected and admired president of Notre Dame university when I was living in Chicago. Father Hesburgh said, "The very essence of leadership is that you have to have vision. You can't blow an uncertain trumpet." I like that quote because it sums up my view of Ray Kroc. As the visionary behind McDonald's Corporation, he hit some sour notes along the way, but he never blew an uncertain trumpet.

Create an environment of teamwork and collaboration. My business career has revolved around working successfully with other people and building teams. I have explained my methods of team building throughout this book, and if I boil them down to one principle, it is to create an environment in which team members are committed to a common goal and are also empowered to succeed individually. The leader's job is to create this environment, and effective leaders begin with the first principle, The Golden Rule. In my career, the person who stands out as the finest example of this principle is Ed Schmitt. Good leaders—and great ones like Ed—respect each person's abilities and limitations, including their own. They communicate their vision with clarity and enthusiasm, and they are willing to explain how the business works and how each worker's job fits into the overall mission. They set reasonable expectations for their employees, provide ongoing training and the tools team members need to meet those expectations, and give workers clearly defined degrees of decision making authority. Good leaders take disciplinary action as and when necessary; as Vernon Winfrey puts it in the context of parenting, "Don't love your kids too much to say 'no.'" Good leaders also give credit by recognizing and rewarding achievement frequently and without favoritism. Good leaders stay close to their employees, without interfering yet providing opportunities for discussion and creative thinking. They understand that creative team solutions may create friction, and they are not afraid of disagreements that allow the cream to rise to the top. They know that when everyone operates in good faith, progress will follow friction.

An effective leader keeps his feet on the ground and his door open, with his lights on—thus being available to everyone on the team. When I was a multi-restaurant owner, I trained my managers to train our employees, but I continued to participate in the motivational sessions. The "we, us, our" training, which unified our teams, would not have been as successful if *I* were absent from the process. Whenever an employee or manager came to me with an idea or a problem, I listened more, talked less, and learned a lot. Priority listening informed my thinking and led to genuinely helpful suggestions and solutions.

My observation of good leaders is that they also stay close to the customer. Customers, after all, are part of the team. Customers are the recipients of a business's product and service, and their reactions ultimately determine whether the business succeeds. Working in D.C. and Chicago, I quickly learned the importance of treating customers and the whole community with respect, regardless of their economic situations. In Nashville, I became actively involved in the community, and I value my civic and cultural interests for raising my awareness and knowledge of the unique characteristics of the city. What I learned through my outside activities flowed into my work, enhancing my understanding of my employees and our customers and making me a more conscientious leader.

In an environment where leaders must work with other leaders, too many cooks can spoil the broth. I was exceptionally fortunate to be part of a group, the first black McDonald's owners, whose need for mutual assistance and support created a bond among them that was stronger than anyone's ego. They formed the Black McDonald's Operators Association in Chicago; then long before their own issues were resolved, they reached out to owners in other markets, with whom they created a national organization. Each of those owners knew that his (and later her) business survival depended almost entirely on self-help and creating an environment that fostered collaboration and teamwork. They regarded their individual successes as mutual. It still amazes me how cohesive our black owners group was under such stressful conditions. Owners didn't make progress at the same pace, yet when one owner got ahead of the curve with his stores, he didn't break away or aggrandize his achievement, and his fellow owners didn't become jealous or discouraged. The real secret to that kind of collaborative environment was each owner's openness to learning from and helping each other. It may have come from desperation in the early days, but as I saw not long ago in New Orleans, sharing both the pain and the gain is still alive in NBMOA.

Respect your shelf life. When I was president of NBMOA, I gave a state of the association speech at the 1981 Houston convention that most attendees still recall. I no longer have a copy of the speech, but I remember beginning by talking about tartar sauce. When tartar sauce sits on the shelf longer than its expiration date, it spoils quickly, emits an offensive odor, and becomes a health hazard. I went on to describe other things that become useless after they pass their shelf life. Relationships, I said, have a life span, and I asked everyone who had been divorced to raise a hand; a lot of hands went up, mine first. Then I said that businesses have shelf lives too, and I cited some well-known examples of negative situations between McDonald's and its franchisees that resulted in owners being pushed out of the company. In every case, one or all the parties had been in denial and ignored signs that their shelf life expiration date was approaching. My point was that we had to be aware of shelf life and be prepared to take timely action, which usually meant developing an exit strategy. For a franchisee to leave a winner, he or she must be willing to face facts, control his reactions, and *choose* to sever ties on his own terms.

I was addressing situations inside McDonald's and specific to black franchisees. We had reached a point in the development of black ownership where some of our members were tired of the constant battle to survive in ailing urban stores, frustrated with the company's continuing refusal to recognize our special issues, and just plain tired of the daily grind without adequate financial rewards. I wanted everyone to be aware of shelf life and ready to transform an ending into an opportunity. When our shoes wear out, I said, we have a choice: Go barefoot or get new shoes.

In business and in other relationships, I believe that we must respect shelf life and not hang on just for the sake of hanging on. Nobody wants to be a quitter, but moving on at the right time is not quitting. When I was a boy and we played baseball in the field adjacent to my house, there were occasions when someone would get angry, throw down the bat, and storm off. That was quitting. But as the sun set at the end of the day and we could no longer see the ball clearly, we all knew that it was time to go home and do other things. That was a realistic response.

The penalties for ignoring shelf life can be terrible. In business, people who have reached their expiration date might be fired, but just as often, they may be subjected to various pressures— increased surveillance by supervisors, increased criticism of their output, being cut out of the loop for routine meetings and communications, consistently being passed over for assignments that he or she normally got in the past, receiving lower performance ratings for trivial reasons. The list of tactics used to push someone out can be lengthy. Most of us also get internal signals that we ignore at our peril. When the habit of procrastinating sets in, when we sense our creativity diminishing, when our performance falls short of our own standards, when we find ourselves involved in more conflicts at work or start to regard our co-workers or employees as interruptions, when we no longer look forward to new challenges—any of these reactions are telling us that it's time to create better opportunities for ourselves.

It takes awareness and a special kind of courage not to overstay one's welcome in any situation. By recognizing the signs and facing them squarely, however, we can take control of the situation.

Once we accept that our expiration date is near—and get over our initial emotional responses—we can think, plan, and act in order to make the change beneficial for ourselves and others. When I resigned my job in McDonald's Chicago regional office in 1975, I was confident that I had done everything possible to improve a difficult situation and that leaving was my most viable option. I was frustrated and didn't have a vision or a strategy. John Cooke convinced me to take a temporary assignment; a couple months later, Ed Schmitt offered me my dream job. I was able to cool down, rediscover why I loved working for McDonald's, visualize my future, and explore my options fully. Thirteen years later, as an owner in Nashville, I was much more attuned to the signs of my impending shelf life expiration with the company. I eased my way out by selling two of my three stores and considering other business opportunities. When the final blow came—the signal from my regional manager that my hope to expand was futile—I was angry, but I was prepared to go. I also knew that my employees wouldn't suffer because I was leaving, and their welfare had played a major role in my planning. My shelf life had expired; theirs had not. A leader never abandons his troops in the middle of a battle.

KATRINA: A TEST OF PRINCIPLES

Late in August 2005, I was working on wrapping up my book when the Gulf Coast was hit by Hurricane Katrina. From the advance reports, everyone knew it was going to be a major storm, but few of us could imagine the devastation it would bring to Mississippi and Louisiana, particularly New Orleans. Before the hurricane landed early on Monday, August 29, hundreds of thousands of people had left the coastal region, and Tennessee, like other states in the region, was gearing up to provide shelter and assistance to evacuees until they could return to their homes. Everyone knows what happened next: the storm; the day-long lull when it seemed that the damage, though severe, was manageable; the first reports that the water in New Orleans was rising. Then came the pictures of families trapped on their roofs by the dirty, rising water rushing through broken levees and more people fighting against the water as they made their way to 'shelter' in the Superdome and the convention center. For so many of these people, there were no longer any homes to return to.

As I watched television and began to take in the scope of the disaster, my mind was on the friends I have in the Gulf Coast region and the safety of the McDonald's owners and their employees there. Calls started coming in from people in other parts of the country who thought I might have some information. Until communications were re-established, however, I and my old McDonald's colleagues were in the dark. Then news began to trickle in: Many stores had been lost or severely damaged, but the Gulf Coast owners were all safe. The immediate concern was for the employees no one could locate, and McDonald's Corporation was helping in the search, setting up a toll-free hot line and a website as a central communications network for owners, employees, and volunteers. Through McFamily Charities, each employee affected by Katrina would receive $500; a contribution of $5,000 would be provided for the burial expenses of any employee who died as a consequence of the storm.

I got a lot more information when I attended the 2005 NBMOA convention in Atlanta in October, by which time most of the Gulf Coast employees had been accounted for, though they were widely scattered at various evacuation sites. I learned that two hundred McDonald's stores had been closed initially and that about half had been reopened, though many were being operated on very limited schedules by greatly reduced crews. I also learned that Ralph Alvarez, chief operating officer of McDonald's USA, Jan Fields, the division president, and Rick Colon, manager of the Dallas region, had gone into New Orleans to assess the situation. Don Thompson, then chief operations officer for McDonald's USA had also taken a team of people to New Orleans as soon as they could get in. Based on what they learned in the Gulf Coast area, the executives had developed a response plan. Given the extent of the damage in New Orleans, it was decided to treat the city as a distinct entity, with Rick Colon in charge, while the New Orleans regional office would continue to manage the remainder of the region.

People throughout McDonald's were anxious to help, so the corporate offices in Chicago coordinated volunteer efforts, sending people in as needed. As of this writing, more than a thousand McDonald's volunteers, from places as far away as Washington state and Oregon, have served in the Katrina effort. McDonald's set up a temporary residential and administrative headquarters to manage and coordinate volunteer efforts, while working closely with its suppliers to restore the supply lines to the affected stores.

In mid-November, two and a half months after the storm, I got my own ground-level view of New Orleans. I was invited to visit by Roland Parrish, a multi-store owner in Dallas and one of NBMOA's division presidents. (When we're together, he refers to himself as Roland II, and for clarity, I'll do that here.) In the NBMOA spirit of self-help, Roland II was taking twelve of his key operational staff to New Orleans to assist his NBMOA brothers and sisters, and he asked me to come along to see the situation and give encouragement to the owners and their people who were rebuilding.

Despite all that I had seen on television, I was unprepared for what I found in New Orleans. The oldest parts of the central city, including the French Quarter, located on the highest ground had survived Katrina and were pretty much intact. But beyond there, the extent of the destruction was hard to comprehend. The eastern suburbs, including the Ninth Ward where the levees first gave way, were basically deserted. Residential neighborhoods that I remembered from past visits were unrecognizable. Many of the structures were rubble, and much of what remained standing, especially the older wooden homes, was clearly beyond repair. There was still a lot of standing water, and the smell of decay was inescapable.

There was also hope. I knew that NBMOA had offered immediate help, including an extraordinary gift of $80,000 to each of its affected members. I have talked with all the black owners in New Orleans, and their accounts are both sobering and uplifting. Chris Bardell, for example, sent his wife and two children to Dallas on the night before Katrina hit. Chris originally intended to stay and ride it out, but as the storm approached, he decided to head north and made it to Shreveport, Louisiana, where a fellow NBMOA member got him a motel room. When he returned to New Orleans, Chris found that two of his six stores in the Bay area were destroyed and three others would require extensive rebuilding. The week after the storm, Chris rented a closed fitness center and turned it into a shelter for his employees, while he helped them find permanent living quarters. He also coordinated assistance with McFamily Charities. Chris credits the money he received from NBMOA for enabling him to pay the $5,000 monthly rent and equip the center for living.

Terry Scott and his family had evacuated before the storm. Katrina and the flooding almost destroyed one of his two restaurants, and the other was severely damaged. The building where both Terry and his wife, an insurance agent, had their offices was also badly damaged. Their house had been flooded, and they'd lost two automobiles. But the worst losses were people. One of Terry's employees and her sister, a former employee, had drowned in their house, along with their aunt and the sister's two children, and Terry handled the funeral arrangements. One of his managers had lost a child in the flooding. While dealing with the emotional stress of these tragedies, Terry and his wife were also tracking down and doing everything they could to assist other employees, pushing their own resources to the limit. Terry praises NBMOA for its contributions to the families of members and employees.

When I talked with Gloria and Kurt Holloway, all of their 130 employees had been located but only six crew members and two managers had returned to work. The Holloways owned two McDonald's restaurants and had reopened one, serving a limited menu and operating just six hours a day. They have no idea when or if their other store might be back in business because there are now no customers in the area and may never be. The couple's home was destroyed, and they commute from a rented duplex in Baton Rouge, a daily drive of more than five hours when they gave rides to their employees. The financial costs of operating again are staggering: The Holloways are competing in a market where wages and salaries have skyrocketed and trained workers are scarce. "It can be numbing," Kurt told me, but with help from other NBMOA members who have—like Roland Parrish—brought in their own employees to assist and from McDonald's volunteers coordinated by Rick Colon, morale in the Holloways' store is high. When I asked Kurt what was the most important business lesson he had learned from the experience, he smiled when he replied, "Value your people, and don't take anything for granted."

As I've heard these and similar stories from the Gulf Coast survivors, I am continually impressed by the optimism and good humor of the owners and their employees. Down in New Orleans, without any guarantees of succeeding, these determined people are digging out, rebuilding, and adapting to a marketplace that changed completely after Katrina. (With so many families gone and local businesses closed, the average customer is now an adult male probably working in the reconstruction of New Orleans.) They know that their lives, their businesses, and their city will never be the same again. They also know that the odds against them are high, but they are optimistic about their chances to succeed. The people I've talked with are deeply appreciative of the help they have received—from McDonald's and NBMOA, private agencies, and individuals across the country who responded to Katrina with funds, material necessities, and outpourings of goodwill. They also know that the ultimate responsibility is theirs.

When you are living something every day, it can be difficult to look beyond the problems of the moment and see the progress you've made. Surveying the damage in New Orleans, however, brought back to me the images of another crisis—the 1968 riots after Dr. King's assassination—and I understood how far we have come. In 1968, McDonald's Corporation had been dismayed and confused by the uprisings in major cities across the country. The white men who had masterminded the phenomenal growth of McDonald's had little notion of how to deal with this kind of crisis and almost no understanding of its predominately black and ethnic urban customers. The temptation to abandon the central cities and retreat to the suburbs was great, but it wasn't Ray Kroc's way to give up once he had started something. So for the first time, the corporation sought direction from its only experienced black supervisor and its black store managers in Washington D.C. As a result, I was recruited as the first black regional consultant in the company and Herman Petty as the first black restaurant owner, and others soon followed us.

Many, many mistakes were made as McDonald's corporate leadership moved toward genuine commitment to diversity, and too many black owners fell by the wayside in the process. BMOA, later NBMOA, had been formed in response to the company's misreading of black owners' unique set of problems. Still, the corporation had moved forward, becoming a powerful example to the rest of corporate America. Although not the first company to integrate, McDonald's high profile certainly made it one of the most influential, especially in the areas of racial, cultural, and gender equity.

Nearly forty years later, in the crisis of Katrina, there had been no bewilderment and no hesitation. Nobody asked, "How do we save our stores?" as they looked at the mostly black faces of the New Orleanians made homeless and helpless by the storm, the floods, and the dismal response of government at every level. Based on what I saw and heard in New Orleans, I imagine that in McDonald's headquarters in Chicago, the first questions were, "What do our people need?" and "How fast and efficiently can we get help to them?" The company's first step in 2005 was to find and safeguard its people and their families, which hadn't been a serious concern in the riot areas in 1968. There had been no dithering and hand-wringing in the McDonald's executive offices after Katrina; there had been no turf battles between corporate McDonald's and NBMOA when NBMOA rushed to aid its members.

My initial reaction when I got to New Orleans last November was a sense of déjà vu. Hadn't I seen this kind of destruction before, in D.C. in 1968? I felt at first that I had come full circle, but I was wrong. We hadn't gone back to our starting point. McDonald's Corporation, NBMOA, every executive, and every franchisee, manager, and employee in the system had been put to the test; in my opinion, they were passing with flying colors. Everywhere I went, I was met by the embodiments of my Standing Up and Standing Out principles. It was an awesome experience.

The future will bring more obstacles, but I am confident that forty years of struggle, conflict, and hard-won successes have prepared the company and its people for the challenges ahead. In New Orleans, I realized that instead of coming full circle, I was witnessing the beginning of a new circle. If Daddy were still with me, I would tell him about everything I saw and learned, and he would chuckle and say, "That's what happens when folks are given the opportunity to do their best. Most of them will live up to your expectations, and a lot of them will exceed your highest hopes."

Index to Names and Locations

Italics indicate photography pages.

INDEX

414